mending the SOUL workbook

for men and women

mending the soul
workbook
for men and women

CELESTIA G. TRACY

Copyright © 2012 by Celestia G. Tracy.

A special thanks to **Heather Campbell**, the finest editor we could find, who painstakingly read through this document numerous times to prepare it for publication. It would not be the quality resource it is without her dedication and sacrifice. And my warmest thanks to **Mandy Finley**, who said yes to a project that was bigger than she—putting her active social life on hold in order to see this workbook through to completion. And finally, my deepest respect and gratitude to the many survivors who have shared their art, stories, poetry, and hearts in the pages of this workbook. Thank you for courageously stepping into truth and staying there in order to walk a path of wholeness and restoration. It's our honor to serve you.

All rights reserved. No portion of this book may be reproduced or transmitted in any form or by any means, electronic or mechanical, including photocopying and recording, or by any information storage or retrieval system, except as may be expressly permitted in writing by the publisher.

Published by Mending the Soul Ministries, Inc., PO Box 97636, Phoenix, AZ 85060.

Unless otherwise indicated, Scripture quotations are from the *Holy Bible,* New International Version®. Copyright © 1973, 1978, 1984, 2011 by International Bible Society. Scripture quotations identified NKJV are from the New King James Version. Scripture quotations identified The Message are from the Message Remix Version copyright © 2003 by NavPress. Scripture quotations identified ESV are from the English Standard Version.

Cover and Graphics by Mandy Finley, www.mandyfinley.com
Photography by Abigail Tracy-Kakeeto, www.aperfectinjustice.com and aperfectinjustice.blogspot.com; Timothy Boyd, Studio B Photography; and Milena Mallory, flyfreephoto.com

Healing Art copyright © James Van Fossan.
To order prints, please contact James at www.jamesvanfossan.com.

To order additional copies of this resource, visit www.mendingthesoul.org.

ISBN 978-0-9849871-1-5

Printed in China

Dedicated to God's shepherds around the world who have followed Christ into the dark, offering to the oppressed His hope in the day of doom.

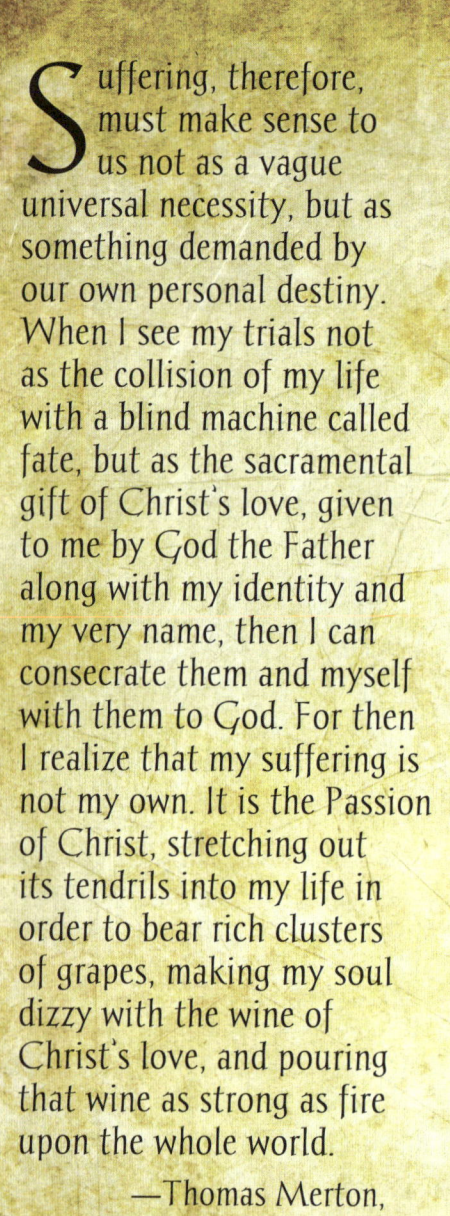

Suffering, therefore, must make sense to us not as a vague universal necessity, but as something demanded by our own personal destiny. When I see my trials not as the collision of my life with a blind machine called fate, but as the sacramental gift of Christ's love, given to me by God the Father along with my identity and my very name, then I can consecrate them and myself with them to God. For then I realize that my suffering is not my own. It is the Passion of Christ, stretching out its tendrils into my life in order to bear rich clusters of grapes, making my soul dizzy with the wine of Christ's love, and pouring that wine as strong as fire upon the whole world.

—Thomas Merton,
No Man Is an Island

Contents

A Word for Leaders 9

Preface 11

Introduction 17

Group Guidelines 25

Chapter One: Three Foundational Beliefs 35

Chapter Two: What Is Abuse and Where Does It Come From? 47

Chapter Three: Profile of Abusers 87

Chapter Four: Portrait of an Abusive Family 103

Chapter Five: Shame 123

Chapter Six: Powerlessness and Deadness 145

Chapter Seven: Isolation 163

Chapter Eight: Facing the Brokenness 181

Chapter Nine: Surrendering to God's Love 199

Chapter Ten: Forgiveness 219

Epilogue 235

Appendix One: For Clergy or Caregivers—How to Respond When a Child Is Sexually Exploited 239

Appendix Two: Is A.A. for You? 240

Appendix Three: Eating Disorder Screening (SCOFF) 242

Appendix Four: Depression Inventory 243

Appendix Five: Feeling Charts 244

Feedback Form 247

The word "mass" is said to be derived from the final sentence of the old Latin rite, *Ite misse est*. In polite English it might be rendered "Now you are dismissed." In more blunt language it could be just, "Get out!"—out into the world which God made and godlike beings inhabit, the world into which Christ came and into which he now sends us. For that is where we belong. The world is the arena in which we are to live and love, witness and serve, suffer and die for Christ.

—John Stott, *Issues Facing Christians Today*

A Word for Leaders

I'm encouraged when men and women complete this study, because it reflects a sacrificial commitment to truth and growth. I know how challenging it is to take a long, hard look at how abuse has impacted you. The truth sets us free, but freedom doesn't come cheap. I'm particularly thankful when *spiritual leaders* complete the workbook. Some do it for their own growth and healing, while others are motivated to help abuse survivors in their congregations. Either way, the potential fruit for this investment is very great.

As a missionary and seminary professor blessed to train Christian leaders around the world and as someone who spent fifteen years as a pastor, I love the church. I love equipping church leaders. You—we—are on the front lines of the battle. And we often feel wholly inadequate to the task of shepherding God's flock—in a very real sense, we are. I love the apostle Paul's reminder in 2 Corinthians 3:5 that as church leaders we're not adequate to claim anything as coming from ourselves, for "our competence comes from God." Our contemporary culture teaches us that effective leaders have their acts together, are powerful and competent, and have the skills to get the job done. But if we're honest and true to Scripture, we know that this isn't entirely true. God does his best work not through our strength but instead through our human weakness. That way He gets the glory! When we are transparently weak, He is shown to be strong (2 Corinthians 12:9).

As you journey through this workbook, it may well open Pandora's Box for you, your family, or your church. Thank you for taking this risk and doing this work. Facing the truth about abuse and the wounds it creates is absolutely necessary—for individual church leaders and for their congregations. I pray that God will give you wisdom and courage for this task. Satan wants to intimidate us—especially regarding painful realities. God wants to set us free and to give us courage to face pain and darkness—first in our own souls and then in the lives of others we shepherd. It has been my greatest joy and privilege to assist spiritual leaders around the world in this process. I continue to marvel at the way God brings beauty out of ashes, joy out of sorrow, and good out of evil. God wants to do this in your life and in your church. Once you have faced what you never thought you could (in yourself or others) and found God's love and grace in the midst of pain and darkness, you and your congregation will never be the same.

God bless you as you use this workbook to guide you through this journey.

—Steven R. Tracy

"Comfort, comfort my people," says your God. (Isaiah 40:1)

Do not remember the former things,
Nor consider the things of old.

Behold, I will do a new thing,
Now it shall
spring forth;

Shall you not know it?
I will even make a
road in the wilderness

And rivers in the desert.
(Isaiah 43:18-19 NKJV)

Preface

You are here, in this moment, reading these pages by God's design. He has brought you to this place for specific redemptive purposes. His voice will speak over your heart as it's laid bare before His Spirit's anointing presence. God is committed to your restoration and is here with you now, bending even closer as you begin your journey.

I have seen his ways, and will heal him; I will also lead him,
And restore comforts to him and to his mourners. (Isaiah 57:18 NKJV)

God's Spirit indwells you and will be prompting your thoughts, feelings, and recovered memories as you make your way through this workbook. Watch for Him, listen to Him, and record all that He brings to mind. Share what you will when you're ready—you're in charge of your healing, and the Lord is your intimate Guide. Each memory is important and deserves your attention and care. Many memories will be beautiful; and as they come to mind, you'll be encouraged because you'll see how God watched over you. Some of your memories, however, will be difficult and extremely painful, evoking deep anger and shame. These are also important for your healing and are mediated by God's Spirit so that you might know true freedom and peace. Allow all your memories to surface so that they can be felt and released. The light of truth will set you free.

Sin multiplies, creating more sin in all of us; and relational damage pushes us towards isolated, numbing paths of death—not life. Abuse mixes things up relationally and creates significant layers of false guilt for outcomes we're not responsible for and shame for sins we didn't commit. At the same time, we can remain numb to the effects of abuse we perpetrate on others and the pain they carry because of us. Either way, confession and forgiveness are gifts granted to us by a loving and merciful God who abundantly pardons and longs to set us free.

Step with me onto the Highway of Holiness where only the redeemed may walk. The Lord has called you by name; you are His. He dotes over you like a lovesick father, delighting in every aspect of your being, because He created you uniquely in His image. He loves you more than you can know and has all sorts of moments planned for just the two of you. If you allow Him, He will be near and show you Himself. He delights in you and has a destiny for you to fulfill. Come. Enter into your healing with joy.

preface

Strengthen the weak hands, and make firm the feeble knees.
Say to those who are fearful-hearted, "Be strong, do not fear!
Behold, your God will come with vengeance,
With the recompense of God; He will come and save you."

Then the eyes of the blind shall be opened,
And the ears of the deaf shall be unstopped.
Then the lame shall leap like a deer, and the tongue of the dumb sing.
For waters shall burst forth in the wilderness, and streams in the desert.
The parched ground shall become a pool . . .

A highway shall be there, and a road,
and it shall be called the Highway of Holiness.
The unclean shall not pass over it, but it shall be for others.
Whoever walks the road, although a fool, shall not go astray.
No lion shall be there, nor shall any ravenous beast go up on it . . .
But the redeemed shall walk there, and the ransomed of the Lord
shall return... with everlasting joy on their heads.
They shall obtain joy and gladness,
and sorrow and sighing shall flee away!
(Isaiah 35:3-10 NKJV)

Awake, you who sleep, arise from the dead,
and Christ will give you light.
(Ephesians 5:14 NKJV)

preface

This workbook is a practical tool to guide you in the interactive process of healing. It's designed to be a supplemental resource to the book *Mending the Soul* by Dr. Steven Tracy and is best utilized in a small group setting. As your abuse took place in relationship, so must your healing. This is why you will benefit the most from this resource if you're able to share your journey with at least one other person—either a counselor, mentor, or close friend. The section on group guidelines will help you get started. I suggest you read the chapters in *Mending the Soul* or listen to the audio presentations of each chapter on CD before beginning the corresponding chapter in this workbook. There is a lot of content in each chapter; therefore, you'll need to move through the workbook at your own pace. It's helpful to approach healing not as a one-time event, but instead as a life-long process of deepening intimacy with yourself, God, and others—this workbook will give you the foundational skills you'll need.

If you're interested in bringing Mending the Soul support groups to your church or school, you'll find the following resources on our website, www.mendingthesoul.org: Church Resource Kit, Clergy Guide, Facilitator Guide, and MTS Basic Training DVDs.

Now let's get started! Read on and see if you can identify with the experiences the survivor describes below:

I only have a vague sense that something is wrong.

I'm not sure what I'm feeling; in fact, I'm not sure that I "feel" at all. Only recently have I discovered that, even though I'm a Christian, I really don't experience joy—I'm not sure I know what joy is, to tell you the truth. I seem to always be tired, and I've been depressed as long as I can remember, though I really don't admit that to myself or to others. I'm not really aware of what's going on inside me most of the time. And what I do realize and acknowledge I never admit to anyone else—too risky. I'm insecure about myself. I consistently feel guilty about most things I do, even for just being me. If people really knew me—my past, my present, and even the thoughts I have—they would find me repulsive. I keep comparing myself to others, and I always come up short. I just feel "different" from everyone else. It feels as if people are looking at me and evaluating me. I sometimes think of taking my own life. I feel worthless and unlovable. How long can I keep wearing this happy face?

Things aren't right in my life. People don't treat me well. They never have. How can I stop it though? I really don't feel as if I have the right to ask them to stop. My whole life I have let people treat me poorly, and there's nothing I can do about it. What makes me think that now, after all this time, I'm going to be able to change one thing? I have a difficult time saying no to anyone who asks for help. In the rare times I do, I feel guilty for it. I allow others to take advantage of me. I don't have a healthy sense of my own boundaries—where I end and where others begin. I feel as if I belong to others. They get to use me any way they want. I don't have choices. I feel powerless to act on what I know is right and true. This makes me feel tired and worn out. What's wrong with me? I feel alone. I'm so insecure about myself that I can't handle criticism in any form. It feels as if people are rejecting me even when they're merely trying to give me feedback. It's this feeling that makes me keep blaming others for things I should take responsibility for. If I admit any responsibility, any weakness, or any sin, then the floodgates will open and I'll be overwhelmed with a sense of shame.

I seem to focus on the way I look. Looking back, I feel as if my value was tied to my physical appearance, from my face, to my body, to my clothes. It's ridiculous that any self-worth comes from my body. My abuser used my body as if it belonged to him—that's what was of value to him. I feel so dirty but also so fixated on my body at the same time. I hate that.

Whenever things start to go well for me, I seem to mess it up. It's almost as if I'm doing it to myself. I don't even follow through on goals that will be good for me. There are things that I do over and over again that I feel guilty about and swear I'll stop. However, the only time I don't feel despair or fear is when I do these

preface

things—anything to make me forget the constant sense of uneasiness inside. Ironically, I even feel guilty when things go well, because I don't think I deserve that either. I walk around saying, "I'm sorry."

Although I have some definite memories of what happened to me, it also seems as if there may have been more. I'm not sure why I've forgotten so much of my childhood. There are sometimes flashes of memory—images I can't quite make out. Sometimes I have a vague feeling of anger, but I'm not sure who I'm mad at or for what. I'm doing better than most people though. Whatever happened to me couldn't have been that bad. At least I'm not crazy.

People have criticized me for not accepting fault and for blaming others for my mistakes and sins. I've gotten feedback that I'm overly critical and seem to hold others in contempt. That seems ironic, because that's what I do to myself. I'm so self-focused that I can't just relax and be in a relationship; I'm constantly comparing myself to others.

I have no real, close friends—I hold people at arm's length. If they get too close and see the truth about me, I'll disgust them and they'll reject me. I'm deathly afraid of real intimacy. I'm not sure I really know what intimacy is. I get bored in relationships. I'm not really comfortable with sex either. It's not related to intimacy in my life. I'm not sure I'm even capable of having intimate, monogamous sex in the context of a loving marriage relationship. Sometimes I substitute other things for intimacy. While these things may not be as satisfying, they seem safer and definitely provide immediate relief.

I'm also suspicious. This is consistent with how I relate to God too. I know He's good, yet I don't really trust Him either. I need a safe place. A group where I can be really honest about myself—my feelings and my needs. I need to know I'm not alone. I need to hear others' stories too. I need to be willing to tell myself the truth about myself and not believe the lies. I need to see myself as a beloved child of God made in the image of God, having great dignity despite my sin. I need to accept the shame that I'm legitimately responsible for and reject the shame that rightfully belongs to my abuser. From God, I need faith, grace, love, forgiveness, truth, strength, and His comforting presence to meet my ultimate needs. I'm desperate for God to reveal Himself to me the way He really is, not the way I've come to believe He is. I need God to teach me He is good, trustworthy, kind, gracious, and loving. I can't know this on my own—I need Him to reveal Himself to me. I want to be connected to Him.

All quotations in this font are journal entries completed by survivors.

Throughout this workbook you will be provided with journaling pages. When there aren't specific instructions, use these pages to record your thoughts, feelings, or needs.

preface

Nothing comes easy, even now, For those who are **broken**,

Who carry shame deep in the marrow.
There is no easy fix.

Each must walk a long journey
To the center and back again.

This I know:
The journey is worth the traveling.

Residual Self-Image

I visited the thrift store, on foot
To exchange some clothes.
I carried them in a green plastic basket.
Unhappy with their fit,
I'd hoped to change my appearance.
Transformation. Rebirth.

I wanted these clothes to fit a certain way,
But they wouldn't.
I was uncomfortable inside them.
They showed too much.
But the threads didn't complain.
Still, I bought all new shirts.
I put them on. The mirror. . .

The clothes fit the same way,
No matter how I wore them
Or in what combination.
I was the same. But they didn't complain.
I tore the shirts in frustration.
In desperation, I ripped from end to end.
I was naked. Alone.

I had vowed I would always change
And now I had nothing. No one.
Would the gentle woman at the register
Please exchange my mirror for a window?

—Mike

Introduction

MAY I ENCOURAGE YOU TO...

Choose Life

Men and women who have lived wisely and well will shine brilliantly, like the cloudless, star-strewn night skies.
And those who put others on the right path to life will glow like stars forever. (Daniel 12:3 The Message)

The first step of healing is making the choice to work through the healing process. It takes courage to face your pain, the resulting damage, and your responses to the ache inside. The process will be difficult at times. However, it's in pain that you'll experience God face to face as He heals your deepest wounds. We're promised that He who has started a good work in us will be faithful to complete it (Philippians 1:6). God is faithful to continue changing us. The steps ahead may seem long and uncertain, but the result of peace and wholeness is worth the effort!

Choose Safe Relationship

It's better to have a partner than go it alone. Share the work, share the wealth.
And if one falls down, the other helps, but if there's no one to help, tough! (Ecclesiastes 4:9-10 The Message)

Don't tackle this workbook alone. You've been on your own for too long now, figuring things out by yourself without safe guides. We understand why you don't trust others with your true self, but you won't heal if you don't begin to trust. Take a risk, one relationship at a time. Safe people won't judge or tell you what to do. They'll listen and feel with you, offering their presence as comfort. They need to carry some of your pain so that their souls are awakened too. You need each other. From this point forward be done with isolation. Growing up alone in your pain has tricked your heart into believing that you're better off figuring it out yourself. You're not. It's one of Satan's first lies.

introduction

Choose Comfort

Blessed are you who hunger now, for you will be satisfied. Blessed are you who weep now, for you will laugh. (Luke 6:21)

God directs you to both receive and give comfort, and when you do, you experience healing—something supernatural occurs. You'll be equipped to offer comfort to others as you experience comfort. So let others in! Soon you'll begin to feel better, and you'll have a sense of how important you are to God.

I will never forget the time someone was sharing and I began to cry. I was confused because I didn't know why I was crying. My friend encouraged me to write about what I was feeling. In my journaling I discovered that when this group member began to share about her abuse, I had felt the same way when I was abused. Her sharing had triggered a deep sadness of my own.

Through learning to trust others and receive their comfort, I have learned to see God in a different way— a way that helps me trust Him and receive His comfort.

Choose Honesty

If you abide in my word, you are truly my disciples, and you will know the truth, and the truth will set you free. (John 8:31-32 ESV)

Good journaling records the real and the ugly—no lying to yourself or anybody else! Pay attention to what's going on inside (your thoughts, feelings, and memories) and write it all down. It's for your eyes only, unless you want to share it. Good journaling will take practice because—chances are—you have survived your pain thus far by distancing yourself from your inner self: distracting, numbing, lying, using substances or people, or running. Now I am asking you to put on the brakes and turn around. Head back into your heart and sit down there. Listen. Feel. Take good notes.

Read Abigail's honest struggle with fear of God:

I grew up in a church that taught that God was displeased with me if I wasn't perfect. I learned that God expected too much and that I could never be perfect. When I was a child, a neighbor sexually abused me. I had learned that I couldn't go to God with my problems (nor could I go to anyone in the church), because no one was safe. As a teenager, I began to act out sexually and was confronted by the elders in our church. I realized I couldn't live up to their expectations of me, so I stopped trying. The next several decades were spent doing whatever I wanted to do, because I knew I was going to hell anyway (according to my church beliefs). I knew I couldn't be good enough to go to heaven, because I'd already tried. My life fell apart due to depression, and I tried to commit suicide. I wanted to end the pain, but God had a plan. He was wooing me back into His arms.

At first, any mention of Scripture literally made me vomit. Eventually, I grew to understand grace and God's unconditional love. My heart began to change, and I began to listen. I began to have hope. He slowly and gently showed me His love. He was so incredibly tender and patient. I couldn't believe He hadn't abandoned me when I was so bad! I realized that Christ had never left me, even during my sinful behavior and rebellion. I learned,

introduction

over time, that He loved me and had my best interests in mind. I learned that I could trust Him. Now, I couldn't live without Him. He's truly my best friend and I'm forever thankful to Him for delivering me from my misery.

Choose Rest

Are you tired? Worn out? Burned out on religion? Come to me. Get away with me and you'll recover your life. I'll show you how to take a real rest. Walk with me and work with me—watch how I do it. Learn the unforced rhythms of grace. I won't lay anything heavy or ill-fitting on you. Keep company with me and you'll learn to live freely and lightly. (Matthew 11:28-30 The Message)

Healing is a bit like dragging your heart to the gym. You'll be exercising muscles that have been dormant for a long time. So expect some significant fatigue. Be gentle with yourself through this process and give yourself some breaks. Your heart and body will tell you what they need.

Choose Vulnerability

[God] reveals deep and hidden things; he knows what lies in darkness, and light dwells with him. (Daniel 2:22)

Being honest with your feelings in the presence of others will be uncomfortable at first. You may find that you're admitting thoughts and feelings to yourself and others for the very first time. The strong feelings and the work required to heal may seem overwhelming. After all, most of us have spent a lifetime trying to avoid the past, running from our pain and anger. However, the only way to leave the pain behind is to walk through it. Be assured that God will be with you each and every step of the way. If you surrender to Him, He will pull the weight. God has deep and hidden things to reveal to you as you wait for Him in the darkness. His words of comfort will turn on the lights, and you'll understand things you have not known before. Daniel's God is your God too.

> Generous in love—God, give grace!
> Huge in mercy—wipe out my bad record.
> Scrub away my guilt, soak out my sins in your laundry.
> I know how bad I've been;
> My sins are staring me down.
>
> You're the One I've violated, and you've seen it all,
> seen the full extent of my evil.
> You have all the facts before you;
> whatever you decide about me is fair. . .
> What you're after is truth from the inside out.
> Enter me, then; conceive a new, true life.
>
> Soak me in your laundry and I'll come out clean,
> scrub me and I'll have a snow-white life.
> Tune me in to foot-tapping songs,
> set these once-broken bones to dancing. . .
> God, make a fresh start in me,
> shape a Genesis week from the chaos of my life.
> Don't throw me out with the trash,
> or fail to breathe holiness in me.
> Bring me back from gray exile,
> put a fresh wind in my sails!
> Give me a job teaching rebels your ways
> so the lost can find their way home.
> Commute my death sentence, God, my saving God,
> and I'll sing anthems to your life-giving ways.
> (Psalm 51:1-15 The Message)

introduction

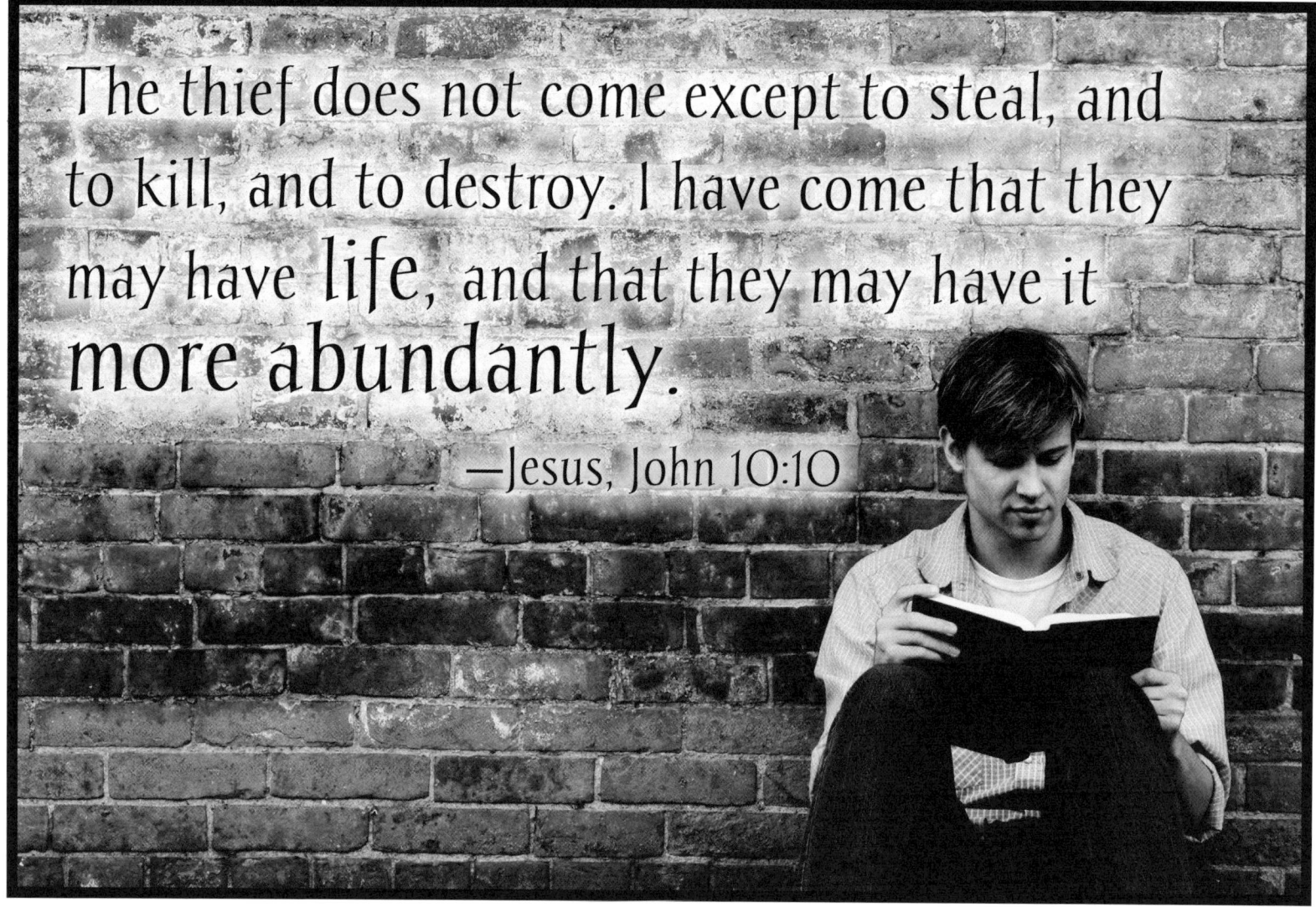

> The thief does not come except to steal, and to kill, and to destroy. I have come that they may have life, and that they may have it more abundantly.
>
> —Jesus, John 10:10

A solitary soldier believed himself a regiment and so he died, as he saw it, a whole army felled with a single ball. Fools are made secure by egotism, but the wise, knowing all their weaknesses, gather into troops to walk through Dante's mind.

—Calvin Miller, *A Requiem for Love*

introduction

You have read about God and His healing power, but perhaps you're uncertain whether or not you know Him on a personal level. Perhaps you are afraid of—or angry with—a God who is referred to as *Father,* because of the abandonment or abuse you suffered from an earthly father. Use this space to record your thoughts and feelings, making specific requests of God.

Speak honestly to Him now...

After practicing my journaling for a while, I found that I needed it to be able to determine what I was feeling and thinking. Soon, my writing became a release for me and even turned poetic. It became a way to express myself creatively.

You would never know after reading my first journal entry that God would turn this confused girl into a writer, but my journals have been used to help several people along the same healing journey. I am thankful for Romans 8:28, where God promises to work out all things for good for His children. He definitely turned my pain into something good to help others.

—Donna

introduction

GOD HAS A PLAN FOR YOU!

God wants to give you life in all its fullness (John 10:10). The Bible tells us that everyone has sinned and falls short of God's standard (Romans 3:23). This sin separates us from God (Isaiah 59:2). But God loves us so much that He made a way to be with us forever. He bridged the gap between man and Himself by paying for our sin through the death of His Son. Jesus Christ died for us on the cross and rose from the dead (John 3:16; 1 Timothy 2:5). He is the only way to God (Acts 4:12; John 14:6). If you believe in Him and ask Him to be your Lord and Savior, He is faithful to forgive you completely and will give you eternal life (1 John 1:9).

Knowing Christ personally gives you the ability to draw upon the strength of the Creator in times of sorrow and trouble. The Bible teaches us that God's Spirit comforts us (2 Corinthians 1:3-4) and helps us to understand Jesus' teachings (John 14:26). Scripture also tells us that Jesus Christ will not lose any who believe in Him but will deliver all of His followers to Heaven (John 6:38-40; 10:27-30; Ephesians 1:13-14; Romans 8:31-39). Once you place your faith in Christ and become a child of God, He promises never to leave you (Hebrews 13:5) but to always be with you (Matthew 28:20).

Because of the healing power of God, we all can experience joy and peace that is beyond understanding, as the Bible describes in Philippians 4:7. As you begin the work of healing, you may question if you'll ever feel relief from the ache in your soul, have the courage to make better choices, or understand more about life. The answer is a resounding *yes!* If you're struggling to find hope, let us who have been on our own healing journeys, offer you our hope. For we have seen the deep recesses of despair and can personally attest to God's miracles of healing. We believe these can happen for you as well.

> "For I know the plans I have for you," declares the Lord, "plans to prosper you and not to harm you, plans to give you hope and a future. Then you will call on me and come and pray to me, and I will listen to you. You will seek me and find me when you seek me with all your heart. I will be found by you."
> (Jeremiah 29:11-14)

If you want to place your faith in Christ, you may begin by praying a prayer something like this:

Dear God,
I believe You sent Your Son, Jesus, to die for my sins. I ask You now to forgive me for the things I have done wrong and be my Lord and Savior. Thank You for saving me, Lord! Amen.

If you prayed this prayer, let us welcome you into the family of God! God's Spirit now lives in you (John 3:1-8), your sins are forgiven (Colossians 1:13-14), and you have eternal life (1 John 5:12-13). You're now God's child. Remember, you can fully trust what He says in His Word. If you've decided to delay this decision, you may come back to this section of the workbook at any time. God is lovingly waiting with His arms open wide. You can come as you are.

introduction

Use this space to write your prayer to God.
Ask Him to guide you through this healing process and to give you a willing heart to hear and do what is necessary for the healing of your soul.

Let us then with confidence
draw near to the throne of grace,
that we may receive mercy and find
grace to help in time of need.
(Hebrews 4:16 ESV)

Come to Me, all you who labor and are
heavy laden, and I will give you rest.
Take My yoke upon you, and learn from
Me, for I am gentle and lowly in heart,
and you will find rest for your souls. For
My yoke is easy, and My burden is light.
(Matthew 11:28-30 NKJV)

The Lord is at hand. Be anxious for
nothing, but in everything by prayer
and supplication, with thanksgiving, let
your requests be made known to God;
and the peace of God, which surpasses
all understanding, will guard your hearts
and your minds through Christ Jesus.
(Philippians 4:5-7 NKJV)

And we know that in all things
God works for the good of those
who love him, who have been called
according to his purpose.
(Romans 8:28)

Dear friends, let us continue to love one another,
for love comes from God. Anyone who loves is a child of
God and knows God. But anyone who does not love does
not know God, for God is love. God showed how much he
loved us by sending his one and only Son into the world so
that we might have eternal life through Him.
This is real love—
not that we loved God, but that he loved us and sent
his Son as a sacrifice to take away our sins.

Dear friends, since God loved us that much, we surely
ought to love each other. No one has ever seen God. But if
we love each other, God lives in us, and his love
is brought to full expression in us.

As we live in God, our love grows more perfect.
(1 John 4:7-12, 17 NLT)

There was never a saint yet who did not have to
start with a maimed life.

—Oswald Chambers

Group Guidelines

> The more facile the expression in words, the less likely is the truth to be carried out in life. There is a peril for the preacher that the listener has not, the peril of expressing a thing and letting the expression react in the exhaustion of never doing it: that is where fasting has to be exercised—fasting from eloquence, from fine literary finish, from all that natural culture makes us esteem, if it is going to lead us into a hirpling walk with God.
>
> —Oswald Chambers

If you decide to do this workbook in a small group, you'll find support when others come alongside you as you face your pain. At the beginning of each meeting, refer to the following eleven guidelines in order to create and maintain relational safety. A MTS small group is not a place to come just to complain or to blame someone for your pain. It's a place where you'll receive support, encouragement, and love. Because the time in a small group is shared with others, you'll find that your sharing time is more limited than it would be in a one-on-one counseling session. Remember that *your group facilitator isn't a professional counselor* and won't have all the answers to your questions, but he or she may refer you to a counselor if you feel a need for therapeutic help. Although this workbook is intended for use in a small group setting, it may be used individually as well. If you're not able to attend a small group, you will want to find a safe person with whom to share some of your insights. A safe person is someone who listens without condemning, keeps your sharing confidential, and supports and guides you toward the love of Christ. Review the guidelines on the following page to understand more about safe relationships.

group guidelines

GROUP GUIDELINES: KEEPING IT SAFE

1. **Attendance**—All participants are encouraged to attend each session to gain maximum benefit for self and others. If absence is unavoidable, the participant is to call the facilitator in advance.

2. **Confidentiality**—Everything spoken in the group stays within the group.

3. **Time-Keeping**—Group will begin and end on time, meeting for two hours each week for a pre-determined duration of twelve to twenty-four weeks.

4. **Prayer**—The group will determine how and when prayer will be experienced, keeping in mind the safety needs of each participant.

5. **Sharing**—All participants are encouraged to share as they are ready—honesty and vulnerability are modeled and encouraged.

6. **Boundaries**—Time is equally distributed among participants, and unnecessary graphic details of abuse aren't shared with the group. This allows the group to maintain a focus on the *effects* of the abuse and not on the *details* of the abuse.

7. **Listening**—Respect is communicated to each participant by attentive listening. No interrupting, talking over, arguing, side conversations, talking on cell phones, texting, or coming late, etc.

8. **No Comparisons**—All abuse is harmful and the damage of any abuse or abandonment is best understood through the effects experienced by the survivor. Don't compare your abuse to others or minimize another's abuse.

9. **Touch**—Our bodies have eighteen square feet of skin. Because skin can't shut its eyes or cover its ears, it's always on. Thus, touch is something we offer and receive as permission is given.

10. **Feelings**—All participants are asked to allow the full expression of feelings. No one is to shut down this process by interrupting or inserting humor. Each participant is allowed to feel and work through his or her feelings as necessary, understanding silence as an important part of group process.

11. **No Advising**—Don't give unsolicited advice—participants and facilitators are there to support and not to fix, rescue, or direct each other.

RESPONSIBILITIES OF A GROUP MEMBER

Assess Readiness

Before beginning a small healing group, it's necessary to ask yourself if this group is right for you at this time in your life. There are several reasons you might want to wait to join a small healing group. For instance, you may find that you aren't ready to deal with the intense emotions that are involved, and you may want to seek professional counseling from a clinician before proceeding. You may find that you aren't able to commit to the work involved, or perhaps you can't do the work required due to illnesses or addictions that need to be addressed first (for example, depression or drug dependency). You may find that you're able to proceed but want to seek additional help for addictive patterns at the same time you're working through this resource. While you must identify and heal the underlying pain that causes addictive behaviors in order to be free of their power, you also need adequate support to do so.

In the box to the right is a set of questions to help you decide whether or not you're ready for a small healing group. These questions can help you determine if you need additional assistance before attending the group, or if you're ready to proceed. As you consider each question, you'll notice areas that guide you to additional questionnaires. Based upon your answers, you'll be more aware of your needs at this time.

> - *Are you struggling with a dependency or addiction to alcohol? (See appendix two: "Is A.A. for You?" or visit www.aa.org)*
>
> - *Are you struggling with a drug dependency or addiction?*
>
> - *Are you struggling with other addictive behaviors?*
>
> - *Are you struggling with an eating disorder? (See appendix three: "Eating Disorder Screening")*
>
> - *Are you able to concentrate on the work required in this book?*
>
> - *Are you able to attend each weekly small group session?*
>
> If you're struggling with an alcohol or drug dependency or addiction, an eating disorder, or a condition that keeps you from concentrating on the work required for healing, it would be better to seek help from professionals who can meet your needs at this time. If you're able to concentrate on the workbook material and attend weekly meetings, you're ready to proceed. Your pastor, mentor, or facilitator may require you to complete an intake form and be interviewed prior to beginning a MTS group. (These forms are included in the MTS Facilitator's Guide.)

Two are better than one, because they have a good reward for their toil. For if they fall, one will lift up his fellow.
(Ecclesiastes 4:9-10 ESV)

group guidelines

Prioritize Safety

Create a safe environment in which everyone feels safe to share. This is achieved in four ways: (1) Listen intently while others share, offering good eye contact and focused attention. (2) Share your honest feelings and experiences—authenticity begets authenticity. Others won't feel safe to share their shameful feelings and experiences if you refuse to be real. (3) Affirm, encourage, and give specific validation after others self-disclose—share with them how their stories have touched you personally. (4) Balance sharing time within the group by inviting quieter members to speak. In summary, emotional safety involves comfort, validation, and empathy (feeling the feelings of others). These are basic relational needs that are a necessary part of healing and must be a consistent part of the group process.

Abuse survivors have differing needs regarding touch—be sensitive to this and talk about your individual needs within the group context. Some people are comfortable with high levels of affection, and others are sexually triggered by any form of touch. Each person has been uniquely impacted by his or her relational history, and you must know this about each other at the beginning. You'll be creating your group's individual culture as you determine the guidelines that will keep everybody feeling safe and comfortable. These safety guidelines will differ from person to person and from group to group.

To ensure group safety, confidentiality is essential. Each member of the group is responsible to handle information in a safe and loving way. There are exceptions to confidentiality that pertain to the facilitator. (See the Facilitator's Guide for further discussion.) For group members, however, it's important to know that what's shared within the group stays within the group. During the first meeting, individual concerns about confidentiality must be shared. As an example, there will be times when a group participant hasn't disclosed to a spouse or significant partner that he or she has joined a support group. That participant then needs to share with the group how he or she would like this handled by the group members. It's the group's responsibility to protect each member of the group. This can only be done as each group member knows the needs of each participant, maintains strict confidentiality, and has agreed to an articulated set of guidelines for group safety.

Finally, all of you, have unity of mind, sympathy, brotherly love, a tender heart, and a humble mind.
(1 Peter 3:8 ESV)

Therefore encourage one another and build one another up.
(1 Thessalonians 5:11 ESV)

group guidelines

Listen Courageously

It's important to turn off cell phones and avoid all other distractions during sharing. One person at a time is to speak without interruption. Be discerning and prayerful about everything you say. During times when painful or intense emotions are being felt, it's often tempting to tell a joke to lighten the mood. This can shut down the group process and invalidate the person who is sharing. Listening isn't just valuable for others, it's a gift we give ourselves as we learn from each other. Listen in order to be changed by what you hear.

Don't Judge or "Fix"

Judging others and giving advice can be tempting during the group process. Every person is in a different place in their recovery and spiritual healing. Some participants will be spiritually mature and fairly emotionally healthy. Others will not be. When someone is given unsolicited advice or a look of disapproval, the group will not feel safe. God uses His Word and His Spirit to convict us individually of the steps we need to be taking toward maturity. Our job is to express the love and grace of Jesus so the group will be a place where others can be honest and feel safe doing so.

Accept people just as they are. If God has used something to help you in the past, it's natural to want to pass this information along. The best way to help someone else is to prayerfully consider what you want to say and then share it as a self-disclosure rather than a directive. For example, "Jill, when I was going through something similar, journaling really helped me" is more effective than, "Jill, you need to journal." Telling Jill what to do might elicit feelings of inferiority in her and places you as an authority over her. Love others and allow God's Spirit to be the one who convicts.

> Having purified your souls by your obedience to the truth for a sincere brotherly love, love one another earnestly from a pure heart.
> (1 Peter 1:22 ESV)

I remember not wanting to go to my group one night. I had a strong urge to stay home, but I went anyway. I remember sitting there listening to the others share, and God spoke to me through these people. Their feelings and thoughts were so similar to what I had been going through that week. I learned more from listening that night than I did by sharing. I was so thankful that I didn't stay home. I have come to believe it was Satan who wanted me to miss such a blessing.

group guidelines

Understand Projection

You might feel uncomfortable or tense around a particular group member—you just don't enjoy being around them. This may be the result of a common defense mechanism known as projection. When we project, we may be repulsed by a characteristic in another person that we find distasteful and are rejecting in ourselves, or perhaps they remind us of a difficult person in our lives. The best way to handle this is to journal. With God's help, writing can reveal the hidden things of the heart that we don't understand (Psalm 44:21). Choose to make this experience more about you than the other person, and allow God to uncover the deeper truths that you've been avoiding. If you need additional assistance with this problem, see your facilitator, pastor, or mentor.

Handle Hurt

Hurting people hurt people. Because of past pain, you may avoid conflict at all costs. Your small group is a safe place where you'll learn how to talk, feel, and deal with uncomfortable things in a direct and respectful way. When it functions well, a small group can replicate a type of healthy family: a group of people who are committed to each other and the group process, who really know each other, and who support each other through a healing journey. Conflict is a natural part of healthy relationships. Your facilitator will help you should any conflict arise.

Support Your Facilitator's Role

Your facilitator isn't a professional counselor. Instead, he or she is a person who has been through a MTS group before you. This person won't have all the answers you're searching for, but he or she can help and guide you along your healing journey. Expect your facilitator to keep the group focused. As problems arise, he or she will refer each participant back to the guidelines in order to maintain safe boundaries. You can best assist the facilitator by doing your part to create a safe environment (as described on page 28), praying for your facilitator, and respecting the facilitator's position of leadership.

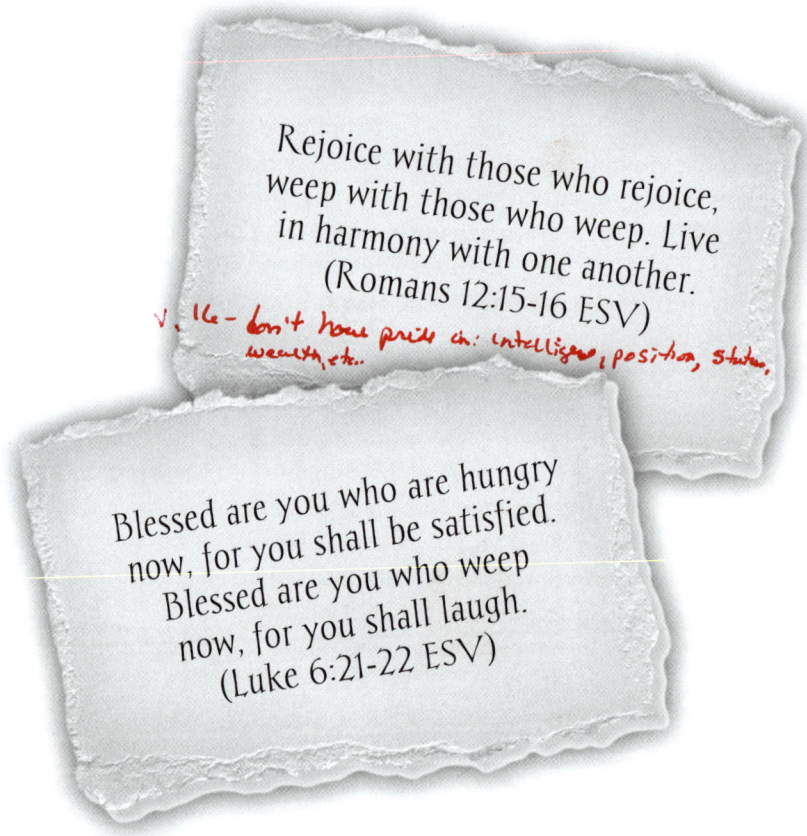

Rejoice with those who rejoice, weep with those who weep. Live in harmony with one another. (Romans 12:15-16 ESV)

Blessed are you who are hungry now, for you shall be satisfied. Blessed are you who weep now, for you shall laugh. (Luke 6:21-22 ESV)

group guidelines

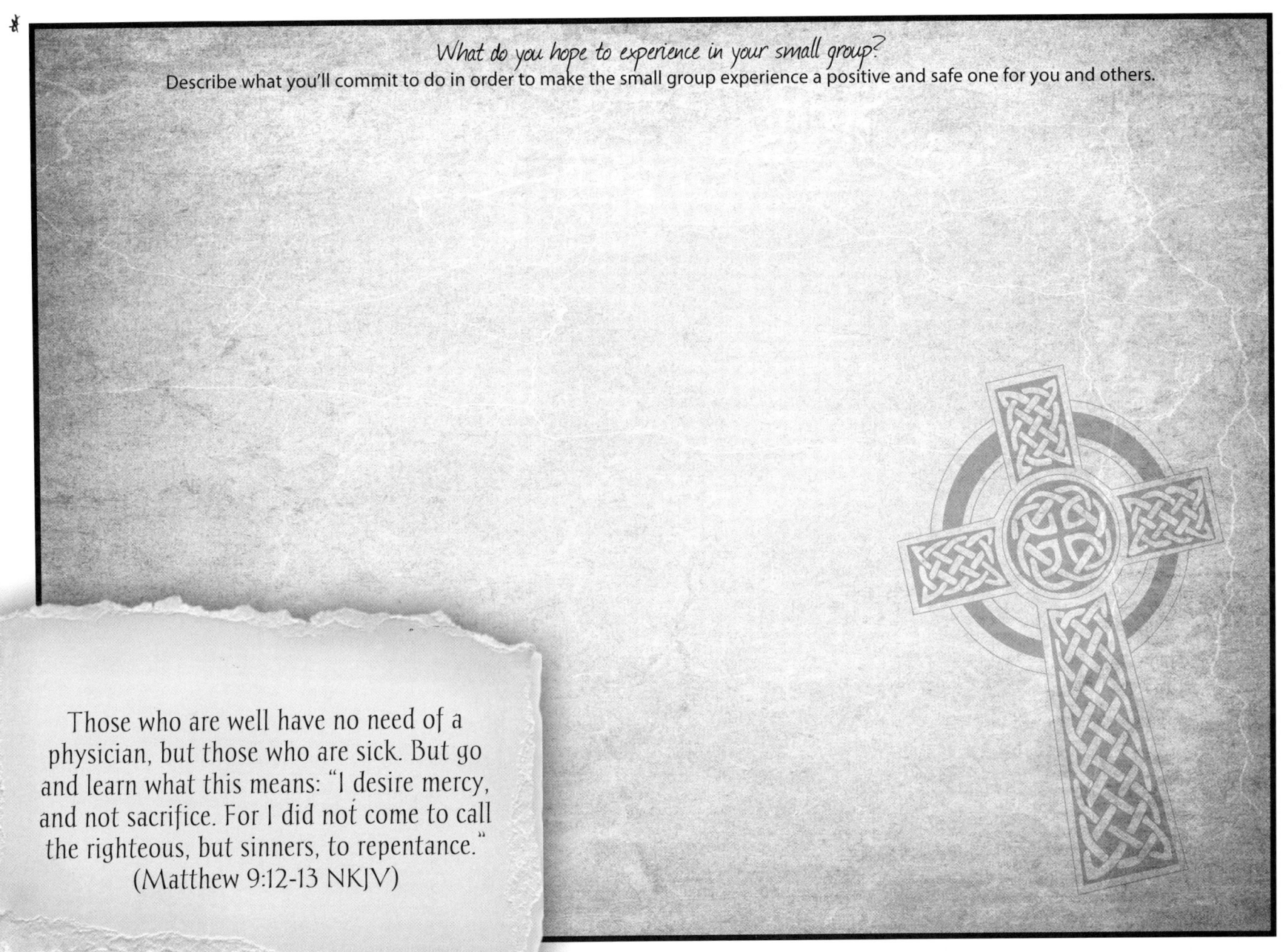

What do you hope to experience in your small group?
Describe what you'll commit to do in order to make the small group experience a positive and safe one for you and others.

Those who are well have no need of a physician, but those who are sick. But go and learn what this means: "I desire mercy, and not sacrifice. For I did not come to call the righteous, but sinners, to repentance."
(Matthew 9:12-13 NKJV)

group guidelines

My Safe Anchor

Draw, collage, or paste an image that reminds you of God's power and goodness to heal. This image will anchor your thoughts to the *truth* of who you are—and who He is—as you begin to work through your memories.

group guidelines

My thoughts and feelings. . .

Chapter One
Three Foundational Beliefs

If you extend your soul to the hungry and satisfy the afflicted soul, then your light shall dawn in the darkness, and your darkness shall be as the noonday. The Lord will guide you continually, and satisfy your soul in drought, and strengthen your bones; you shall be like a watered garden, and like a spring of water, whose waters do not fail. Those from among you shall build the old waste places; You shall raise up the foundations of many generations; and you shall be called the Repairer of the Breach, The Restorer of Streets to Dwell In. . . Then you shall delight yourself in the Lord; and I will cause you to ride on the high hills of the earth.
(Isaiah 58:10-12, 14 NKJV)

THE BEST PLACE TO BEGIN A HEALING JOURNEY IS WITH THE TRUTH ABOUT OUR LIVES.

In an effort to survive, most of us automatically hold on to the good of what we have experienced and bury the bad. God, in His foreknowledge of sin, gave psychological defenses to help us endure childhoods that too often include abuse and abandonment. These defenses function like switches that turn off memories of past events too painful to experience or events we were too powerless to control and too vulnerable to prevent. These defenses deny or minimize the severity of childhood pain and push it away from our conscious minds. God's word is explicitly clear regarding the importance of inner honesty: what we don't reveal can't be healed.

chapter one
My timeline

This is the beginning of your story. It is uniquely yours. You will be adding layers to it as you work through this book.

Birth

chapter one

Begin by placing upon the timeline below five to ten of the most significant events of your life.

Include the positive, life-giving experiences and also the painful secrets of your past. It will be difficult to even write these down, but this is an important first step in your healing. You may use words or sketch these memories with symbols or stick figures. Place the positive memories above the line and the painful memories below the line.

Present

chapter one

ABUSE IS RAMPANT

It's normal for those of us who have suffered deep pain to feel that we're alone or that we're different—that nobody else can understand what we've experienced. But while everyone's experience is unique, it's by no means true that you're alone in what you experience. Sadly, abuse is as old as mankind. Because of sin and its effects, there will always be neglect and abuse. Abuse occurs in all cultures and throughout all strata of society.

What are you feeling as you get to know others who can relate to your pain?

ABUSE IS PREDICTABLE

The Scriptures teach that people are totally depraved. All human beings are sinful from the moment of conception. King David, the same person that God described as *"a man after [His] own heart" (1 Samuel 13:14)*, had this to say about himself: *"Surely I was sinful at birth, sinful from the time my mother conceived me" (Psalm 51:5)*. The apostle Paul tells us that this is true of all humanity: *"Therefore, just as sin entered the world through one man [Adam], and death through sin, and in this way death came to all people because all sinned" (Romans 5:12)*.

In the Old Testament, Isaiah had this to say about mankind approximately seven hundred years before Christ: *"We all, like sheep, have gone astray, each of us has turned to our own way; and the Lord has laid on him the iniquity of us all" (Isaiah 53:6)*. Genesis 3 is the account of man's fall into sin, and in the very next chapter, the first murder occurs. A short three chapters after the fall, God had this to say about mankind: *"The Lord saw how great the wickedness of the human race had become on the earth, and that every inclination of the thoughts of the human heart was only evil all the time" (Genesis 6:5)*.

This means that all people have the potential to commit evil acts of cruelty. The doctrine of universal sin does not mean that all people are abusive, only that all of us are capable of being abusive.

chapter one

GOD IS OUR HEALING REDEEMER

You may be asking, *Where was God when this happened to me? Did He then or does He now care about the pain I experienced?* If you've had these or similar thoughts, let it be a comfort to know you're not alone. Often Christians believe that having such questions is ungodly or sinful. God, however, is not threatened by our questions or doubts. In fact, Scripture gives many examples of godly believers who've poured out their hurts, questions, and feelings to Him. Note, for instance, the way the following godly believers cried out to God:

> *Be merciful to me, O God, be merciful to me, for in you my soul takes refuge; in the shadow of your wings I will take refuge, till the storms of destruction pass by. I cry out to God Most High, to God who fulfills his purpose for me. He will send from heaven and save me; he will put to shame him who tramples on me. God will send out His steadfast love and his faithfulness! My soul is in the midst of lions; I lie down amid fiery beasts—the children of man, whose teeth are spears and arrows, whose tongues are sharp swords. Be exalted, O God, above the heavens! Let your glory be over all the earth!* (Psalm 57:1-5 ESV)

> *When he opened the fifth seal, I saw under the altar the souls of those who had been slain for the word of God and for the witness they had borne. They cried out with a loud voice, "O Sovereign Lord, holy and true, how long before you will judge and avenge our blood on those who dwell on the earth?"* (Revelation 6:9-10 ESV)

> *When the righteous cry for help, the Lord hears and delivers them out of all their troubles. The Lord is near to the brokenhearted and saves the crushed in spirit. Many are the afflictions of the righteous, but the Lord delivers him out of them all. He keeps all his bones; not one of them is broken. Affliction will slay the wicked, and those who hate the righteous will be condemned. The Lord redeems the life of his servants; none of those who take refuge in him will be condemned.* (Psalm 34:17-22 ESV)

> *As a deer pants for flowing streams, so pants my soul for You, O God. My soul thirsts for God, for the living God. When shall I come and appear before God? My tears have been my food day and night, while they say to me all the day long, "Where is your God?"* (Psalm 42:1-3 ESV)

Ps. 42:4,5 (notes)
1 Peter 1:7
James 1:12

I knew I would need someone to pray with me and be available by phone as I needed support. I was pretty scared to begin this process. My sponsor had been through a group herself, so she was a great comfort. She already knew what I was feeling.

chapter one

Within my earthly temple there's a crowd; there's one of us that's humble, one that's proud.
There's one that's broken-hearted for his sins, there's one that unrepentant sits and grins.
There's one that loves his neighbor as himself, and one that cares for naught but fame and self.
From much corroding care I should be free, if I could once determine which is me!

—Edward Sanford Martin, *My Name is Legion*

Rom. 7:15-21, 24-25 — not spiritual struggle before conversion but conflict between old and new.

In the space provided write a prayer to God that conveys your true feelings to Him about your abuse.
Be honest with Him. This is your starting place.

Healing Redeemer

chapter one

Sometimes it's hard to believe that God actually understands what we're going through. It can be even more difficult to believe that He cares for us and can actually empathize with us. God has revealed to us, however, through Scripture and through His Son that He is deeply moved by human suffering. In fact, one important implication of Jesus coming to earth and living and suffering in a human body is that He's experienced the pain of growing up in a broken world and has fully felt the effects of abuse. Right before His crucifixion His pain was so intense that He sweated droplets of blood.

> For we do not have a high priest
> who is unable to sympathize with our weaknesses,
> but one who in every respect has been tempted as
> we are, yet without sin. Let us then with confidence
> draw near to the throne of grace, that we may receive
> mercy and find grace to help in time of need.
> (Hebrews 4:15-16 ESV)

> He was despised and rejected by men;
> a man of sorrows, and acquainted with grief;
> and as one from whom men hide their faces
> he was despised, and we esteemed him not. Surely he
> has borne our griefs and carried our sorrows; yet we
> esteemed him stricken, smitten by God, and afflicted.
> (Isaiah 53:3-4 ESV)

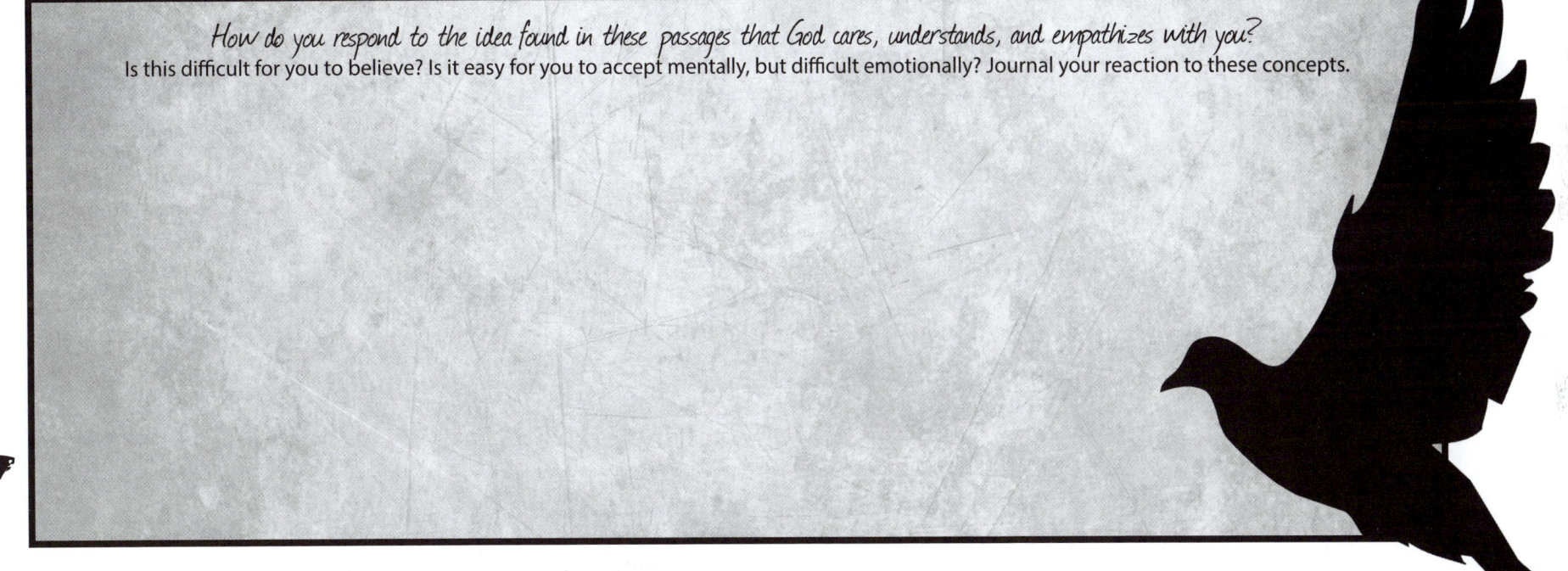

How do you respond to the idea found in these passages that God cares, understands, and empathizes with you? Is this difficult for you to believe? Is it easy for you to accept mentally, but difficult emotionally? Journal your reaction to these concepts.

chapter one

esp vs. 46-42

As you begin this healing journey, you may feel a sense of hopelessness—a sense that things will never improve or that you can never change. You may feel overwhelmed, scared, and alone. These feelings are normal. In truth, you're embarking on a difficult journey. However, there's hope. You're not alone. The Bible describes a God who is deeply committed to healing and redeeming the broken at the greatest cost to Himself (Exodus 2:23-25; 12:1-42; Romans 5:8). In fact, God is even more committed to your healing than you are! He desires to walk alongside you in this journey. He desires to be your helper. This offers tremendous hope to those who are willing to put their trust in Him and deal with Him honestly. *Christ, the Lamb of God, our Passover*

Not only does God desire your healing, it's His specialty. God delights in creating good out of evil and healing out of suffering. Not everything is good, but God has promised to work everything together for good (Romans 8:28). After Joseph had suffered many years of abuse because of his brothers, he could still say at the end of his life: *"You [my brothers], intended to harm me, but God intended it for good to accomplish what is now being done, the saving of many lives"* (Genesis 50:20).

On a scale of one to ten, rate your hope that things can change for you. Journal whatever doubts you have that God can bring about healing in your life.

My sense of hope: 1   2   3   4   5   6   7   8   9   10

When all the nation had finished passing over the Jordan, the Lord said to Joshua, "Take twelve men from the people, from each tribe a man, and command them, saying, 'Take twelve stones from here out of the midst of the Jordan, from the very place where the priests' feet stood firmly, and bring them over with you and lay them down in the place where you lodge tonight."

Then Joshua called the twelve men from the people of Israel, whom he had appointed, a man from each tribe. And Joshua said to them, "Pass on before the ark of the Lord your God into the midst of the Jordan, and take up each of you a stone upon his shoulder, according to the number of the tribes of the people of Israel, that this may be a sign among you.

When your children ask in time to come, 'What do those stones mean to you?' then you shall tell them that the waters of the Jordan were cut off before the ark of the covenant of the Lord. When it passed over the Jordan, the waters of the Jordan were cut off. So these stones shall be to the people of Israel a memorial forever.
(Joshua 4:1-7 ESV)

chapter one
stone of remembrance

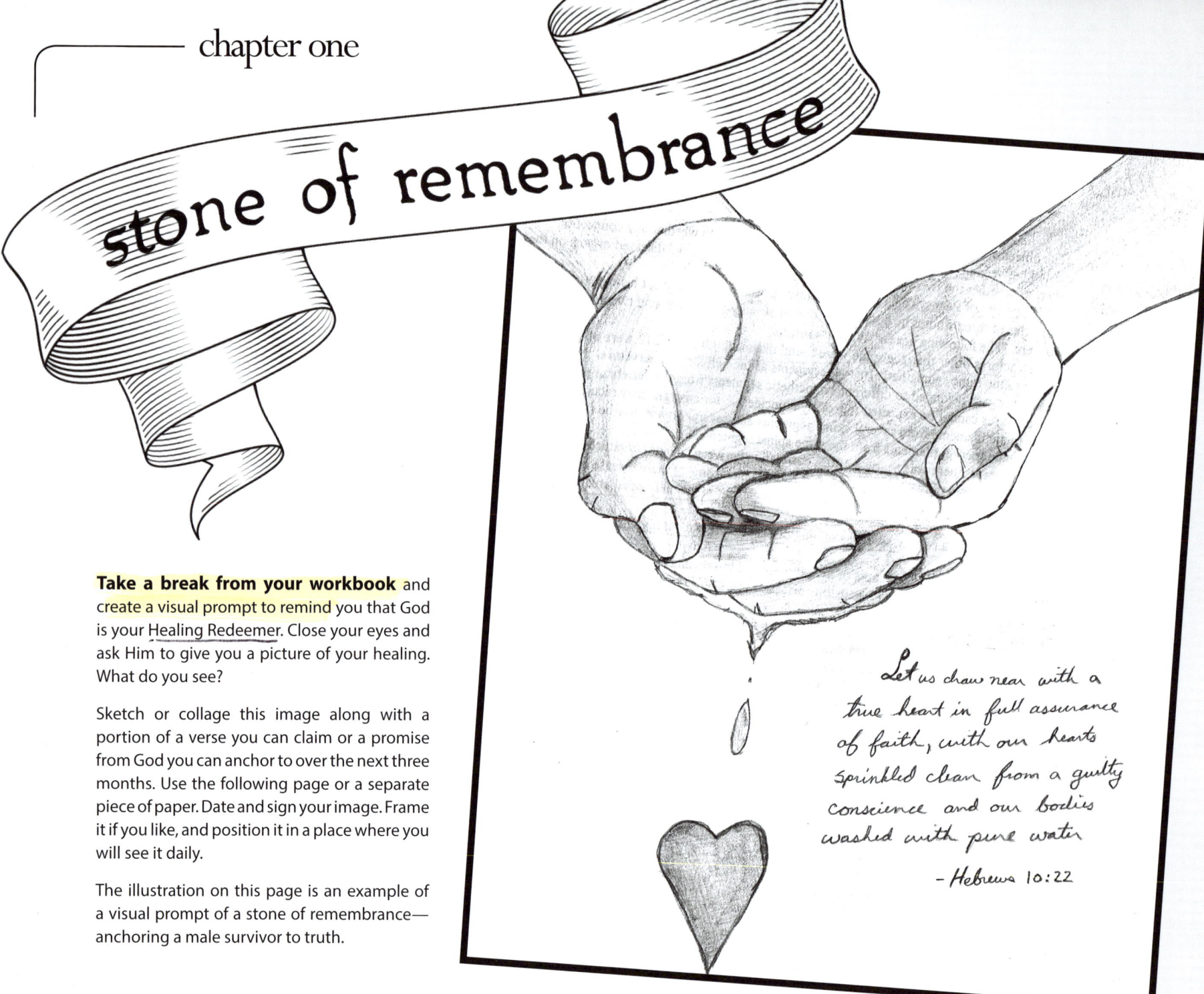

Take a break from your workbook and create a visual prompt to remind you that God is your Healing Redeemer. Close your eyes and ask Him to give you a picture of your healing. What do you see?

Sketch or collage this image along with a portion of a verse you can claim or a promise from God you can anchor to over the next three months. Use the following page or a separate piece of paper. Date and sign your image. Frame it if you like, and position it in a place where you will see it daily.

The illustration on this page is an example of a visual prompt of a stone of remembrance—anchoring a male survivor to truth.

Let us draw near with a true heart in full assurance of faith, with our hearts sprinkled clean from a guilty conscience and our bodies washed with pure water
— Hebrews 10:22

chapter one

My Stone of Remembrance

Chapter Two
What Is Abuse and Where Does It Come From?

In your relationships with one another, have the same mindset as Christ Jesus:

Who, being in very nature God, did not consider equality with God
something to be used to his own advantage; rather,
he made himself nothing by taking the very nature of a servant,
being made in human likeness. And being found in appearance as a man,
he humbled himself by becoming obedient to death—even death on a cross!

Therefore God exalted him to the highest place
and gave him the name that is above every name,
that at the name of Jesus every knee should bow,
in heaven and on earth and under the earth,
and every tongue acknowledge that Jesus Christ is Lord,
to the glory of God the Father.

Therefore, my dear friends. . . continue to work out your salvation with fear and trembling,
for it is God who works in you to will and to act in order to fulfill his good purpose.

Do everything without grumbling or arguing, so that you may become blameless and pure, "children of
God without fault in a warped and crooked generation." Then you will shine among them like
stars in the sky as you hold firmly to the word of life.
(Philippians 2:5-16)

chapter two

We must first understand the character of God before we can comprehend our own exquisite, original design. And in chapter two of *Mending the Soul*, Dr. Tracy states that we must know what it means to be created in the image of God before we can understand abuse and how it affects us. He writes,

> *The unpleasant truth is that abuse has profound, wildly irrational consequences. It tears the soul. The only way we can truly understand the effects of abuse is to clarify what it means to be a human being made in the image of God. To understand the devastating impact of abuse, we need to understand the manner in which abuse perverts the image of God in humans.*

Abuse profoundly mars our ability to see ourselves as God designed us: beings uniquely created in His image. Abuse is doubly damaging as it not only distorts our perception of ourselves but also distorts our perception of God our Creator. This incorrect view of God damages the intimacy He intended for us to enjoy with Him.

Once upon a time, I was a little girl.
I have seen pictures, torn and faded, so I believe it—mostly—
that I had shiny cheeks and sparkling eyes, that I delighted in
puppets with silly voices, and mussed my piggy tails as soon as
I escaped out the front door...

eternal spirit - capable of personal fellowship w/ our Creator
body -
soul - non-physical part of man   mental, physical, spiritual
spirit

> *How did the abuse you experienced make you feel about yourself?*
> Write down the messages that your abuser gave you about your worth.

chapter two

Paste here a picture of yourself as a young child.
What do you see in the picture that hints at your original, exquisite design in the image of God?

List at least ten characteristics of yourself that you can discern from this picture.

1._____

2._____

3._____

4._____

5._____

6._____

7._____

8._____

9._____

10._____

chapter two

GOD'S RELATIONAL IMAGE
WHY I DESIRE YET FEAR INTIMACY

Abusers distort the relational aspect of the image of God by distorting the nature of true intimacy, and one of the most common reactions to abuse is the fear or avoidance of intimacy. Before sin entered our perfect world, God described our built-in longings for human intimacy when He said, *"it is not good for the man to be alone"* (Genesis 2:18). Our desire for close relationships reflects God's image in us and thus isn't sinful or selfish. In the beginning of creation, Adam and Eve experienced this perfect intimacy, with God and each other. The Genesis account describes their closeness by declaring that *"Adam and his wife were both naked, and they felt no shame"* (Genesis 2:25). This is one of the most beautiful descriptions of soul-satisfying human intimacy in all of Scripture. Tragically, this relational intimacy was shattered as described in the very next paragraph of Genesis, when Adam and Eve sinned. While all sin creates shame and hiding, abuse victims experience some of the greatest amounts of shame and isolation. However, unlike Adam and Eve who felt shame for their own sin, abuse victims feel shame for another's sin. The shame from abuse often creates social isolation. Abuse survivors find it difficult to trust others and may have some superficial friendships while keeping the most significant members of their family at arm's length. In this and other ways, the relational aspect of the image of God is distorted.

How has your abuse affected your relationships?
Rate the intimacy level of your significant relationships on a scale of one to ten.

| 1 | 2 | 3 | 4 | 5 | 6 | 7 | 8 | 9 | 10 |

"No one really knows who I am!"   "My close friends sort of know me."   "My close friends totally know me, and I feel safe with that."

Then the eyes of both were opened, and they knew that they were naked. And they sewed fig leaves together and made themselves loincloths. And they heard the sound of the Lord God walking in the garden in the cool of the day, and the man and his wife hid themselves from the presence of the Lord God among the trees of the garden.
(Genesis 3:7-8 ESV)

chapter two

Can I Be Naked?

Can I be naked? Could we take it? Could we stand the rift,
If you knew what it meant to be me? Baby, can I be naked?

If I were to stand before you naked, and you saw each curve, dip, and wrinkle
Each dimple, pimple, hair, and crinkle
Would you still love me? Would you still love me?

If I stood before you naked, with my war scars bared, with my stretch marks
And that which was once rich and dark having been faired
Would you make love to me? Would you make love to me?

If I were to stand before you naked, with my heart on my sleeve
Wearing nothing but a list of my bereaved
Vulnerable to you and a contradiction to all you have conceived and believed
Would you cover me? Would you cover me?

If I stood before you naked, all my conscience bared,
With my thoughts, ambitions, and prejudices with their ugly heads reared
And you saw for all my bravado that I am just a little child scared,
Would you still care for me? Would you still care for me?

If I were to stand before you naked, with no secrets and no lies
If you could see my soul and marry my spirit by the meeting of our eyes
Would you shield me? Would you shield me?

If I stood before you naked, all my disguises removed,
Stripped of my circumlocution and could only tell the truth
If this were my fate, if in my haste, I am subject to wait
If my emotions are real and every casual word I am doomed to feel,
Would you protect me? Would you protect me? Can I be naked?

—Therosia

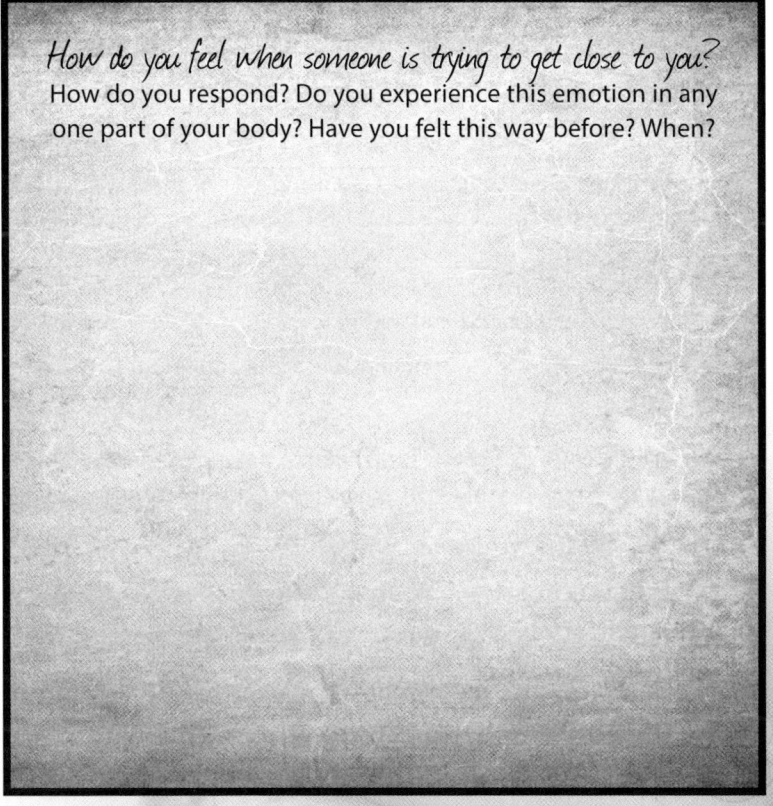

How do you feel when someone is trying to get close to you? How do you respond? Do you experience this emotion in any one part of your body? Have you felt this way before? When?

chapter two

GOD'S ORIGINAL RELATIONAL DESIGN
SECURE ATTACHMENTS

When you were born God pre-programmed you to bond with one significant person: your first primary caregiver—probably your mother. Ideally, this was your first interactive love relationship. This mother-child attachment bond shaped your developing brain and influenced your self-esteem, relational expectations, and your ability to attract and maintain successful relationships. As an infant you couldn't reason, plan, or speak; therefore, you were completely dependent upon nonverbal communication to get your needs met. An attuned caregiver understood your nonverbal signals and consistently responded to your cries, meeting your physical and emotional needs. This first bond determined how you would relate to other people throughout your life, because it established the foundation for all future verbal and nonverbal communication.

Conversely, if you grew up experiencing confusing, neglectful, frightening, or otherwise broken emotional interactions throughout your first five years, you probably grew into adulthood experiencing difficulties understanding, expressing, and containing your feelings in relationship with others. There can be many causes for disrupted early attachments such as physical neglect; emotional neglect or abuse; a young or inexperienced mother; a depressed mother; a family member who struggled with addiction; frequent moves or placements; an inconsistent caregiver; a separation from the primary caregiver due to death, divorce, adoption, illness, etc. Any one of these can produce unhealthy, insecure relational patterns in adulthood such as avoidance, self-focus, emotional distance, fierce independence, anxiousness, fearfulness, insensitivity, developmental delays, learning disabilities, etc.

Because all successful adult relationships depend upon nonverbal forms of communication, these early broken attachments must be "repaired" in later relationships. (See *Forever and Always: The Art of Intimacy* by Tracy and Tracy for a couples' template for forming emotional bonds.) Once we recognize and understand how our first interactive relationships were disrupted, we can begin to reconstruct new connections through healthy nonverbal and verbal communication skills that will produce attuned attachments and satisfying adult relationships today—relationships that are full of safe nurturing touch, emotional connections, play, focused attention, and laughter.

He was so good at illness, a whole disorder has been named for him, Munchausen's syndrome, otherwise called factitious illness, the patient faking not for money but for things beyond weight, beyond measure . . .
Perhaps I was, and still am, a pretender,
a person who creates illnesses because she needs time, attention, touch, because she knows no other way
of telling her life's tale.

—L. Slater, *Lying*

chapter two

My bedroom was small and cold. There was a hole in the window, and the night air always seeped in. Those thin walls knew so many secrets: the good, the bad, the ugly. They cried with me and watched with glee as my heart was restored by the affections of my Father—both God and my physical father. My dad worked at the church as a youth pastor and commuted over a hundred miles to Bible college many days of the week. He left before dawn, whizzing away in his tiny blue hatchback before my eyes ever saw the light of day. I can hear him stirring in the kitchen; the "clink, clink, clink" of cereal hitting a bowl. I can hear him humming "Jesus Freak" and picking up his keys delicately as not to wake us. I still remember feeling his goatee on my forehead. He would come in my room and kiss me before he left for school. He thought I was asleep. Little does he know that his whiskers had touched the very inside of my soul and remain forever etched there like a handprint in a concrete slab.

Houses hold us, and all that is dear in our worlds. I slipped in, and felt the walls curve to cup me, and smelled roasted chicken and other just general living odors, sweat and steel wool pads leaving swaths of blue soap that are beautiful. A home has many purposes, but it should primarily be a place where you can cry and run a good fever.

—L. Slater, *Lying*

My closest or most bonded relationship is...

chapter two

In the space below, describe your relational pattern during different stages of your life. Did you seek out relationships, or did you wait for people to pursue you? Did you avoid relationships? Did you keep your relationships shallow, or did you attempt to get close to people? If you can remember your approach to relationships before the abuse, pay particularly close attention to that stage of life. How did you change after the abuse began?

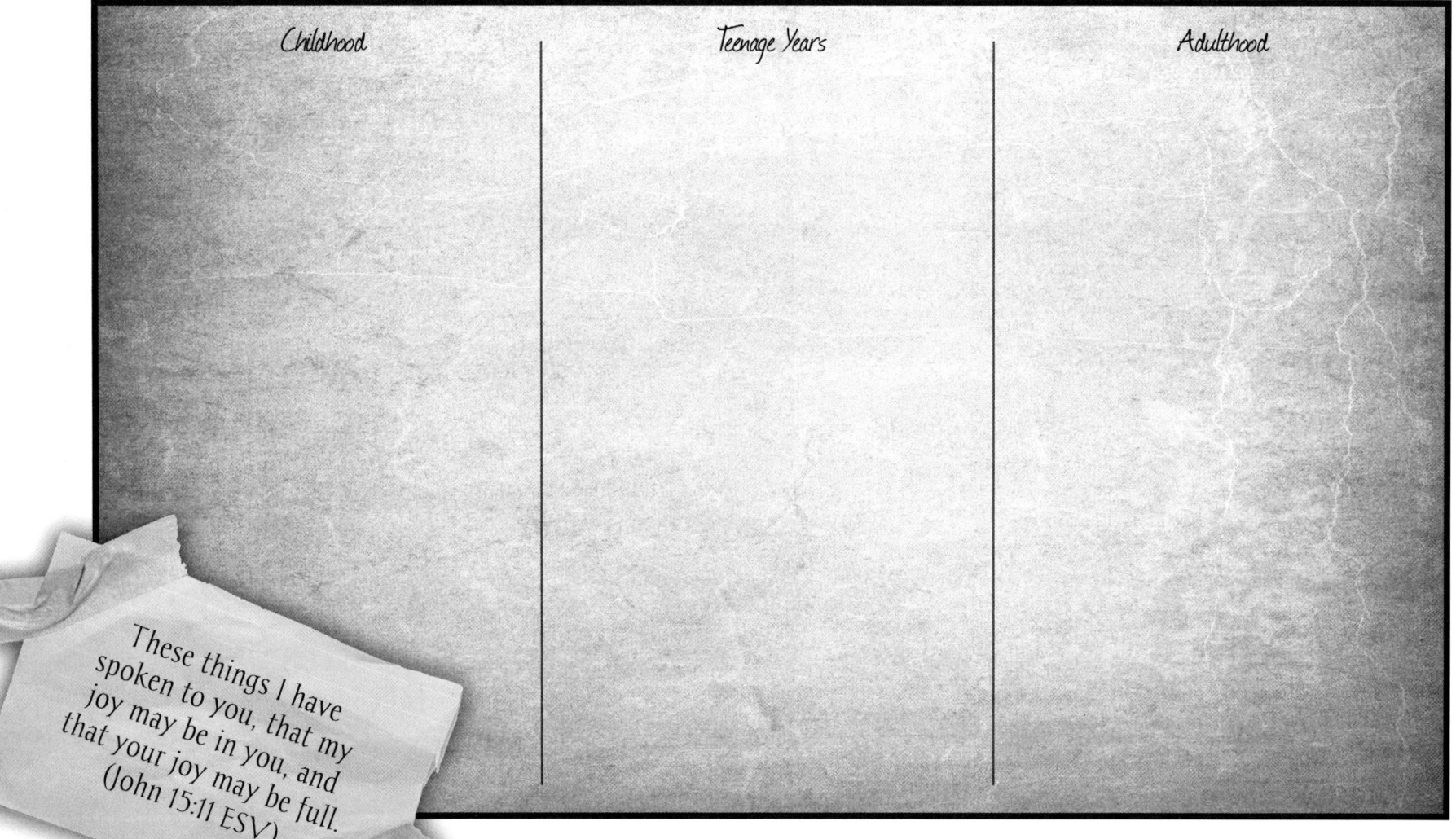

Childhood	Teenage Years	Adulthood

> These things I have spoken to you, that my joy may be in you, and that your joy may be full. (John 15:11 ESV)

GOD'S VISIBLE IMAGE
LOVE DISTORTED

We're meant to display the characteristics of God to each other in relationship. God intends for us to see Him in each other by the way that we live our lives and relate to others. Abusers distort the visible aspect of the image of God by demonstrating character qualities to their victims that are quite the opposite of God's qualities. It's so sad when children, who are looking to receive good things from their parents or adult authority figures, instead receive the evil of abuse. Survivors of abuse all too often have seen the image of Satan rather than God in the destructive behavior of their abusers.

The many forms of abuse represent a sad perversion of the God-given roles within the family and the church. Fathers, who are not to "exasperate [their] children; instead, bring them up in the training and instruction of the Lord" (Ephesians 6:4), are too often the primary source of their children's anger. Husbands, who are supposed to "love [their] wives, just as Christ loved the church and gave himself up for her" (Ephesians 5:25), too often physically and verbally abuse their wives. Mothers, who are supposed to nurture their children, sometimes do great damage to them through hurtful words or through neglect of their needs. Pastors and church leaders, who are supposed to "be shepherds of God's flock . . . not because [they] must, but because [they] are willing, as God wants [them] to be. . . not lording it over those intrusted to [them], but being examples to the flock" (1 Peter 5:2-3), sometimes use their spiritual authority not to mirror Jesus but to instead manipulate, shame, and dominate those in their care. Sadly, we sometimes look to our relationships to see something of God, and to our surprise see sin instead. This can have disastrous effects on our ability to trust people.

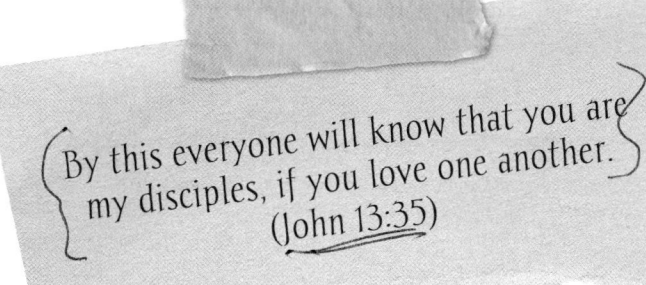

By this everyone will know that you are my disciples, if you love one another.
(John 13:35)

chapter two

Violation

Violation, a touch unbidden,
Forced down with hard hands—angry, white hands.
I was never asked. I had no say.
I had no chance.

The hands push harder
So nothing in me pushes back
My fight turns inward,
Raging deeply, unseen unceasing.

Even now the fight wells up
Unbidden from within,
Pulled to the surface with white hands

I remember it all, yet startlingly little of it.
It is as if my heart went white,
Somehow snow blind, lost in drifts of blizzard,
Just like that, lost to whiteness.

Webbing voices, sounds, mostly sounds,
All dark and breathing
Calm of the lake outside,
Warm breath of breeze in the summer leaves.
Juxtaposition of violence and peace.
Hellish, touching raw.

—Anonymous

chapter two

Write down your view of God that was shaped as a result of the things your abuser said and did. What role did the abuse and abuser play in creating this view? Don't be afraid of what God will think. First, He already knows your deepest beliefs about Him, and second, He is compassionately aware of the abuse that has created the distortions. It's essential that you take accurate stock of your feelings, thoughts, and beliefs so that you can trace their roots. This will enable you to see how your beliefs are connected to your abuse and why those beliefs are actually lies fed to you by your abuser and by Satan. In time you'll be able to use biblical truth to challenge and correct your faulty beliefs.

Identify someone in your life who was kind to you, tried to protect you, or did good for you in some way.
Write what you learned from that person about who God is.

My friend's dad always looked at me as though I mattered. He listened to me and seemed to take me seriously. He's embedded in my memory as a good man.

GOD'S FUNCTIONAL IMAGE
NURTURE EXCHANGED FOR DOMINATION

In describing the effects of sin on the human race, God said to Eve, "Your desire will be for your husband, and he will [harshly] rule over you" (Genesis 3:16). Abusers distort the functional aspect of the image of God by using their "authority" to dominate rather than nurture—to selfishly take instead of to lovingly serve. This can occur in the context of husband-wife, parent-child, pastor-parishioner, or any other relationship where there exists an inequality of power or authority. It's understandable that survivors of abuse commonly either fear authority figures (by developing a highly pleasing personality) or feel a strong need to be in control and so rebel against them.

Due to our distorted concept of authority and power, we must observe how God exercises His authority over His creation. We must look to Scripture and see what Jesus said regarding these things. What feelings have you developed about authority and submission? When you hear the word "authority," what do you think and feel?

> [Jesus] said, "You've observed how godless rulers throw their weight around, how quickly a little power goes to their heads. It's not going to be that way with you. Whoever wants to be great must become a servant. Whoever wants to be first among you must be your slave. That is what the Son of Man has done: He came to serve, not be served—and then to give away his life in exchange for the many who are held hostage."
> (Matthew 20:25-28 The Message)

chapter two

Must go to Scripture, to see how God expects authority & power to be used.

Has authority been abused in your life? How?

Based on the actions of the person who misused his or her power, what can you infer about their understanding of authority and submission?

chapter two

Draw a picture of your family of origin.

chapter two

As children, we naturally believe our childhood experiences are normal and therefore learn to define love by what we feel and see. The relational patterns (both good and bad) that we experience and observe become embedded within our personalities. These perceptions later influence our behavior in relationships. It's crucial that we examine these deeply embedded distortions in order to experience real intimacy with God and others. As you reflect upon your drawing on the previous page, respond to the following questions:

Did you feel seen or heard?

Were you given permission to communicate hurt?

How was anger communicated?

Who comforted you?

What did you see modeled between your father and mother?

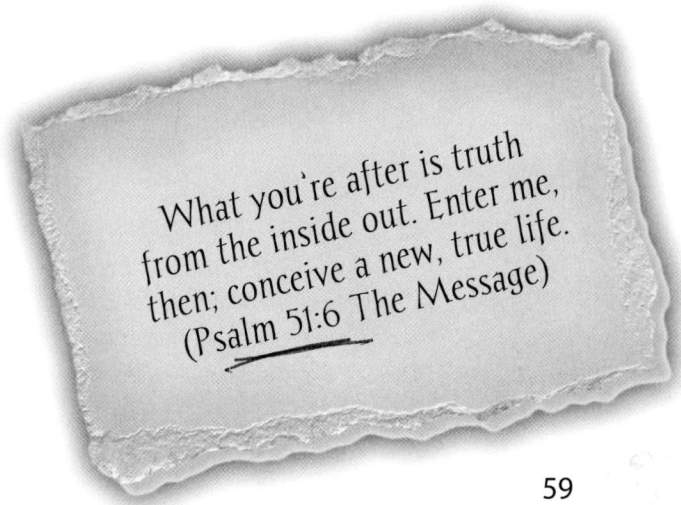

What you're after is truth from the inside out. Enter me, then; conceive a new, true life. (Psalm 51:6 The Message)

chapter two

SIX ABUSES THAT WARP THE LIKENESS OF GOD IN US

All abuse and neglect distorts the image of God in us, which is why it's so damaging. Because abuse is so disturbing it's often minimized or denied, hence clear definitions are critical. On the following pages are brief descriptions of six kinds of abuse: verbal and emotional abuse, physical abuse, neglect, spiritual or religious abuse, sexual abuse, and narcissistic systems. (For a much fuller discussion, see chapter two of *Mending the Soul*.) As you read the descriptions of abuse on the following three pages, highlight the portion of the description with which you identify. As you work through the remaining portion of this chapter, you need only complete the exercises within the sections of abuse that pertain to you.

I Hurt

I hurt beyond words as I speak my truth.
I have been molested. I have been raped.
I have been abandoned. I have been violated.
I have been betrayed. Something inside of me bleeds
Still wringing out new pain from old wounds.

Fresh cut, fresh bruise, fresh wound.
There is no shifting from past to present.
It feels all one, a hollowing out of flesh.
Scraping, always from the inside out,
As if some strange gourd,
cleaned out for second carving.

I have been molested. I have been raped.
I have been abandoned. I have been violated.
I have been betrayed.

My truth is another stabbing, another shattering,
Another subtle tethering from past to present.
I sense longing deeply
To be cut loose this once,
So healing can come.

chapter two

Give it a Name...

If your pain remains undefined, it's much easier to deny what happened to you, which makes it difficult to heal. But if you can name the problem, you can take steps to overcome it. Comparing your relational experiences to God's original design for you is the only way you can expose distortions within your belief system about God, others, and yourself. *As you read the descriptions, highlight any phrases you identify with.*

Verbal/Emotional Abuse

Verbal/emotional abuse is made up of a series of incidents that occur over time. Emotional abuse is much more than just verbal insults. Instead, it's characterized by repeated incidents—whether intentional or not—where a person is insulted, degraded, humiliated, threatened, isolated, deceived, or controlled. Verbal abuse is "a form of emotional maltreatment in which words are systematically used to belittle, undermine, scapegoat, or maliciously manipulate another person (*Mending the Soul*, 34). Scripture tells us that our words are extremely powerful and can give life or tear down (Proverbs 18:21). In a figurative sense, verbal/emotional abuse is a distortion of the command to "be fruitful" (Genesis 1:28), for our words are to give life—not destroy (James 3:5-9). Emotional abusers systematically weaken their victims in order to gain control and strengthen themselves. They seek to destroy what matters most to their victims (pet, work, appearance, family, friends, etc.). In summary, relational pain is created when one person seeks to maintain control of another through power posturing, verbal attacks, deceit, over-dependency, abandonment, or threats of abandonment.

Physical Abuse or Domestic Violence

Physical abuse is called *domestic violence* when someone causes—or attempts to cause—bodily injury to a family member or to someone who lives in his or her household. It's also considered domestic violence when the abuser doesn't injure his or her victims but instead asserts control with threats of imminent physical harm. It involves the occurrence of any of the following:

- Causing or attempting to cause physical or mental harm to a family or household member
- Placing a family or household member in fear of physical or mental harm
- Causing or attempting to cause a family or household member to engage in involuntary sexual activity by force, threat of force, or duress
- Engaging in activity toward a family or household member that would cause a reasonable person to feel terrorized, frightened, intimidated, threatened, harassed, or molested

Most common are sexual assault, assault or battery, physical harm or serious injury, threats of harm, harassment, stalking, trespassing, damage to property, kidnapping, and unlawful restraint. These definitions are much broader than most people realize, because they involve the act of violence and the psychological torture involved in threats of harm. Physical abuse perverts the God-ordained responsibility for humans to care for God's creation (Genesis 1:26-28). It also perverts God's mandate for parents and spouses to nurture, protect, and love vulnerable family members (Ephesians 5:22-30; 6:1-4; Colossians 3:18-21).

chapter two

Neglect

Neglect is "the failure of a parent or guardian to provide a minor with adequate food, clothing, medical care, protection, supervision and emotional support" (*Mending the Soul*, 30). *Neglect is the most frequently reported form of child abuse (60% of all cases) and also the most lethal.* Neglect is the failure to provide for the shelter, safety, supervision, and nutritional needs of a child. Child neglect may be physical, educational, or emotional: Physical neglect includes refusal of or delay in seeking health care, abandonment, expulsion from the home or refusal to allow a runaway to return home, and inadequate supervision. Educational neglect includes allowing chronic truancy, failing to enroll a child of mandatory school age in school, and failing to attend to a special educational need. Emotional neglect includes such actions as marked inattention to the child's needs for affection, refusal of or failure to provide needed psychological care, spouse abuse in the child's presence, and permission of drug or alcohol use by the child. As with physical abuse, neglect is a perversion of the functional aspect of the image of God's creation; this is especially true when a parent neglects his or her own child (Genesis 1:26-30; 1 Timothy 5:8).

Spiritual or Religious Abuse

Spiritual abuse is an "inappropriate use of spiritual authority" such as the Bible or church tradition in order to "force a person to do that which is unhealthy." Spiritual abuse typically involves a "forceful or manipulative denial of that person's feelings and convictions" for the self-advancement of the abusive spiritual leader (*Mending the Soul*, 32). Jesus explicitly condemns this in Matthew 23, when he indicts the Pharisees for the hypocritical misuse of their authority. In addition to power posturing, spiritual abuse involves performance preoccupation, unspoken rules, layers of legalism (seeking to earn God's favor and forgiveness on the basis of rigid rule-keeping), and rigid fundamentalism (harsh and unfair scrutiny of others in light of a strict standard that the one judging does not live up to). Spiritual abuse is typically experienced with other forms of abuse, and often produces the highest levels of toxic shame.

Sexual Abuse

Child sexual abuse is defined as "the exploitation of a minor for the sexual gratification of another person through sexual contact or sexual interaction" (*Mending the Soul*, 27). With adults or children, there are three interrelated factors that distinguish sexually abusive acts from non-abusive acts (the presence of any one of these factors raises concerns that the sexual interaction was abusive): power differential, knowledge differential, and gratification differential. Sexual abuse covers a much broader spectrum than most people realize. It's not merely unwanted intercourse but is any exploitative sexual contact (groping or sexual touching over one's clothes, fondling one's genitals, etc.) or interaction (photographing a nude child for one's own sexual purposes, exposing a child to pornography, discussing explicit sexual activity with a minor for one's own sexual gratification, etc.). Furthermore, when adults place children in adult roles they're not mature enough to assume, such as confidant or caregiver, it often results in symptoms similar to those of victims of direct contact sexual abuse. (These differentials will be explained later in this chapter.) Adults can also sexually abuse other adults by demanding unwanted or bizarre sexual acts, physically attacking sexual body parts, treating another as a sex object, waking a spouse for sex on demand, and other related actions. Sexual abuse in marriage is a gross distortion of the beautiful, God-ordained "one flesh" sexual union God intended between a husband and a wife (Genesis 2:24).

Self-love

Narcissistic Families: The Other Kind of Pain

Narcissistic families are emotionally neglectful and often appear "perfect" from the outside. These families operate according to an unspoken set of rules that block children's access to their parents while allowing the parent(s) to mistreat, neglect, or abuse the children at will. Children from these families feel invisible—not seen, heard, or nurtured. Adult children of narcissists have many symptoms of neglect and emotional abuse but have difficulty identifying the deeper cause of their pain. Narcissistic families effectively hide their pain, thus making it more difficult to acknowledge or understand.

My thoughts and feelings...

Wheel Of Abuse

Shade in the areas on the wheel that describe a form of abuse you have experienced or are currently experiencing.

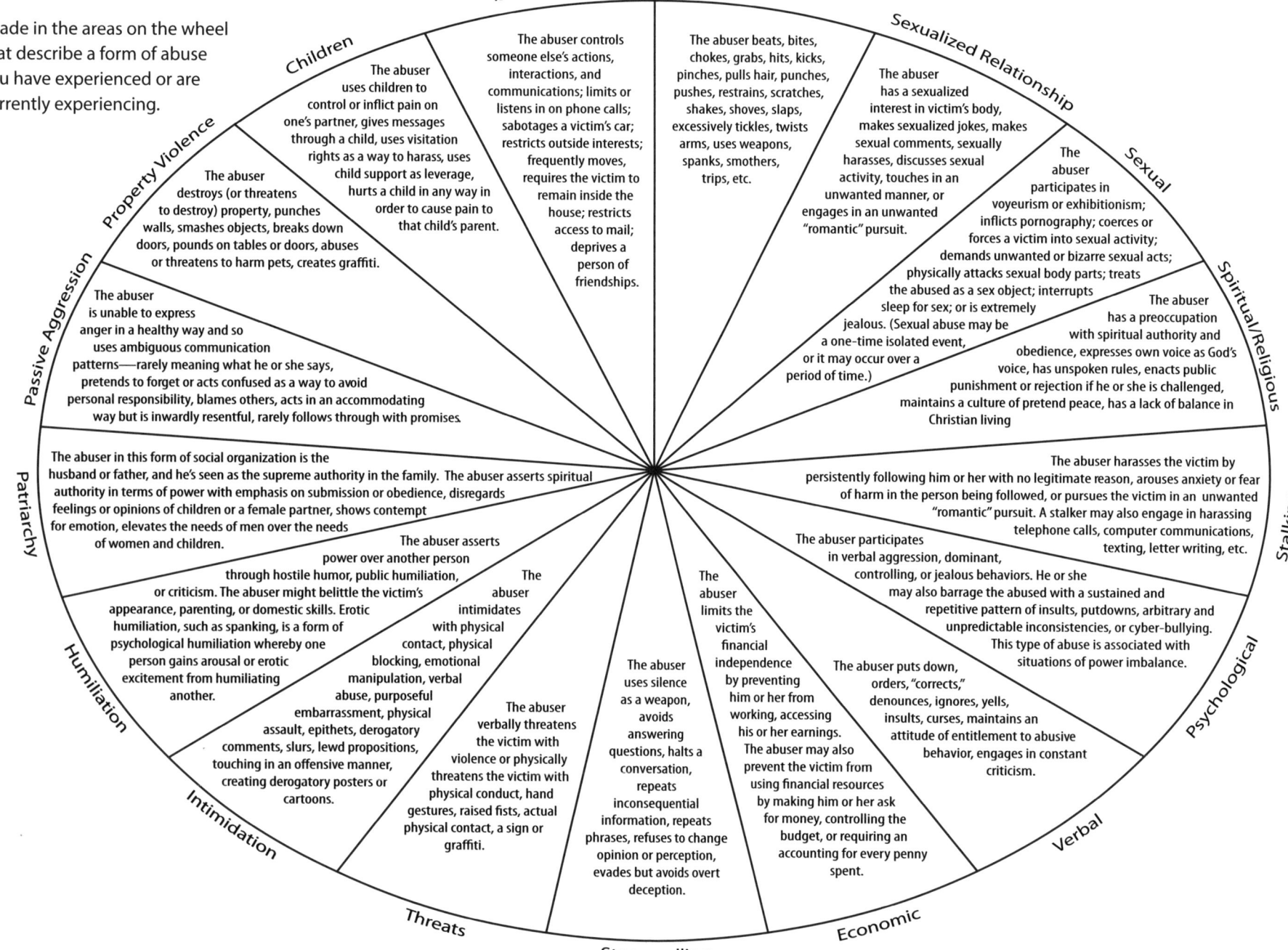

chapter two

I feel like our peaceful home is being infiltrated by evil from the scorpion house.

This scorpion house was drawn by a single mom who was trying to protect her two little girls from the poison of her ex-husband. Even though they were divorced and she didn't live with him, his verbal and emotional abuse—communicated over the phone and via email—was making her physically sick and was also creating symptoms of trauma in her girls. Like the scorpion, his "venom" was invisible, yet lethal. His words, rages, and attempts to control were like the poison of the scorpion's sting. He was out of the house and yet, through his tongue, just as with the tail of the scorpion, he stung again and again—in an attempt to destroy his victims. After drawing this scorpion house, the young mother recognized her need to establish emotional safety for herself and her girls, and she began to set bigger boundaries to limit his psychological control. Today she is happily married to a man who loves and cherishes her. She found healing, and you can too.

chapter two

A FURTHER EXPLORATION

The following exercises will probably be the most difficult in this workbook, but they can also be the most helpful as they guide you through the "truth-telling" process. Before proceeding, reflect on your pace of recovery. For some people, it's overwhelming to think of multiple abusers at one time, and it's most helpful to do this chapter with one person in mind at a time. At a later date, you may go back through this chapter and focus on another relationship where you've experienced deep pain. For others, it feels best to think of the whole of their life and what they've experienced, even if they're processing the damage done by several people. You set the pace for your healing. We're all different—you know best what will be most helpful for you at this time.

Verbal/Emotional Abuse

Emotional abuse can be one of the more damaging forms of abuse because of its subjective and often subtle nature. Words can strike to the very core of who we are with force for either good or evil. Just as with God's words by which worlds were made, our words carry great power, which can be wielded destructively to cause feelings of worthlessness, isolation, and hatred in others. The temptation is to minimize verbal abuse because it creates no physical pain and leaves no physical scars. The thought is, "If there are no bruises, it wasn't abuse." However nothing could be further from the truth. Therefore, the first step in dealing with verbal abuse is to recognize it for what it is.

I experienced ___*verbal*___ abuse when _____ said _____
                                          Name of Abuser(s)   Detailed form of Verbal Abuse

How did writing this sentence make you feel? Include both positive and negative feelings.

Reflect on the ways you have experienced verbal abuse. For example, was it directed at your intellect, such as, "You are stupid?" Was it directed at you physically, such as, "You are ugly," etc.? Record some of the specific things you recall being said to you.

Reflect on the ways you responded to verbal abuse. What beliefs about yourself or others did you develop as a result of those messages? Can you recognize ways that those beliefs affected your behavior, your relationships, etc.?

How have these messages shaped your behavior?

chapter two

Physical Abuse or Domestic Violence

Physical abuse can come in the form of child or domestic abuse and is the injury or destruction of what should have been nurtured, sustained, and enhanced. God has created us with longings for love, nurture, and protection—so physical abuse is especially damaging. Love and affection is given and received through relational vulnerability, thus making the betrayal of a family member that harms instead of helping that much more destructive. As a result of this betrayal, survivors often commit to never be vulnerable to anyone again—closing themselves off from love and intimacy.

Identify which type(s) of physical abuse you have experienced or are experiencing.

- ☐ Threats
- ☐ Shoves
- ☐ Pinches
- ☐ Slaps
- ☐ Scratches
- ☐ Punches
- ☐ Bites
- ☐ Kicks
- ☐ Hair pulling
- ☐ Being shaken
- ☐ Being grabbed
- ☐ Being thrown against a wall
- ☐ Being choked
- ☐ Being tied up
- ☐ Being cut
- ☐ Being stuck with pins
- ☐ Being stepped on

- ☐ Being poked
- ☐ Being burned
- ☐ Being locked in a room or car
- ☐ Being pushed from a car
- ☐ Being held at knifepoint
- ☐ Loaded gun pointed at you
- ☐ Unloaded gun pointed at you
- ☐ Harmful substances thrown
- ☐ Deprived of food or drink
- ☐ Deprived of sleep
- ☐ Denied medical treatment
- ☐ Poisoning
- ☐ Drugging
- ☐ Humiliation
- ☐ Causing to be naked
- ☐ Attempting to drown
- ☐ Being suffocated

- ☐ Harm of pets
- ☐ Destruction of property
- ☐ Assault with inanimate objects
- ☐ Assault with deadly weapons
- ☐ Stalking
- ☐ Intimidation
- ☐ Emotional abuse
- ☐ Other _____
- ☐ Other _____
- ☐ Other _____

I experienced _*physical*_ abuse when _____ did _____
  Name of Abuser(s)   Type of Abuse

We are broken ones,
all. With smudged
cheeks and
ravaged hearts.

We are longing ones,
all. Straining for love
and wholeness.

We are human and
hurting, all. Our
destiny, tied up
in bundles of pain,
We long for release,
for our kindness
deserved,
for endless sky.

We are humans,
all, too.

chapter two

How did you feel when writing about physical abuse?
What fears did you have as you put your abuse into words?
Were there any positive feelings?

Conviction = the state of being convinced of error or compelled to admit the truth

If you're feeling convicted of past abuse that you've committed against another, allow this feeling to come. Use it to push you towards confession and repentance. This is God's *only* remedy for a guilty conscience. The feeling of legitimate guilt is His gift to you so that you will take Him up on His offer to "cleanse you from all sin" and make you righteous (in right standing) in His sight. Be honest and record your prayer—make it right with God. Then, make things right with others.

chapter two

Neglect

Neglect is abusive because it results in confusion, loss of trust in others, and difficulty trusting one's own perceptions. When a parent fails to provide for the needs of his or her child, the child inevitably begins to doubt whether his or her needs are valid. This can lead victims to despise their desires or to feel that they're not worthy of having their needs met. Survivors of neglect are thus forced into a cruel emotional dilemma: either my caretaker is evil for failing to meet my needs (which is a reality that can be nearly impossible for a child to face), or I'm bad for desiring anything. Often children will view themselves as selfish rather than label the caregiver as abusively neglectful. All the while, Scripture says that these neglectful abusers are "worse than an unbeliever" (1 Timothy 5:8).

> *The most serious finding of the last ten years concerning the effects of trauma is that neglect appears to be the most pervasive and persistent form of it when considering implications with a lifelong trajectory. Neglect affects every aspect of the developing neurological system. (Ziegler, Traumatic Experience and the Brain)*

If you've suffered neglect from a caregiver, you'll need to work especially hard at identifying the things that happened to you (or didn't happen in this case) as abusive. Your longings and desires to have the affection, acceptance, and protection of your caregivers were good. They are God-given. However, you may just be starting to see them that way. Ziegler concludes:

> *Neglect over-develops neural networks related to survival (as does abuse and/or trauma), the brain's prime directive. Lack of response to any basic need initiates responses in the lower, more primitive regions of the brain that first develop in the child. These responses are either over-activation (the fight response) or under-activation (the flight response, which can result in dissociation or mental processes shutting down and the child or adult "checking out"). If neglect is chronic, the child's brain arrives at the conclusion that it is trapped and there is no way out. This initially increases the heart rate, blood pressure, stress response, and production of the chemical cortisol, which kills neurons.*

Identify the areas of neglect you have experienced.

For each type of abuse you identify, in the space provided indicate the severity of the neglect by writing a number from one to ten, with 1 being least severe and 10 being most severe.

- ____ Lack of adequate clothing
- ____ Lack of adequate food or drink
- ____ Inadequate shelter
- ____ Inferior living quarters compared to siblings
- ____ Refusal of schooling
- ____ Insufficient medical care
- ____ Insufficient dental care
- ____ Lack of protection from physical danger
- ____ Lack of protection from abusive parent
- ____ Lack of protection from family member
- ____ Lack of parental supervision
- ____ Lack of physical touch
- ____ Lack of verbal affirmation
- ____ Lack of instruction in basic life skills
- ____ Lack of emotional support
- ____ Lack of verbal interaction
- ____ Failure to provide meals
- ____ Failure to provide basic hygiene or dental care
- ____ Insufficient personal hygiene items
- ____ Lack of basic housecleaning
- ____ Lack of attention due to alcoholism or drug abuse
- ____ Extreme failure to provide stability
- ____ Left unattended
- ____ Being ignored
- ____ Keeping secrets or being asked to lie

I experienced ___*neglect*___ abuse when _____
                                            Name of Abuser(s)

did _____
        Detailed Form of Neglect

chapter two

How did you feel when writing about neglect?
What fears did you have as you put your abuse into words?
Were there any positive feelings?

If we claim that we're free of sin, we're only fooling ourselves. A claim like that is errant nonsense. On the other hand, if we admit our sins...he won't let us down; he'll be true to himself. He'll forgive our sins and purge us of all wrongdoing. (1 John 1:8-9 The Message)

Godly sorrow produces repentance leading to salvation, not to be regretted; but the sorrow of the world produces death. (2 Corinthians 7:10 NKJV)

Dear God,
I admit that . . .

chapter two

Spiritual or Religious Abuse

In their book *The Subtle Power of Spiritual Abuse*, David Johnson and Jeff VanVonderen point out the following four characteristics of a spiritually abusive system:

- Power posturing
- Performance preoccupation
- Unspoken rules
- Lack of balance

Power posturing involves a leader who is preoccupied with spiritual authority and continually asserts his spiritual authority over others. The leader constantly reminds the congregation that he's the spiritual leader and they are to submit to his authority. He claims that to fail to obey him is to fail to obey God. Spiritual abusers are arrogant, prideful, selfish, oppressive, and hypocritical as opposed to the gentle, godly servanthood that Jesus modeled (Matthew 11:29) and prescribed (Luke 22:24-27). Power-posturing leaders seek their own gain and are committed to their own agendas at everyone else's expense. They will employ dishonest and manipulative tactics to accomplish their goals while ruthlessly denying any accusations brought against them and deflecting any criticism back on the person bringing it.

> After Jesus washed His disciples' dirty feet He said to them, "Do you understand what I have done to you? You address me as 'Teacher' and 'Master,' and rightly so... if I, the Master and Teacher, washed your feet, you must now wash each other's feet. I've laid down a pattern for you... If you understand what I'm telling you, act like it—and live a blessed life.
> (John 13:14-17 The Message)

Inversely, Scripture is quite clear that church leaders are not to be power brokers. Instead, they are to be gentle, humble servants (1 Peter 5:2-3; Matthew 18:1-6).

Performance preoccupation is when the measure of one's spiritual maturity is based on external performance or how well one follows the rules as opposed to inner character. Jesus spoke out strongly against this approach in the Sermon on the Mount (see Matthew 5:21-6:4). Jesus' harshest rebuke was reserved for the Pharisees who showed preoccupation with outward performance at the expense of people (Matthew 23:4, 23; Colossians 2:16-23).

Unspoken rules are not directly communicated in spiritually abusive ministries. However, these "sacred" rules exist, and disobedience to them is punished. Unspoken rules could include prohibitions against discussing certain subjects, prohibitions against disagreeing with the leaders, and an inordinate value placed upon loyalty and praise of the leader.

Lack of balance can take the form of either extreme objectivity or extreme subjectivity. An example of extreme objectivity would be the refusal to respect anyone who doesn't have a formal degree in theology or subscribe to the "right" doctrinal formulations. This can take the form of refusing to acknowledge or give credence to any emotional aspect to spirituality. An example of extreme subjectivity is when spiritual leaders make the claim that "God has spoken to them" (making them "prophets") about His will regarding someone else's life. Any questioning of the leader is then equated with questioning God.

If a Christian leader causes another Christian to stumble, sin, feel defeated instead of edified or uplifted, or be pushed farther away from Christ instead of drawn nearer to Him, then spiritual abuse has occurred. Likewise, any time Christians are given the message that they're only good enough for Christ if they perform for the church leader (legalism), spiritual abuse has occurred.

chapter two

Spiritual abuse is particularly damaging because it poisons the very resources designed by God for our growth. Because Scripture, prayer, preaching, and Christian fellowship have been perversely used to harm spiritual abuse victims, they have a hard time trusting or utilizing resources they need for recovery and healing. Describe in the boxes below how the religious organization in which you were involved displayed each of the following characteristics:

Power Posturing	Performance Preoccupation	Unspoken Rules	Lack of Balance

I experienced ____*spiritual*____ abuse when _____ did _____
                                                    Name of Abuser(s)   Detailed form of Spiritual Abuse

chapter two

Journal how spiritual abuse has affected you. Are there spiritual activities that you find it difficult to perform? How has the abuse affected your ability to trust other spiritual leaders? How has it affected your view of God?

Authority. I was afraid of it and resented it. Authority was intimidating—and it became my aim to get around it.

Look, whenever you are asked by the pastor to do something in church it is as though God Himself was asking you to do it. The pastor's eyes told me he was serious.

Idolatry is putting anyone or anything in place of God.

chapter two

Reading your thoughts . . .

I wanted to read your thoughts, because I thought it might help me better understand. I wanted you to speak your mind, but the decibels never rang louder than zero. I had this sneaking suspicion that your mind-life and your word-life were two separate worlds, guarded by demons of past wounds and inertia. If I asked, I feared punishment or rebuke, sometimes both together—wrapped into a thorny ball, thrown into my hands with a laugh. Condemnation was your middle name, one kept skillfully masked under a porcelain veneer of a smile, as venomous words seeped like iodine from the corners of your mouth. I look at you in the eyes and open my mouth to speak, to defend myself, and nothing comes out. Decibels misplaced. I don't think I will ever find them.

At night, I dream of violence. Somehow, the soft environment of false pretense always became violent when I slept. A cosmic battle was taking place during dreams. I harnessed guns and weapons that I wouldn't likely touch in real life. A remnant of the spiritual battle I'm engaging? Or a dark reminder that life is filled with pain? I'm not sure.

Am I crazy? I feel as if I'm on The Truman Show and I just reached the edge of my world with a horrific realization that everything I've known has been manicured and fake. But I have no other reference point, so the mental going is slow. That's why people stay here for so long: all of their input sensors have continuously lied to them about who they are and where they have been. How do you escape from that? In some ways, I feel bad for them and hope that by divine intervention they will see light breaking in through their vinyl skies.

The fruit of the Spirit is quickly diffusing out of me like a soda with a loose lid. Indeed, I am 100% responsible for my response. But right now I need to let it out. I need to feel angry. I need to grieve the loss that I've experienced. It's been a subtle slow death, a grooming to become docile and without opinion, in their words a "kid" whose "mother would call if something went wrong" (I am a grown adult) and a "poor thing," one who acts outside authority—one who needs therapy. I feel that I have been humiliated and then expected to put my hand to the plow and never look back. But this is a death plow. Death to all that is creative—all that is me. And I refuse it.

A few months ago, some people prophetically spoke into my life. They told me to embrace my identity in Christ as a powerful woman of God, putting off the cultural labels and downgrades that women too often accept without thought. It's hard to do in a patriarchal environment. I kept trying to earn my right to minister for over a year. Did the early apostles earn their right to minister? No. The people saw that they had been with JESUS. And I can say that I have seen Him; He Himself has revealed His heart to me. He is the good shepherd, and he laid down His life for me. I know it. My heart longs to teach and to speak words of life. Instead, my words have been repressed and locked away. I feel fear more than freedom. Words of life have been replaced with ones of death and defeat. But I can see breakthrough coming. Only a few more weeks of this. Then recovery.

I still wait for the day that I will be able to understand, to read your thoughts. For now, I will have to settle for leaving you to your psychotic world unattended—for others to silently bear the brunt of your hypocrisy. And I hear it clearly—<u>the mouth of Jesus—saying to me, "I am not like them."</u>

chapter two

Sexual Abuse

One of the most powerful and beautiful aspects of being a person made in the image of God is the possession of healthy sexuality. It's through our sexuality that we are drawn into intimate relationship, and it's through sexual intimacy that we demonstrate the image of God. It's also through the sex act that we're able to procreate. Thus, the ability to engage in sexual relations, reproduce, and demonstrate the intimacy of the Trinity is one of the greatest privileges and blessings God gives to husbands and wives (Psalm 127:3-5). But the inherent power of sex can produce just as much destruction and pain as it does pleasure and life. Sexual abuse is never minor—it's always very damaging. Even when sexual abuse doesn't involve intercourse, force, or physical violence, it's still very serious and harmful.

Sexual interactions are abusive when at least one of the following factors are present:

- **Power differential.** This exists when the offender controls the victim and the sexual encounter isn't mutually conceived. Relational power can derive from the role relationship between offender and victim: for example, when the abuser is a teacher, parent, minister, or coach. Power can also derive from the larger size or more advanced capability of the offender, in which case the victim may be manipulated, physically intimidated, or required to comply with the sexual activity. Power may also arise out of the offender's superior capability to psychologically manipulate the victim (which in turn may be related to the offender's role or superior size). The offender may bribe, cajole, or trick the victim into cooperation.

- **Knowledge differential.** This exists when the offender has a more sophisticated understanding of the significance and implications of the sexual encounter. Knowledge differential implies that the offender is older, more developmentally advanced, or more intelligent than the victim.

- **Gratification differential.** This exists when the offender is attempting to sexually gratify him or herself. The goal of the encounter is not mutual sexual gratification, although perpetrators may become aroused by attempting to arouse their victims. Alternatively, the abuser may delude him or herself into believing that the goal is to sexually satisfy the victims. Nevertheless, the primary purpose of the sexual activity is to obtain gratification for the perpetrator.

For years as a grown man, I've carried the humiliation of knowing it was a man who abused me. I knew that I belonged to God. But I didn't realize how distorted my view of masculinity had become as I considered the Father and His Son in Scripture. My male perpetrated sexual abuse distorted how I saw God, and it also distorted how I thought He saw me. It made prayer difficult . . . I thought if God can't stand to look upon sin, how could He possibly stand to look at me? I tried to imagine some deserted, God-forsaken place and what that might look like. Then I began to imagine a God-forsaken man and what he might look like. That's when I started thinking that Jesus might be able to understand me!

Chapter Two

Acts of Sexual Abuse

Noncontact acts

- Abuser makes sexual comments to a child or adolescent
- Abuser exposes intimate parts to a person—sometimes accompanied by masturbation
- Abuser is voyeuristic—such as a stepfather watching his stepdaughter shower
- Offender shows a child pornographic materials
- Offender asks child to undress or masturbate

Sexual contact

- Offender touches a child's intimate parts (genitals, buttocks, breasts)
- Offender induces the child to touch his or her intimate parts
- Abuser engages in frottage (rubbing genitals against the victim's body or clothing)

Sexual contact with digital or object penetration

- Offender places finger(s) in child's vagina or anus
- Offender induces child to place finger(s) in offender's vagina or anus
- Offender places instrument in child's vagina or anus
- Offender induces child to place instrument in offender's vagina or anus

Oral sex

- Abuser engages in tongue kissing
- Abuser engages in breast sucking, kissing, licking, biting
- Abuser engages in cunnilingus (licking, kissing, sucking, biting the vagina or placing the tongue in the vaginal opening)
- Abuser engages in fellatio (licking, kissing, sucking, biting the penis)
- Abuser engages in anilingus (licking or kissing the anal opening)

Penile penetration

- Abuser induces or forces vaginal and anal intercourse.
- Abuser induces or forces intercourse with animals

If you experienced sexual abuse, look at the descending continuum of types of sexual abuse below and identify the forms of sexual abuse you experienced.

Most Severe
- ☐ Intercourse
- ☐ Attempted intercourse
- ☐ Oral sex
- ☐ Genital contact
- ☐ Breast contact
- ☐ Intentional sexual touching of buttocks or thighs
- ☐ Simulated intercourse
- ☐ Touching of clothed breasts
- ☐ Sexualized relationship
- ☐ Sexual kissing
- ☐ Deliberate exposure to pornography or sexual activity
- ☐ Exhibitionism
- ☐ Sexual conversations with a minor
- ☐ Sexual nickname

Least Severe

I experienced ____*sexual*____ abuse when _____
             Type of Abuse   Name of Abuser(s)

did _____
                    Detailed Form of Sexual Abuse

From the U.S. Department of Health & Human Services

chapter two

Grooming and Sexual Abuse

Although there will be a whole chapter devoted to the topic of shame, there are some unique ways in which shame can arise from sexual abuse. These are worth focusing on now. With the exception of forcible rape, the abuser must figure out a way to secure some type of compliance from the victim. This compliance creates a false sense of shame in the sexual abuse victim. Understanding that sexual abusers tend to use the same pattern or process in performing their abuse allows the victim to place the blame for compliance on the abuser. The abuser is the adult. That adult abusively grooms the child for later, more overt forms of sexual abuse. The adult abuser knows exactly what he or she is doing; the child is merely responding in the only way he or she can—as a child lacking a mature perspective and personal power in the relationship.

Sex offenders groom in a gradual, calculated way that separates the victim from peers or family by engendering in the child a sense that he or she is special to the offender. This explains how victims can appear "complicit" in the abuse. Forensic psychiatrist Dr. Michael Welner explains the six stages that can lead up to sexual molestation. (For more information see http://www.oprah.com/child-sexual-abuse-6-stages of grooming):

Stage 1: Targeting the Victim. This is based on the child's vulnerability, emotional neediness, isolation, and lower self-confidence. Children with less parental oversight are easier targets.

Stage 2: Gaining the Victim's Trust. Trust is gained by watching and gathering information about the child, getting to know his or her needs, and carefully meeting them. Offenders mix effortlessly with responsible caregivers, because of their warmth and interest.

Stage 3: Filling a Need. The child's needs are met in idealized ways that place the offender in a "special" role in the child or adolescent's world. Gifts, extra attention, or affection may distinguish one adult in particular and should raise concern and greater vigilance.

Stage 4: Isolating the Child. The "special" relationship with the child is used to create situations in which they are alone together such as babysitting, tutoring, coaching, and special trips. This isolation further reinforces a special connection and dependence. Parents may unknowingly feed into this through their own appreciation for the unique relationship.

Stage 5: Sexualizing the Relationship. At a stage of sufficient emotional dependence and trust, the offender subtly sexualizes the relationship. The child's defenses are gradually lowered through talking, pictures, even creating situations (such as going swimming) in which both offender and victim are naked, stimulating the child's God-given curiosity. In time, the child comes to see himself as a more sexual being and to define the relationship with the offender in more sexual and "special" terms.

Stage 6: Maintaining Control. Secrecy, threats, and blame are used by the offender to entangle the child in the relationship and maintain the child's compliance, thus furthering the abuse.

chapter two

How Could it Be Abuse if I Experienced Pleasure?

Unlike with other forms of abuse, victims of sexual abuse may experience pleasure, which can be extremely troubling and confusing. Physical pleasure is a biological—not moral—response to sexual activity. Pleasure doesn't negate the fact that the experience was abusive! God has made our bodies with an intricate system of nerve endings and pleasure receptors, which are stimulated by touch—this process is largely involuntary. Because we experience emotional pleasure through affectionate touch, many survivors have great pain and confusion over the fact that the very abuse that caused such shame also produced some physical or emotional pleasure. This is not uncommon and doesn't mean the individual asked for the abuse or is responsible for it.

It's difficult to describe the paradoxical experience of ambivalence. To have one strong emotion (terror) and another equally powerful feeling (desire) seems inconceivable. The apparent contradiction adds to the confusion. How can one hate and want the same person? How can one equally enjoy and despise the sexual pleasure experienced during the abuse? These conflicting emotions makes the victim feel powerless, crazy, and ashamed.

To add to the complexity, there are times when the child will feel betrayed by his or her own body, because he or she is powerless to stop the abuse or even the physiological response to it. A man told me about the times he was masturbated by his mother. She came to his bed late at night, long after he had gone to sleep. She would rearrange the covers and scratch his back. If he was lying on his side, she would stroke his penis. Many nights he would feign sleep and turn on his side when she entered the room. He hated himself for feeling aroused and would occasionally feel overwhelming guilt and then turn away from her touch. Other times he allowed himself to be aroused to orgasm. Afterward, he would hate himself for his sick response and failure of resolve. Sensual arousal, sexual pleasure, and even orgasm may occur when a child or adolescent is abused, even if there was a strong effort to avoid the sensation.

> *Reflect on the stages of grooming.* How does this affect your view of who is to blame for the abuse? Think of the planning and purposefulness with which your abuser acted.

chapter two

A Healthy Parental Response if a Child Has Been Sexually Abused

1. Prayerfully gather your thoughts. Sexual abuse is one of the most disturbing disclosures a parent can receive, but panic will prompt harmful responses. Remember that God's presence, power, and love doesn't change in the midst of suffering and evil (Psalm 46:1-2). Ask God for wisdom and courage (Psalm 23:4; 34:4-8).

2. Calmly and gently talk to your child. Sexually abused children have experienced great trauma. They feel great shame often coupled with fear. Therefore, your calm and loving response is critically important for your child.

3. Honestly share your own sorrow over the abuse. Let the child know how sad you are that this was done to them. Let them know that God is also sad and grieves over their abuse. It hurts God when his children suffer (Hosea 11:8; John 11:35).

4. Assure the child that is wasn't his or her fault. Shame causes abused children to feel as if they are responsible for the abuse. Additionally, perpetrators often tell children it's their fault. It may take a very long time for the child to truly believe the abuse wasn't his or her fault, so repeated verbal assurances from parents are very helpful.

5. Assure the child that you will get him or her help. Abused children don't expect parents to have all the answers or to fix every problem. They just need to know that parents will boldly pursue getting the help that's needed.

6. Contact law enforcement and report the abuse immediately. If the perpetrator is a family member, Child Protective Services should also be contacted.

7. Don't immediately confront the perpetrator. While this is often the first thing parents attempt to do, it can easily backfire. First of all, for the sake of the legal investigation, it's important for law enforcement to be the first ones to interview the perpetrator. Secondly, parents need time to work through the complex issues and intense feelings. Otherwise, they might act and speak in ways that are counterproductive and even destructive.

8. Protect the child from the perpetrator and, if necessary, the extended family and the community. It's the parents' responsibility to protect the child from the perpetrator. That person should have no contact with or access to the child whatsoever. Parents must establish whatever boundaries are necessary with the extended family or community to protect the child. Furthermore, if family, church, or community don't accept these boundaries or seek to minimize or deny the abuse, then parents need to protect the child from those individuals as well. Their denial can be very damaging to the child. Denial and victim blame are some of the most common responses to sexual abuse and are strongly condemned by God (Proverbs 17:15).

9. Seek professional help. Sexual abuse is confusing, complex, and deeply damaging. It is advisable to find a Christian counselor experienced in dealing with sexual abuse.

10. Respect your child's privacy. Scripture tells us that there is a time to speak but also a time to be silent (Ecclesiastes 3:7). Sexual abuse is one of the most shameful things that can happen to a child, and often people don't know how to respond to an abuse report. Therefore, be very careful and selective in speaking about the abuse to other people, especially if the child is present.

11. Be patient. Sexual abuse creates soul damage that generally takes considerable time to heal. Remember that God is infinitely committed to the well-being and healing of his children (Romans 8:28, 31-37; Philemon 1:6). Prayerfully commit the pain caused by abuse to God and entrust healing to Him (Psalm 18:1-6; 1 Peter 5:7). Trust Him to work in His wise way in His time.

chapter two

Did you disclose your abuse? How did your parent or caregiver respond?

Come to Me, all you who labor and are heavy laden, and I will give you rest. Take My yoke upon you, and learn from Me, for I am gentle and lowly in heart, and you will find rest for your souls. For My yoke is easy and My burden is light.
(Matthew 11:28-30 NKJV)

Blessed are those who mourn, for they will be comforted.
(Matthew 5:4)

chapter two

[handwritten: self-love]

Narcissistic Families: The Other Kind of Pain

Children from narcissistic families attempt to earn love, attention, and approval by satisfying their parents' needs. The parents, because of internal or external stressors (mental illness, physical disability, single parenting, poverty, selfishness, immaturity, etc.), are primarily involved in getting their own needs met. Thus, children grow up without the ability to recognize their own feelings and needs and develop an overly dependent relational style—based on the validation of the people around them—or a fiercely independent pattern of relating. (For further discussion of narcissistic families see Pressman and Pressman, *The Narcissistic Family*). Following are some common dynamics from this dysfunctional, intergenerational system (think of these in degrees of dysfunction on a spectrum depending on the level of narcissism in the parents):

- **Image of perfection**—children are taught to fear the opinions of other people
- **Secrets**—Parents' failures or children's unmet emotional needs are hidden from the outside world
- **Lack of emotional intimacy**—parents cannot feel and show their children empathy or unconditional love; they are critical, harsh, and judgmental

- **Adultified children**—Parents are concerned about their own needs and fail to meet children's needs
- **Unspoken rules**—Children are valued for what they do rather than for who they are—which internalizes shame
- **Triangulated communication**—Indirect communication patterns: lack of respectful honesty and family members talk about each other but don't confront directly, which results in passive-aggressive behavior, tension, and mistrust
- **Unclear boundaries**—Children's privacy and other boundaries aren't respected
- **Closeness of siblings not encouraged**—Children are pitted against each other and compete for parents' attention, there are constant comparisons, certain children are favored and other children are scapegoated as a result of parent's projected negative feelings
- **Narcissistic or codependent parents**—When one parent is narcissistic, the other parent commonly revolves around him or her to keep the marriage intact. Many times, this parent has redeeming qualities to give to the children, but is tied up meeting the needs of the narcissistic spouse. This often leaves the children's needs unmet
- **Denial of feelings**—Children are taught to repress and avoid feelings, which are considered weakness or at best ignored; narcissistic parents aren't in touch with their own feelings and project them onto others, resulting in a lack of accountability and honesty
- **Covert versus overt**—Violent and abusive homes are obvious or overt while emotional, psychological, and neglect abuse is often hidden and covert, resulting in *more* damage to the children

> Beware of mirrors, they lead us not to see ourselves but love ourselves like poor Narcissus, who grasping at his image died. They say that floating in the water just above his wide-eyed, silent face there was a butterfly. Had he let it lead him into wonder, he might have loved science, not himself, and lived to cure the world of plague.
>
> —Calvin Miller, *A Requiem for Love*

chapter two

The Spirit of the Sovereign Lord is on me, because the Lord has anointed me to proclaim good news to the poor. He has sent me to bind up the brokenhearted, to proclaim freedom for the captives and release from darkness for the prisoners. . .
to comfort all who mourn.
(Isaiah 61:1-2)

Check the following characteristics that you identify with:

- ☐ Chronic need to please
- ☐ Inability to identify feelings, wants, or needs
- ☐ Need for constant validation
- ☐ Lack of self-confidence
- ☐ Indecisive
- ☐ Anxious
- ☐ Chronic depression
- ☐ Diminished focus or control
- ☐ Unassertive
- ☐ Inner feelings of chronic rage
- ☐ Guilt for angry feelings—repress anger
- ☐ Easily defeated
- ☐ Relationally passive
- ☐ Difficulties trusting others
- ☐ Suspicious and sometimes paranoid
- ☐ Poor interpersonal boundaries—inappropriately self-disclosing and trusting
- ☐ Chronically dissatisfied and lingering feelings of emptiness
- ☐ Unskilled at communicating negative feelings and thus intimacy needs
- ☐ Mood instability—especially in communicating anger—repressed, then explosive
- ☐ Passive-aggressive
- ☐ Pathologically driven to appear successful

Be sure to read

This has been a difficult chapter—you've accomplished a lot. Answering these questions is one of the biggest victories you've experienced thus far, because it's the beginning of *really* dealing with your past. Until you admit the truth of your pain and its source, you remain cut off from those parts of yourself, and thus cut off from others and even God. So, celebrate the success of being here—a place of real dealing and feeling.

chapter two

My thoughts and feelings...

Mercy and truth have met together; righteousness [justice] and peace have kissed. (Psalm 85:10 NKJV)

Meditate on Jesus
Our suffering Savior
Who carried…

Chapter Three
Profile of Abusers

. . . our pain and disfigurements, all the things wrong with us. We thought he brought it on himself,
that God was punishing him for his own failures. But it was our sins that did that to him,
that ripped and tore and crushed him—our sins! He took the punishment, and that made us whole.
Through his bruises we get healed.
We're all like sheep who've wandered off and gotten lost.
We've all done our own thing, gone our own way.
And God has piled all our sins, everything we've done wrong, on him, on him.

He was beaten, he was tortured, but he didn't say a word.
Like a lamb taken to be slaughtered and like a sheep being sheared,
he took it all in silence. Justice miscarried, and he was led off—
and did anyone really know what was happening?

. . . The plan was that he give himself as an offering for sin
so that he'd see life come from it—life, life, and more life.
And God's plan will deeply prosper through him.

Out of that terrible travail of soul, he'll see that it's worth it and be glad he did it.
Through what he experienced, my righteous one, my servant, will make many "righteous ones,"
as he himself carries the burden of their sins. . .
He took on his shoulders the sin of the many,
he took up the cause of all the black sheep.
(Isaiah 53 The Message)

On Left: Francisco de Zubaran - Bound Lamb or Agnus Dei 1630

chapter three

REASONABLE AND BIBLICAL RELATIONAL EXPECTATIONS

It's hard to make sense of our experiences, especially when they involve neglect or abuse. Victims usually blame themselves for their abuse because offenders don't accept responsibility for harming and causing pain—which automatically shifts the shame and blame onto their victim. In order to tease out our relational responsibilities, it's important to understand what God intends for us to experience (and not to not) in our significant relationships. Of course, no one person can be everything we need or love us perfectly—only God can offer that kind of unconditional love. What are we to expect in our close relationships (1 Corinthians 13)? Lundy Bancroft has spent the past fifteen years specializing in preventing and healing domestic abuse, and he offers many practical resources to support women in abusive relationships. Following are some reasonable and biblical expectations for every significant relationship. These can serve as a lens in evaluating your own relationships. There's space after each expectation for you to record your response:

1. To be treated with respect. No partner, spouse, parent, teacher, or pastor has the right to call you names, humiliate you, mock you, berate you, or demean you in any way. It doesn't matter if he or she's furious at you or feels that you were disrespecting him or her. There's always another option. *Do you feel better or worse about yourself in this relationship?*

2. To feel safe. If you're worried that you might be hurt physically or sexually—even if you haven't been—or if your partner behaves in ways that lead you to have unwanted sexual contact with him or her, you're not in a safe relationship. You should be able to trust financially and have your emotional and personal boundaries respected. *Can you completely trust your partner? Why or why not?*

3. To have possibilities expanded, not diminished. Sacrifices are mutual, opening the doors to new opportunities within the relationship; dreams and goals are mutually supported; finances are shared; and family and friendships mutually enjoyed. *Is your relationship broadening your horizons, or is it narrowing them?*

chapter three

4. To enjoy passion and intimacy. Monogamy should enhance rather than deaden sexual energy and help to keep passion alive. When two partners mutually commit to deepening emotional connections, the relationship will grow more dynamic and enjoyable. *Can you completely trust your partner to be faithful, sexually and psychologically?*

5. To feel loved the majority of the time. Even in conflict God intends for you to feel loved and respected. It's normal for relationships to go through stressful seasons and to require intentional restructuring at times; however, it's God's intention for you to feel loved even when you're disappointing your partner or making mistakes within the relationship. *Do you feel that your partner likes you? Do you feel loved most of the time? Are you known?*

A prosecuting attorney familiar with many men accused by the criminal justice system of beating their wives wrote the following:

Despite being charged with a crime, virtually all of these men view the assault as being the fault of the woman. On one occasion I was asked by a judge to speak to a man who was brought to the court from the jail after being arrested for beating his wife. As I spoke to him it was as if the case had nothing to do with domestic violence. I asked, "So, if I understand you correctly, you are arrested and in court today because your wife is writing unauthorized checks on your business account?" Faced with the obvious absurdity implicit in my question he then conceded that he was accused of domestic violence. When I inquired about what had happened he began to describe the anger his wife caused him to feel. Again, I asked him, "Let me see if I understand you—it is your wife's fault that you hit her?" Not even recognizing the sarcasm in my question, he responded as if he had finally found someone who understood and agreed with him. "Yeah! That's right," he responded. I inquired further. He began to explain that he believed his wife was trying to take over his business behind his back, and she knew if she kept writing these checks it would make him angry, and thus she was trying to get him in trouble. Again I tried to clarify by summing up: "I see, she's trying to trick you into hitting her. She's purposely writing these checks with the goal of getting you mad, so she can get you to hit her, so she can call the police, so she can get you put in jail, so she can take over your business while you're in jail?" He believed he had found someone who truly understood. He never sensed any irony or sarcasm in my questions. This man had been convicted of multiple domestic violence charges in the past, including spousal rape.

This profile applies to abusers of all types: sexual abusers, verbal abusers, spiritual abusers, child abusers, physical abusers, etc. These abusers are all incredibly adept at convincing their victims that they're at fault—at making them feel powerless, unsafe, alone, and ashamed. To describe or define something is empowering. Those who have been abused often lack a sense of power in their lives. In this chapter we pray that you'll receive empowerment from describing and defining your abuser. In the process you may experience a tremendous amount of fear, so take a moment now to ask God to graciously provide the courage to face your fears as you continue down His healing path.

chapter three

THE BANALITY OF EVIL

Evil people don't look evil they look like everybody else (*Mending the Soul*, pg 39). No one—including the victim—wants to believe someone is capable of performing a despicable act. Hence, when a victim discloses to others the truth of the abuse, often he or she is not believed. *I have had the opportunity to see countless people charged with the most heinous crimes stand before a judge. There truly is no "look." They don't come from certain neighborhoods or from certain professions. They often are otherwise good, upright people in many ways.* (Maricopa County Attorney)

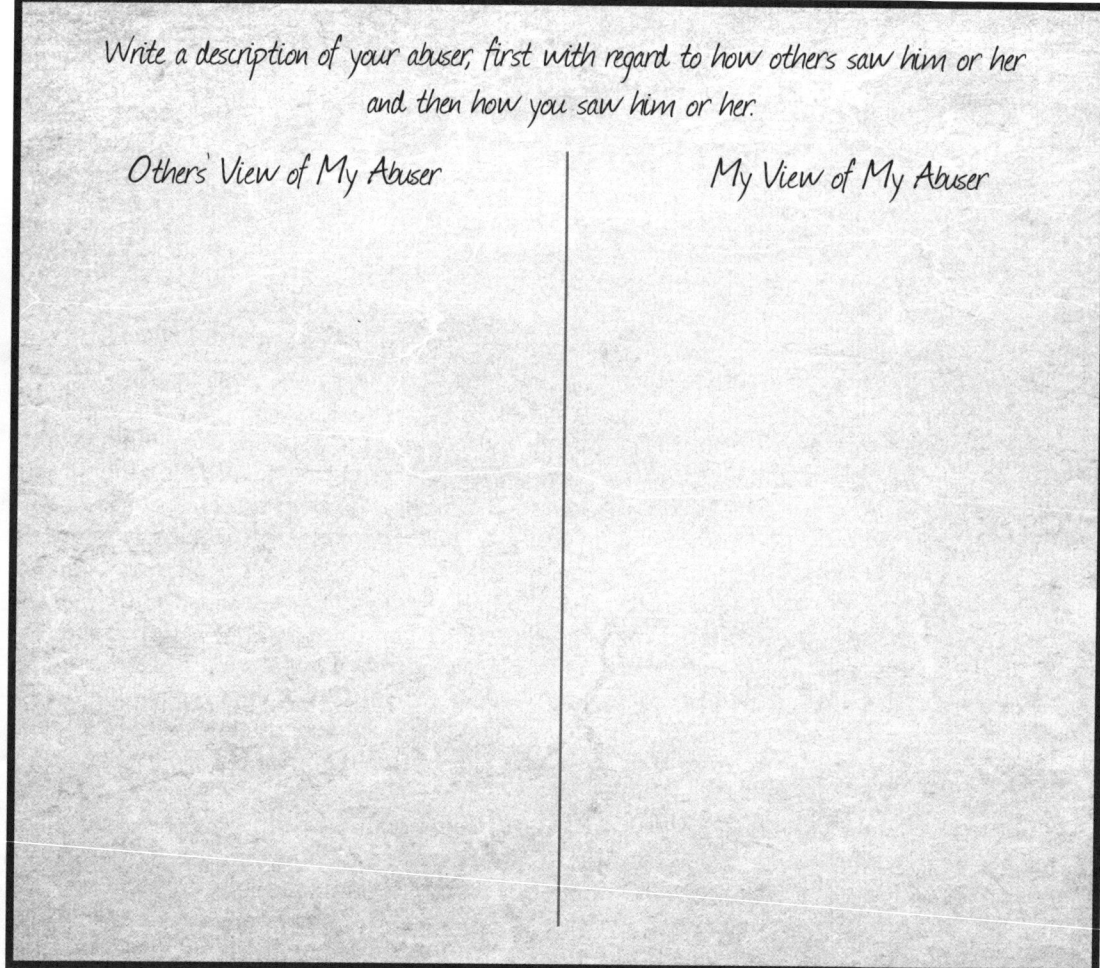

> Again I saw all the oppressions that are done under the sun. And behold, the tears of the oppressed, and they had no one to comfort them! On the side of their oppressors there was power, and there was no one to comfort them.
> (Ecclesiastes 4:1 ESV)

Write a description of your abuser, first with regard to how others saw him or her and then how you saw him or her.

Others' View of My Abuser	My View of My Abuser

chapter three

ABUSE CREATES AMBIVALENCE

am·biv·a·lent [am-biv-uh-luhnt]

The coexistence within an individual of positive and negative feelings toward the same person, object, or action, simultaneously drawing him or her in opposite directions.

Abuse creates ambivalence. On one hand, we hate what our abuser has done to us or those we love, and we hate many of his qualities. On the other hand, there may be other aspects of his or her personality or life that we enjoyed. While an abuser has many evil qualities, he or she probably was not completely evil. He or she may have been generous, humorous, charming, affectionate, and even kind in some ways. He or she may have paid attention to you when others did not. This creates an emotional dilemma. You may feel guilty for actually enjoying or liking the abuser in many ways—*how could I actually like someone who did those things to me? How sick am I that I actually enjoyed some of what he or she did to me?* And then, at the same time, you may feel guilty for hating the abuser; after all, look at all of the good qualities. *Everyone else seems to adore this person. Is it not wrong for me as a Christian to hate? Am I not supposed to forgive? What am I supposed to feel?*

Psychological ambivalence creates an emotional double bind that can effectively shut a person down. If we experience affection from a person and feel affection in response, then we're responding in the way God designed us. If we experienced abuse and feel anger, then we're responding in the way God designed us. The fact that the positive and negative events came from the same person won't affect our emotional responses to the positive and negative events. There need be no guilt for feeling either emotion. Both are simply responses, which is what emotions are. Knowing this about the nature of emotions will not, however, resolve your ambivalence. You still have to process the events and let yourself feel the emotions. In time, as you allow Scripture to shape your core beliefs and allow the Holy Spirit to heal your soul, you will increasingly feel the appropriate response to a given experience (you'll not feel numb at pain, laugh at a painful memory, etc.).

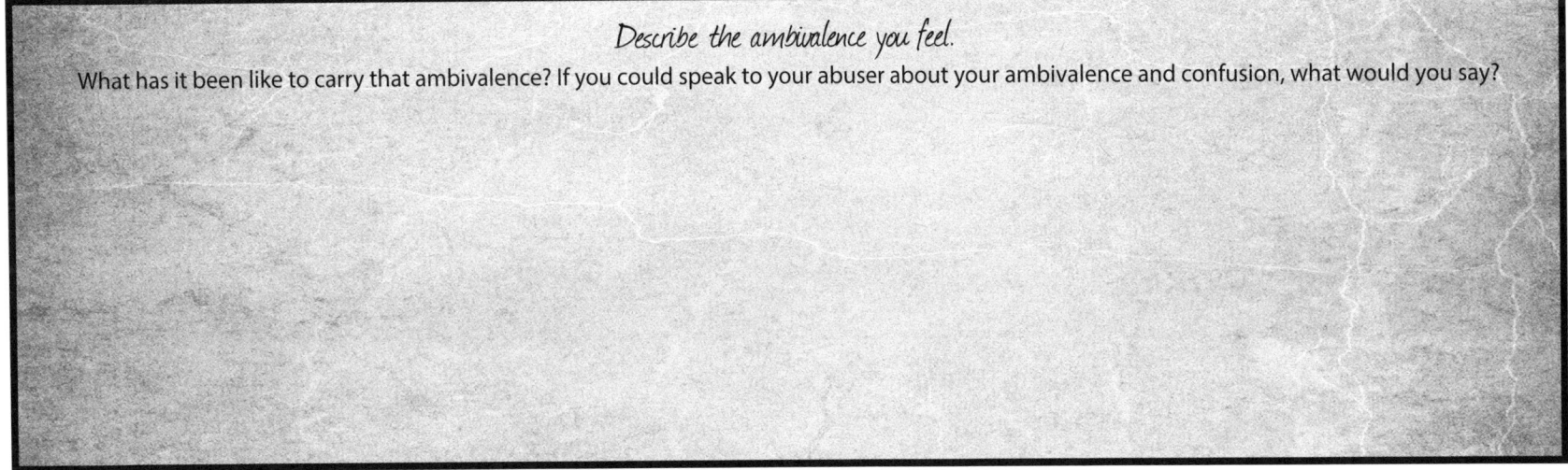

Describe the ambivalence you feel.
What has it been like to carry that ambivalence? If you could speak to your abuser about your ambivalence and confusion, what would you say?

chapter three

	Negative Aspects	Positive Aspects
Record as many of the positive and negative traits of your abuser as you can think of. Don't pause to evaluate, simply write.		
Observe the lists. What do you feel when you focus on the negative aspects? The positive aspects?	*How these make you feel:*	*How these make you feel:*

All I want, Jesus, is more and more to abandon everything to You. The more I go on, the more I realize I don't know where I am going. Lead me and take complete control of me. "Teach me to do thy will, for You are my God."

—Thomas Merton, *A Year with Thomas Merton*

chapter three

FOUR PRIMARY CHARACTERISTICS OF ABUSERS

In chapter three of *Mending the Soul*, Dr. Tracy describes four characteristics of abusers: pervasive denial of responsibility, bold deceitfulness, harsh judgmentalism, and calculated intimidation.

Pervasive Denial of Responsibility

Abusers characteristically show utter unwillingness to accept full responsibility for their behavior (*Mending the Soul*, 39). Those who work with abusers find this to be one of their most distinctive characteristics. Abusers are extremely creative in the lengths they will go to deny responsibility for their actions, even when caught. There are different ways one can refuse to accept blame. Following are some examples:

1. Denial. This happens when a person takes the position that the event did not occur: *You're lying!* One facet of denial is its power over others—it's painfully difficult to confront someone you have a relationship with when they are abjectly denying any wrongdoing. This is especially true when the abuser seems to be a good person. This might help to explain why survivors of abuse rarely disclose and are even more rarely believed.

2. Justification. This happens when a person admits the event(s) occurred but attempts to argue that it wasn't wrong: *Okay, I did say that, but I was only teasing!*

3. Rationalization. This happens when a person admits the event(s) occurred and admits that it was technically wrong, but then he or she offers an excuse, motivation, or explanation for the behavior, showing it to be acceptable after all: *Okay, it was wrong of me to say something like that, but you really upset me!*

4. Minimization. This happens when a person admits the event(s) occurred, admits that it was technically wrong, and admits that he or she had no excuse, but then attempts to maintain that it wasn't as bad as the accuser says it was. In essence, the abuser concedes all the accusations but attempts to make punishing him or her seem unjust. A sophisticated abuser tries to make his victim seem like the bad one for getting him or her "in trouble." One can minimize the frequency: *I only did it once*. Or one can minimize the severity: *I only slapped her*. Or one can minimize actions: *You're too sensitive!*

5. Blame shifting. This happens when a person admits the event(s) occurred, admits it was wrong, offers no excuse, and does not minimize, but insists the victim is to blame: *Okay, I did touch her sexually, and I now understand how that was wrong, because she did say no. But she seduced me. Have you seen the way she dresses?*

When a person refuses to accept full responsibility for his or her actions, the blame is inevitably projected onto the victim. False blame quickly turns into toxic shame for both the abuser and the victim, because abuse (perpetration and victimization) violates the human dignity that comes from being a divine image-bearer. An abuser's toxic projection of shame creates long-term suffering for his or her victims.

chapter three

Bold Deceitfulness

Abusers are skilled at deceiving others about their own character. They often spin a web of deceit around themselves so as to appear kind and innocent. They may go to great lengths to do chores for their neighbors, participate in community service, or engage in time-consuming religious activities to the extent that no one would believe they could ever abuse a child or beat their spouse.

For instance, teachers and coaches who are arrested for child sexual abuse are often highly popular and have a large group of defenders, even after they're convicted. In several instances, they had been awarded teacher of the year honors. The hard-to-see reality is that they weren't only dedicated teachers, they were destructive child molesters as well. Often a child or adolescent whose father or mother beats or molests him or her will have numerous family, friends, and neighbors say how wonderful they believe his or her parent to be. Bold deceitfulness is a common characteristic of all abusers.

Were you or others deceived by your abuser? How?	Did your abuser deny responsibility for his or her actions?
What methods did he or she use?	How did this impact you? Others?

chapter three

Harsh Judgmentalism

This abusive trait is perhaps the most ironic. The abuser has committed despicable acts against others, acts that produce such inner shame in the abuser that he or she feels compelled to engage in pervasive denial of responsibility. Nonetheless, this person has the nerve to be highly judgmental of much lesser wrongs committed by others. Jesus said in the Sermon on the Mount, "Do not judge, or you too will be judged" (Matthew 7:1). Abusers instead adhere to the twisted motto, "Harshly judge so that you will not be judged." In his book *Understanding Child Molesters*, Eric Leberg explains how this dynamic works in the mind of the abuser:

> *Because the offender is still minimizing his guilt, he will desperately try to maintain secrecy through aggressive verbal taunts and accusations that sidetrack all meaningful discussion. The offender is often extremely well prepared to taunt aggressively and accuse others for the simple reason that during the time that he has been grooming and molesting, he has been justifying his own behavior by watching for every misdeed in those around him. Thus, he will remember the number of times that the wife refused his demands for sex, the times she got intoxicated, or the times she didn't clean the house to his satisfaction or forgot his birthday wishes or left her dirty socks on the floor. He'll remember the times the children fought, disturbed his sleep, came home late, did poorly in school, wasted their allowance, spilled milk during dinner, or failed to take his advice "when they knew they should have." To each of these events he will attach some value judgment that, although it may be absurd, again deflects the discussion away from his sexual abuse of his child or children.*

Harsh judgmentalism is a defense strategy that shifts attention away from the abuser's moral fault by focusing on the victim's supposed faults and projects the abuser's own shame onto the victim.

> A person who is willing to allow others to suffer to whatever degree is necessary in order to protect their own image or sense of well-being is a person of the lie...evil.
> —M. Scott Peck

chapter three

God stands squarely on the side of the oppressed. He's outraged and proclaims judgment on those who harden their hearts to the pain of others, do not plead the cause of the fatherless, or defend the rights of the needy (Jeremiah 5:28). Hear His invitation into a life of peace through the pathway of a repentant heart:

> O Lord, are not your eyes on the truth?
> You have stricken them, but they have not grieved; you have consumed them, but they have refused to receive correction. They have made their faces harder than rock; they have refused to return.
>
> "Your ways and your doings have procured these things for you. This is your wickedness, because it is bitter, because it reaches to your heart."
>
> Stand in the ways and see,
> and ask for the old paths,
> where the good way is, and walk in it;
> then you will find
> rest for your souls.
> (Jeremiah 5:3; 4:18; 6:16)

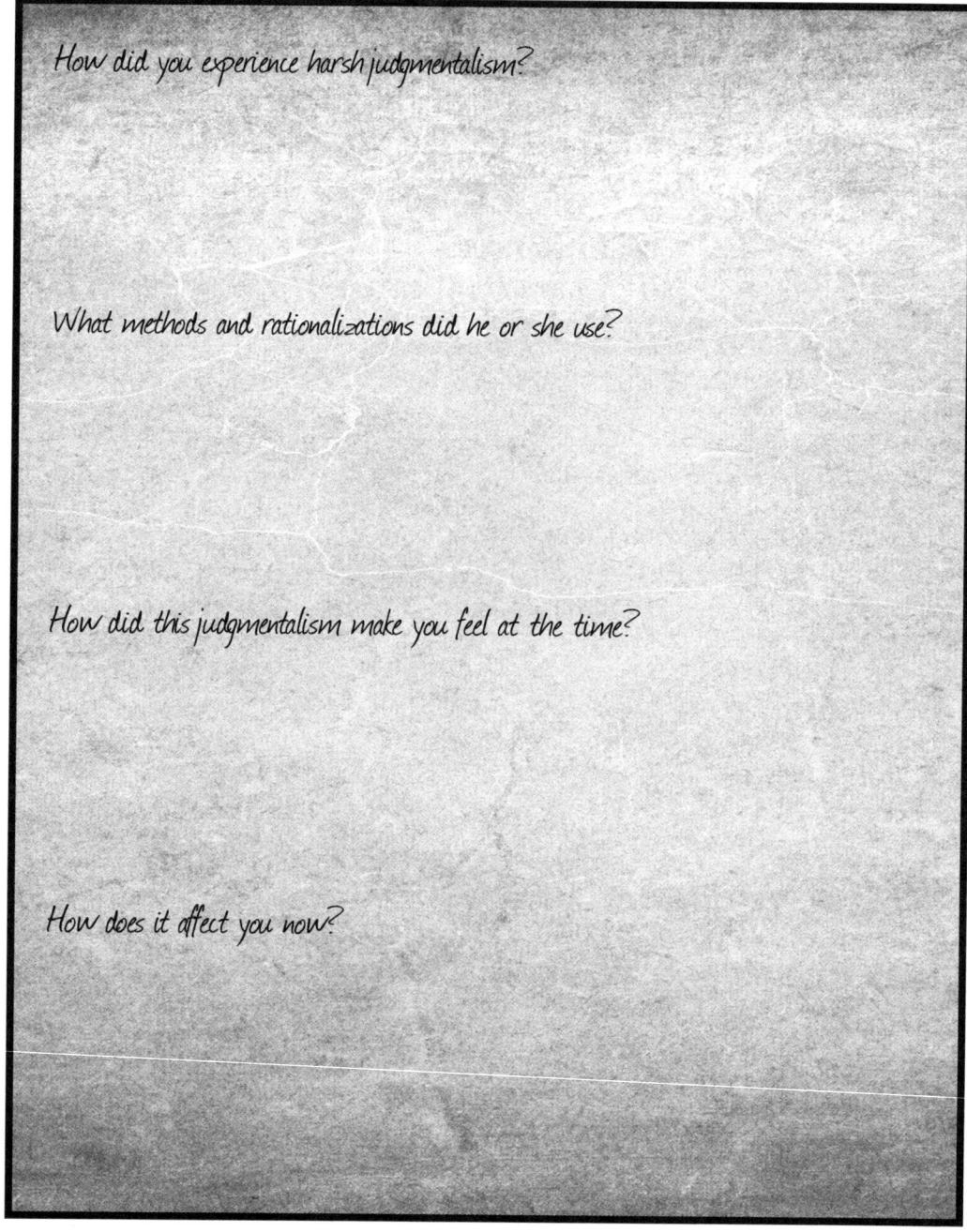

How did you experience harsh judgmentalism?

What methods and rationalizations did he or she use?

How did this judgmentalism make you feel at the time?

How does it affect you now?

chapter three

Calculated Intimidation

Calculated intimidation is a sly strategy used to intimidate victims into silence and submission, allowing abusers to continue to abuse. It also creates much additional trauma to the victim. Abusers use a wide variety of strategies. They might make implied or mild threats: *If you tell, I won't be your friend anymore.* Or they may use explicit threats: *If you tell, I'll kill you,* or *If you tell, I'll molest your little sister.* Abusers often take advantage of their victims' weaknesses and vulnerability in making threats that they can't actually carry out but are frightening enough to achieve the desired effect of silencing the victim.

My mother hurt me deeply, but everyone else thought she was great. It left me feeling really stupid at first. In time, I became resentful and angry.

[My parents] focused on me. That's what happens in dysfunctional families, one person gets focused on and absorbs all the craziness. I was that person.

—L. Slater, *Lying*

There are many wickedly cunning ways an abuser can intimidate his or her victim into not disclosing the abuse, therefore the list below is by no means exhaustive. Check off any of the ways your abuser used calculated intimidation to keep you from disclosing the abuse.

- ☐ Threatening to hurt a loved one
- ☐ Threatening to injure you
- ☐ Threatening to kill a loved one
- ☐ Threatening to kill you
- ☐ Threatening to withhold finances
- ☐ Threatening to abandon you
- ☐ Threatening to send you away
- ☐ Threatening to have you put in jail, an orphanage, or otherwise sent away
- ☐ Shaming
- ☐ Threatening shame
- ☐ Threatening to hurt or kill pets
- ☐ Convincing you no one would believe you
- ☐ Intimidating loved ones into being too afraid to protect you
- ☐ Threatening to molest a sibling
- ☐ Convincing you that disclosure would break up the family
- ☐ Equating silence with loyalty
- ☐ Blackmailing with special attention
- ☐ Blackmailing with special privileges
- ☐ Blackmailing with gifts
- ☐ Blackmailing with "love"
- ☐ Other _____
  _____
  _____

chapter three

God of My Sorrow

Oh God of my sorrow, familiar with grief
Please acquaint yourself with me

Hearken to my voice, its flicker of sound
Bottle my tears before I drown

I am wrought with grief, yet you know it so well
Together in pain we can both dwell

Hold my head in your hands, allow me to weep
Draw me to you, for I am as a lost sheep

But found in your arms the shepherd made lamb
The scars of your sorrow are etched in your hands

I'm not okay, nor will I soon be
But I know joy ever true
As you weep here with me

Survive this with me and I will know pain
For to know it is to know you
Oh, Lamb who was slain

—Mandy

> You realize, don't you, that you are the temple of God, and God himself is present in you? No one will get by with vandalizing God's temple, you can be sure of that. God's temple is sacred—and you, remember, are the temple. (1 Corinthians 3:16-17 The Message)

I wrote this poem after a breakup of sorts. I was frustrated at my relational pattern of reading into guys' behavior and being led on, and this time I cried for about a month straight. It felt good to release the emotion, but I felt like I would never heal. Today I can say that through the violent suffering of Jesus, I found comfort in my time of sorrow. He made sure I knew that he understood my pain and beyond.

chapter three

My Abuser's Profile:

Write a thorough description of your abuser, including how he or she displayed the banality of evil, a pervasive denial of responsibility, bold deceitfulness, harsh judgmentalism, or calculated intimidation.

What does the Lord require of us? To act justly: as Christians we have the responsibility to respond on behalf of the oppressed. To love mercy: as Christians we are uniquely poised to provide protection for the abused and hope for change for the abuser. To walk humbly with our God: as Christians we walk with Him and care for His children as He has cared for us. (Micah 6:8)

—Nancy A. Murphy

> Fret not yourself because of evildoers...For they will soon fade like the grass and wither like the green herb. Trust in the Lord, and do good; dwell in the land and befriend faithfulness. Delight yourself in the Lord, and He will give you the desires of your heart. Commit your way to the Lord; trust in him, and he will act. He will bring forth your righteousness as the light, and your justice as the noonday.
> (Psalm 37:1-6 ESV)

chapter three
BELIEVE IT. SPEAK IT. FEEL...

Read and reread Isaiah 53 at the beginning of this chapter. Allow the words to soak in until you can feel them; connect to the truth of them. Jesus loves you intimately and exquisitely; He's taken up your cause! Any other voices that disagree—from inside your head or outside—are lies, lies, lies! You're God's beloved, and He laid everything down on your behalf, including His own son. *Use this page to journal your reflections on the suffering Savior who took all of your sins upon Himself.*

chapter three

My thoughts and feelings...

May those forced to travel at night take comfort here. May those who yearn for God learn that God is passionately yearning for them. As we all stumble falteringly forward together through the darkness, may the God who is hurrying toward us, rushing like a mother runs at the sound of cries, find us all quickly.

—Jonathan Montaldo

Chapter Four
Portrait of an Abusive Family

Raw Iron

"Stick by my side," he says out loud to his brother, as they grasp in the darkness looking for the others.
"We'll find something soon," he whispers from within, as the feeling of death creeps in beneath his skin.

He staggers to his feet to get any sort of bearing, getting no sympathy from the night, as the cold is uncaring.
"I'm falling apart man," he hears his brother's voice. "We're out here dying alone, and there is no other choice."

Where is there refuge when we were both left behind? How can one take shelter from destruction inside the mind?
Their feet dig deep and heavy into the muddy brown soil, parallel to the weight of their spirits in the midst of this toil.

"I'm broken too, my brother, and I'm getting more lost," speaking of the abandonment, of God, and the cost.
In the still silence of night, in the deepest of dark, they cry out for God's salvation to deliver a spark.

A merciful, loving God attentive to their heartfelt broken cry, calls for the dawn's breaking light to take its place in the sky.
Take warmth my sons; the long night has been broken. Let your footing be made steady; let your joy be awoken.

I did not bring you out here just to leave you to die. I am molding you to my purpose; I am making you mine.
You are as raw iron to be smelted and shaped into a likeness to have my mantle draped.

I will temper you both into a defensive sword to stand for the broken, the weak, and the poor.
"Rise up from your grave," God said, " and drink from my well. I will encamp among the broken, and with the humble I dwell."

With a renewed spirit, they both stood once more, equipped with a hope and a fire not seen before.
As iron sharpens iron so does one man sharpen another. A mission in hand, he prepares for war alongside his brother.

To combat solitude and the abandoned bride and express the hope of God in which they reside.

—Jay M.

chapter four

Typically, abuse doesn't occur in a vacuum; there's a context. The context is often the dynamics of a person's family of origin, which fostered an atmosphere that allowed—and sometimes even encouraged—the abuse. It's often the dynamics of a family of origin that kept the abused from being believed and protected. Sadly, the effects of these dynamics can be as—or even more—damaging than the abuse itself. It's often very difficult for abuse victims to recognize the unhealthy family dynamics they experienced growing up, for this was generally the only family system they've known.

It's rare to find a family that will label itself as dysfunctional, let alone abusive. This is especially true of the parents in the family system. For parents to admit their families are flawed, the parents have to concede that they're either the perpetrator of the abuse or that they failed to protect their children from the abuse. Living in a family system in denial of its most basic reality—the abuse in its midst—will inevitably produce profoundly negative effects in the family members. Those who grow up in a family where abuse takes place are taught not to trust feelings and intuitions. They're also taught not to express feelings or, even worse, not to feel feelings. They're taught not to speak truth. They're taught to absorb guilt and shame that is not theirs. They're taught not to talk about the obvious. These, and more, are the sad realities of abusive families. While all families are unique, there are recurring characteristics of abusive families—traits that are common to most or all abusive families.

There are no assumptions, no givens
You can't choose your family.
As if speaking this can make it all better,
As if that is explanation enough.
I have no assumptions about what should have been.
Assume you will be loved, because children should be.
Assume your father will love and protect you.
Assume your mother will be able to love you.
Assume you are safe and that life is good.
Assume that innocence is yours.
Assume that you will be okay.
God pushes me to pursue freedom,
His hand at the small of my back,
a nudge and a whisper,
gently prodding forward, cajoling,
as if I am a frightened animal
being coaxed from my box.
And I step, just a little—

I balk and back away,
even from His gentle hand.
What the hell happened to me?
What makes me feel like curling up
as if I am a child of five, maybe six,
alone and frightened? I hear my child voice
telling me to be afraid, very afraid—
there is no one to trust, no one to help—
no one safe.
And I don't know why I am afraid now,
but I never doubt my fear when it speaks.
That is where I live now,
in the skin of a child
cowering in some corner,
uncertain what is so frightening,
other than everything is,
and that is reason enough
to be afraid.

chapter four

In *Mending the Soul* Dr. Tracy outlines fourteen characteristics common to abusive families. We're not able to develop all of these here, so you're encouraged to read chapter four of *Mending the Soul* for a complete explanation of these characteristics, which are found in King David's family (2 Samuel 13).

Abusive families usually possess some or all of the following fourteen characteristics. Can you relate to any of them?

- ☐ Parents don't value family members equally.
- ☐ The needs of individual family members are highly expendable.
- ☐ Reality is difficult to discern.
- ☐ The victim is made responsible for meeting needs they can't legitimately meet.
- ☐ Appearances are deceptive.
- ☐ Vulnerable family members aren't protected.
- ☐ There's no straightforward, healthy communication.
- ☐ Power is used to take advantage of weaker family members.
- ☐ There's emotional instability.
- ☐ Victims are shamed, blamed, and demeaned.
- ☐ There's social isolation and a lack of intimate relationships.
- ☐ There are strict codes of silence, especially if the abuser is a family member.
- ☐ Proper, healthy emotions are distorted or destroyed.
- ☐ The wrong people are protected.

These fourteen traits can be synthesized into five important areas of family function and dysfunction. We'll be examining each of these in this chapter:

- Power
- Relationships
- Reality
- Emotions
- Communication

The body is a dwelling place, a shelter for the mind.
A transient and restless camp for the refugee kind
There is nowhere I can travel that it does not follow me,
For the soul inside this body is longing to be free.

chapter four

EXPLOITATION OF POWER IN FAMILIES

Authority is delegated from God to humankind to accomplish good (Romans 13:1-4). God gives parents authority over their children to accomplish good in their children's lives (Ephesians 6:1-4). Husbands are given authority in the marital relationship in order to sacrificially love, protect, provide, and nurture their wives (Ephesians 5:25-27). Unfortunately, many of us don't experience protection, love, or nurture from our fathers or husbands. Many experience just the opposite.

Jesus taught us to pray that God's will would be done on earth the same way it is accomplished in heaven (Matthew 6:10); God doesn't desire for people to perish (2 Peter 3:9), yet we know that some do. Similarly, God's design for authority isn't accomplished on earth the way it is in heaven.

This human distortion of God's intentions began in the Garden of Eden. After Adam and Eve disobeyed God by eating the forbidden fruit, chaos ensued. Their relationship with God changed (Genesis 3:8); their relationship with each other changed (Genesis 3:7); their relationship with the earth changed (Genesis 3:17-19). Because of sin, God predicted an abuse of power taking place within relationships. The potential for the abuse of authority by sinful men is part of the curse. Sadly, this is what many of us know firsthand.

Of course, all of us sin and are sinned against in this post-Eden world. The healthy individual once made aware of his or her hurtful behavior desires to make it right—seeking to repair the relational breach as quickly as he or she is able. Therefore, we must think about families and other relational systems on a continuum from healthy and functional to dysfunctional or abusive:

| Nurturing and Safe | Covertly Narcissistic | Overtly Abusive |

<< ——————————————————————————————————————— >>

Fear of being alone: It is powerful, nuclear. I still am moved by it. What am I to do now that I've survived? Who am I if I am not struggling? Who am I if I am alive and out of danger?

Power wasn't exploited in my family, in fact it seemed non-existent. I have difficulty with the concept of abuse when there was no apparent intent, yet I am angry! The neglect just left me feeling at odds with everyone, including myself.

Abusive or Narcissistic Families Exploit POWER
By Creating Powerlessness: *I can't stop this pain!*

When a person's power is exploited by an abusive family system, it creates in the victim a terror of being powerless. The victim feels helpless to stop suffering—their own or someone else's. When a child grows up in a family where he or she is unable to communicate pain in a way that elicits comfort or expresses hurt and need, he or she grows into an adult who is unable to relationally connect. The reality of powerlessness as a child creates the belief of powerlessness as an adult. Healing is basically relearning to feel, to express, and to need in a community of safe people, where nurture and comfort are the norm.

Think about your present sense of personal power in your significant relationships.
Describe how empowered or disempowered you felt as a child in your family of origin. Then describe what level of power you experience in your relationships today. How might you currently be compensating or protecting yourself in your present relationships to avoid feeling powerless again?

Then (during the abuse) | *Now (after the abuse)*

How do you currently compensate in relationships to avoid feeling powerless?

chapter four

By Creating Fear or Distrust of Authority: *I stay under the radar!*

In the space below describe how you responded to unjust or uncaring authority figures as a child. How did you respond when you were with them? How did you respond behind their back? How has this impacted you? How do you respond today?

As a child	Now

By Creating Rebellion: *No one can tell me what to do!*

Are you inwardly or outwardly rebellious? Why or why not? Give examples.

As a child	Now

chapter four

Abusive or Narcissistic Families Lack Intimate RELATIONSHIPS

If you struggle to maintain intimate relationships, the task is to figure out why. A person's childhood provides important clues to the problem. Every one of us relates off of scripts or relational templates we experienced or saw modeled as children. If these relational patterns aren't exposed and examined, we'll be hard-pressed to change many of the negative patterns. Some have terrible stories of abuse and neglect, which makes it easy to understand the struggle to create and maintain intimate adult relationships. However, others have seemingly uneventful childhoods that are devoid of conflict, abuse, or addiction. In these homes not only was there the absence of anger and conflict but also the absence of love, the absence of comfort, the absence of emotion, the absence of acknowledgement, the absence of . . .

Intimacy is basically the freedom to know and be known within the colorful differences that make us both God-like and human. It's the freedom to make mistakes, the freedom to feel, to differ, to speak, to offer opinions in an atmosphere of mutuality and respect. Dr. Harriet Lerner astutely observes, "the level of underground anxiety or emotional intensity in a family determines how much freedom individuals have to discover, clarify, and express their own truths—and how accurately they will see themselves and others" (*The Dance of Deception*).

An abuser isn't concerned with the needs of others—especially the needs of the victim. He or she is merely concerned with satisfying himself or herself. That's the nature of abuse. Often this isn't difficult for us to discern; however, what can be difficult is how other family members—or the family as a group—also considered your needs expendable. Often other family members knew—or should have known—of the abuse and still failed to protect. There are reasons behind their failure to protect. Those reasons are most likely some form of self-protection on the part of the other family members. Therefore, your need to be protected, believed, and supported was jettisoned in order to serve other family members' needs for financial security, reputation, safety, etc.

Identify the basic needs that were unmet by your family. Check all that apply.

- ☐ To be protected
- ☐ To be believed
- ☐ To be nurtured
- ☐ To be comforted
- ☐ To have appropriate physical touch
- ☐ To have physical needs met
- ☐ To be esteemed
- ☐ To be respected
- ☐ To be known
- ☐ To be shown kindness
- ☐ To be allowed to express individuality
- ☐ To be a child
- ☐ To be shown affection
- ☐ To be allowed to express emotions

> My eye wastes away because of affliction. Lord, I have called daily upon You. Will You work wonders for the dead? Shall the dead arise and praise You?
> (Psalm 88:9-10 NKJV)

chapter four

Draw or collage a picture of yourself as a child in your family of origin here or on a separate sheet of paper. Put in as much detail as possible. What does your family portrait communicate to you?

chapter four

Now draw your current family—if you're single draw your significant relationship(s) or community.
What does your current family portrait communicate to you? About you? What do you want to change?

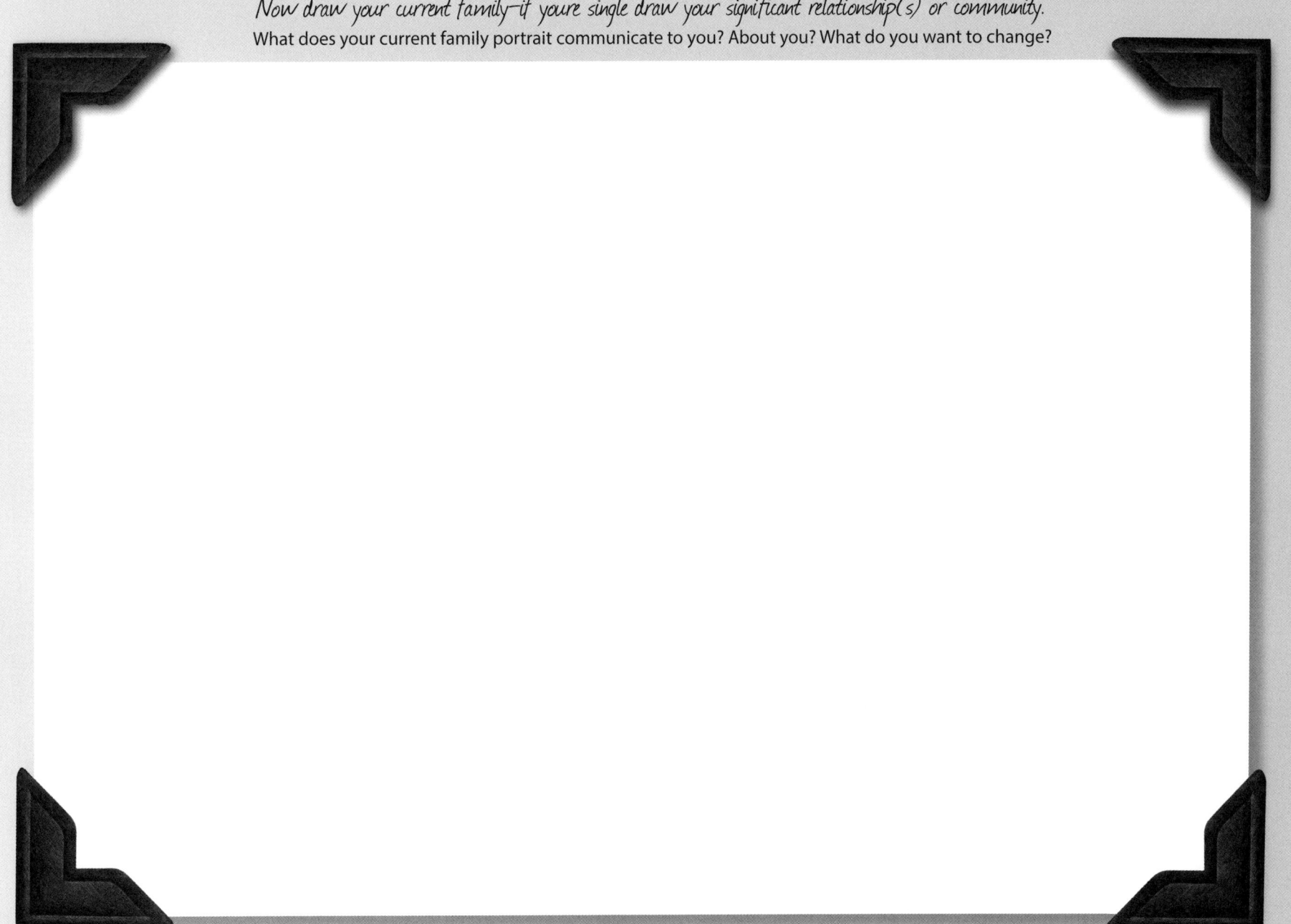

Children shouldn't have to look out for their parents; parents look out for the children. (2 Corinthians 12:15)

When our needs go unmet for significant periods of time, we feel pain and suffer loss. In healthy families when a member hurts, others are there to acknowledge the pain and offer comfort. In unhealthy families (abandoning, narcissistic, or abusive) pain is unacknowledged, unexpressed, and thus experienced alone, without comfort. If this emotional neglect continues, the soul eventually dies, and hope is lost. These losses deserve to be grieved: remembered, felt, and expressed in a context of relational comfort. I believe the best way to do this is in a letter or prayer to God—be completely honest about what you're feeling and wanting.

Below are the words of a young man who survived atrocities of both abuse and neglect on the streets of Portland. Today, he's finding healing in a small Mending the Soul group in his loving church. He poignantly describes how he's mourning the loss of his friends who are still on the streets. He offers them true intimacy through emotional and physical touch in a context of prayer—he asks God for their healing. He writes:

Joey sat across the room from me while I turned up the worship music. Within a few minutes the room fell into a peaceful silence. I looked up at Joey and could see shame and pain in his eyes. I looked away to give him some space and to make him feel safe. The atmosphere of the room was such that I began to quietly pray in front of him. Courage rose up within me. I remembered the loving and gentle care you and Pastor Steve had shown me while consoling me during my heartbreaking moments. Steve placed his hand upon my heart and head while you wrapped your arms around me in a tight, safe embrace. I copied this model after getting up slowly. Once I was standing next to him, I gently placed my hand over his heart and my other hand on his head. I leaned over and whispered into his ear my prayer to the Lord. I declared truths over him, binding lies and releasing truth. I prayed: "Rise up Nathan and find to courage to fight. Heal his heart, Lord, for it is broken. Heal his mind from damage due to drugs." I continued to pray, asking the Holy Spirit to come and heal him. I couldn't see his face, yet I saw him wipe his eyes. I could tell his heart was impacted by the presence of God, worship music, and healing touch. Wow! My heart was overcome with joy, as I knew the Lord had touched his heart. I knew then that this is what I want to do for my friends who are chained to the hustle lifestyle. I want so much for them to experience the healing power of the King of Kings; Lord of Lords; Savior; and Jesus, Son of the Living God. His power can and will overcome the darkness that shrouds them. Not by my might, but by His. I want to see the day when each one of them is singing in victory to the Lord and praying for those hurting. I know deep within my heart that the eyes of the Lord and heaven saw this. I'll continue to petition before our King for their freedom and mine.

chapter four

How were your unmet needs met by others? Or were they?

What strategies did you develop to take care of yourself?

Are any of these strategies maladaptive (worked at the time, but relationally destructive today)?

Do you recognize any relational patterns today that might be connected to your early unmet needs?

chapter four

Abusive or Narcissistic Families Deny REALITY

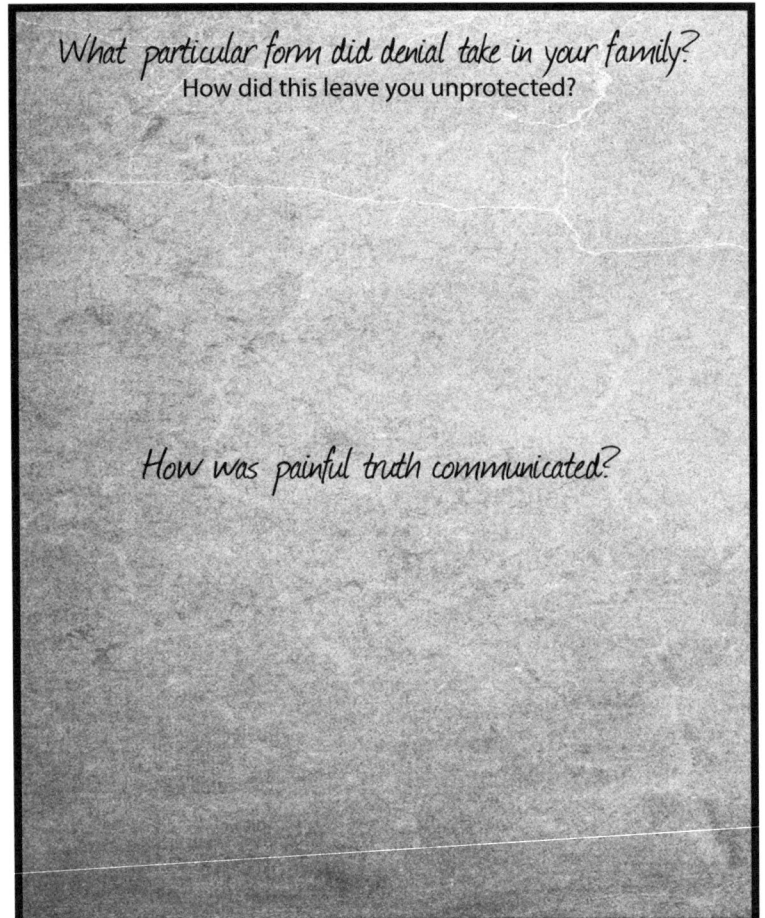

What particular form did denial take in your family?
How did this leave you unprotected?

How was painful truth communicated?

As we discussed in chapter one, denial is a common defense mechanism—a distortion of reality—that everyone uses to some degree. It's an automatic response to avoid something uncomfortable. When families deny the reality of pain it can take various forms:

Outright verbal denial. This is when one claims that no abuse has occurred or denies that the event(s) constitutes abuse. The reasoning given by family members to deny abuse can be downright outrageous: ignoring details, believing a person who is a demonstrated liar, giving no weight to survivor's accounts, ignoring blatant physical evidence, etc.

Obtuse failure to observe. This is when family members fail to pick up on what should be obvious clues, fail to follow up on unusual events, fail to follow up on statements made by the victim, believe the abuser's denial without sufficiently questioning it or giving proper weight to what the victim has said, see evidence of more minor abuse and fail to investigate whether greater abuse is occurring, etc.

Silence. This is when one admits to oneself that abuse has occurred but doesn't talk about it or allow it to be discussed, subtly sending the message: *"We don't talk about this."*

Minimizing: This is when a family member attempts to characterize the abuse as *"not that bad"* or *"only once in a while."* This also is when a family member accuses the survivor of exaggerating the abuse or making too big a deal out of it.

Woe to those who call evil good and good evil, who put darkness for light and light for darkness, who put bitter for sweet and sweet for bitter! (Isaiah 5:20)

chapter four

When the reality of abuse is denied, intense pain and confusion are created for the victim and those who love him or her. A child or adult survives in the midst of this distortion of reality by maintaining a semblance of control or distancing or dissociating from feelings—especially panic and fear. In short, when families don't talk, feel, or deal with the pain in their midst, some form of dissociation is the result. There are three general forms of dissociation:

1. Repressing, projecting or rationalizing the difficult feelings that are causing pain.

2. Using a substance to alter the painful feelings: alcohol, sugar, nicotine, drugs, or caffeine.

3. Maintaining a level of negative excitement that keeps one unaware of deeper fear. The brain has an ability to build a protective armor by producing adrenaline, endorphins, and melatonin to chemically block the perception of pain.

> From prophet to priest, everyone deals falsely. They have healed the wound of my people lightly, saying, "Peace, peace!" when there is no peace.
> (Jeremiah 6:13-14 ESV)

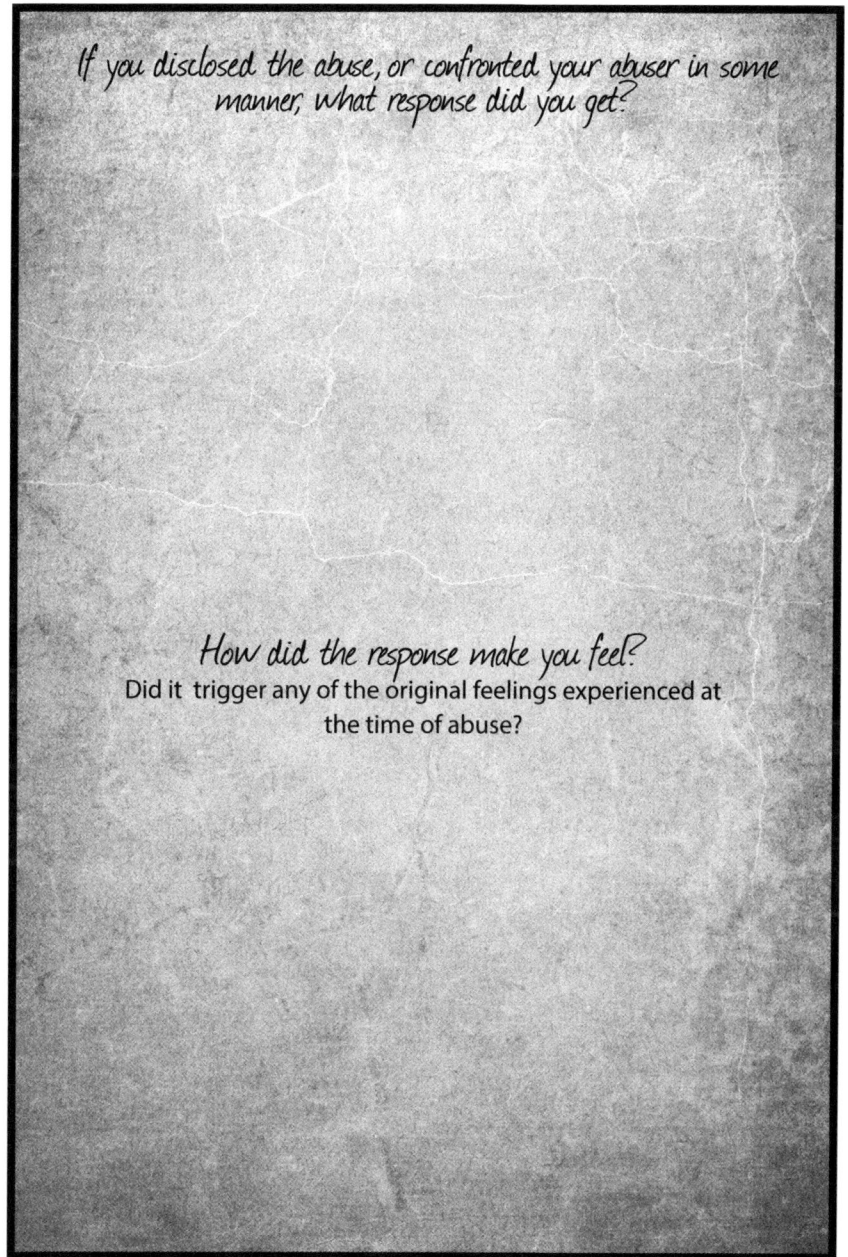

If you disclosed the abuse, or confronted your abuser in some manner, what response did you get?

How did the response make you feel?
Did it trigger any of the original feelings experienced at the time of abuse?

chapter four

Abusive or Narcissistic Families Distort EMOTIONS

Abusive families discourage the experience and expression of emotions. These emotions are simply too threatening. If the victims and witnesses to the abuse actually expressed the true emotions they were feeling, it would be obvious to outsiders that something was gravely wrong. In no time the abusers would be found out. The abuser can't allow this to happen. If the abuse is being labeled as insignificant, then the victim shouldn't be crying, shouldn't be angry, shouldn't be depressed, etc. One way or another it's communicated that any display of emotions is off limits.

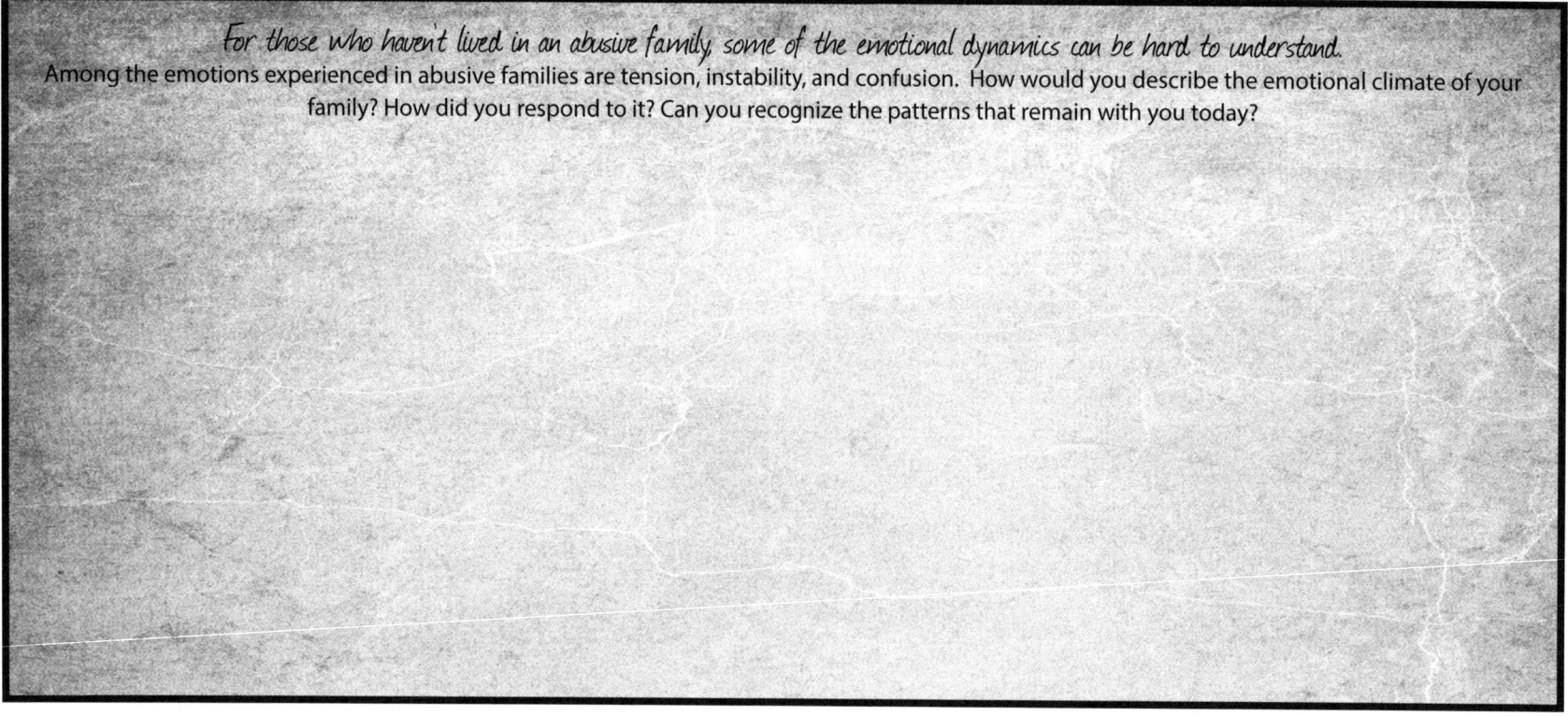

For those who haven't lived in an abusive family, some of the emotional dynamics can be hard to understand. Among the emotions experienced in abusive families are tension, instability, and confusion. How would you describe the emotional climate of your family? How did you respond to it? Can you recognize the patterns that remain with you today?

I'm listening now. I think it is my greatest glory. There is so much to be heard. I have spent my life talking within, with no one in particular listening. My outward silence was deafening..

chapter four

Draw a picture of yourself as a child (or describe yourself).
How did you split from your real self: the child who was experiencing the pain but was not able to talk about it or feel?

Me on the inside as a child:	Me on the outside as a child:
Me on the inside today:	Me on the outside today:

This was the beginning of your "false" or created self—the self who would seek safety from pain or abandonment.
This false self can become so prominent and real that you lose your true sense of identity, forgetting who you really are.

chapter four

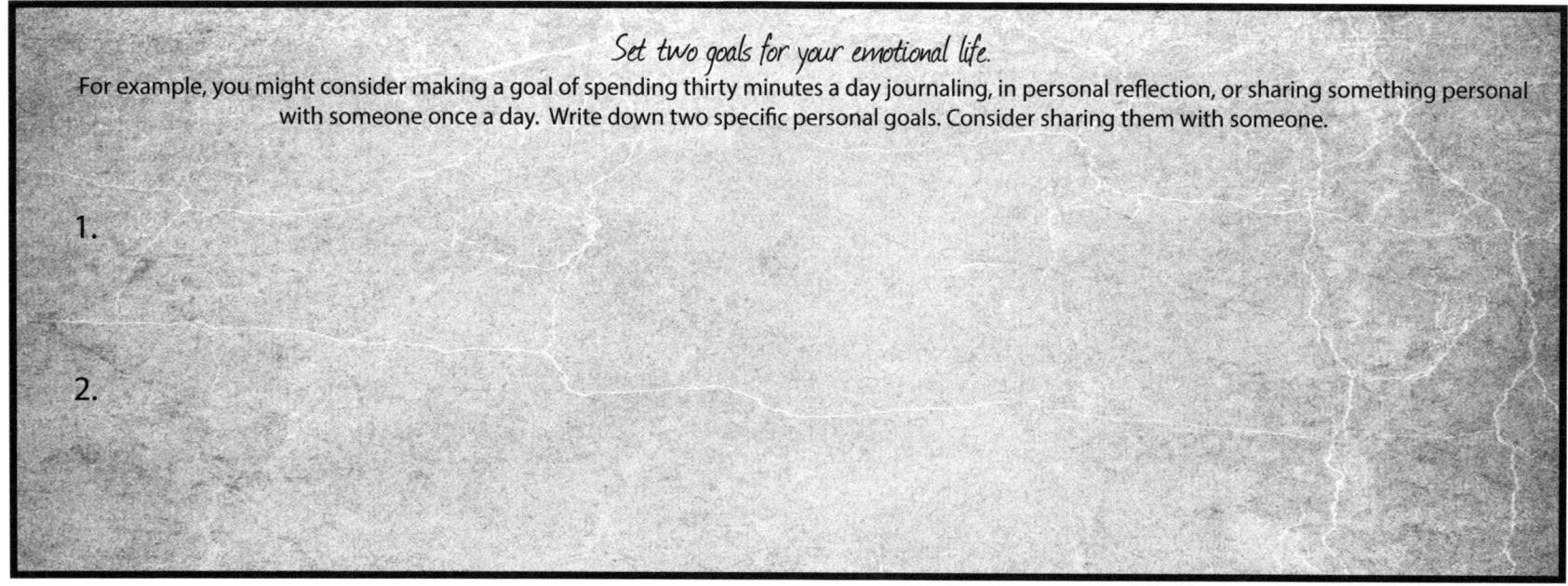

Set two goals for your emotional life.
For example, you might consider making a goal of spending thirty minutes a day journaling, in personal reflection, or sharing something personal with someone once a day. Write down two specific personal goals. Consider sharing them with someone.

1.

2.

The world of the traumatized child is one of constant stress and intense energy, which help the child adapt for survival. With a poor ability to understand feelings and limited cognitive judgment, the child cannot determine the risk at any one time; the abused child lives in a constant state of vigilance as if she were in her own private war zone. Without the ability to use reason, the traumatized child has the unending experience of being vulnerable and helpless, a very frightening combination.

—Dave Ziegler, *Traumatic Experience and the Brain*

No more lies, no more pretense. Tell your neighbor the truth. In Christ's body we're all connected to each other, after all. When you lie to others, you end up lying to yourself.
(Ephesians 4:25 The Message)

chapter four

Abusive or Narcissistic Families Distort COMMUNICATION

Certain patterns of communication are seen repeatedly in dysfunctional and abusive families. These result in family members feeling insecure, devalued, and unconfident.

Secret Keeping versus Truth Telling

Abuse functions like the "emperor's new clothes" in abusive families. It's there for all to see, but it's not acknowledged, because of fear. This code of silence protects the abuser and re-victimizes the child. Secrets like these are deadly. An abusive family will confuse the concepts of privacy and secrecy. Dr. Harriet Lerner deals with this distinction in her book *The Dance of Deception*:

> *My right to privacy includes my right to control access to a certain amount of emotional and physical space that I take—correctly or not—to be "mine." Privacy protects me from intrusion and ensures my separateness as a human being among others . . . I do not seek privacy in order to fool others or engage in acts of deception. Rather, I seek privacy primarily to protect my dignity and ultimate separateness as a human being. . . . Secrecy always involves the intention to hide or conceal information from another person, just as lying always involves the intention to convince another of what we ourselves do not believe to be true. . . . As I see it, however, privacy shifts into secrecy when an act of deliberate concealment or hiding has a significant impact on a relationship process. Secrecy, as I define it here, is deliberate concealment that makes a difference.*

The abusive family will try to convince you that the abuse is private, that it's no one else's business. *"What happens in the family, stays in the family,"* they'll say. Rules around secrecy are spoken and unspoken, often resulting in painful consequences if they're broken.

> *Concealing something important takes attention and emotional energy that could otherwise serve more creative ends. When we must "watch ourselves," even when we do so automatically and seemingly effortlessly, the process dissipates our energy and erodes our integrity. (The Dance of Deception)*

> *Secrets divide us into insiders and outsiders, but they do more than that. The number and types of secrets we keep from one another define our relationships. They touch on how much we trust and distrust each other, how we gauge each other in terms of strengths and weaknesses. Secrets can also help us to define ourselves. What is it about our history that is so painful, so threatening, so shameful, that we need to conceal it? Keeping secrets can create an atmosphere of tension, which is relieved when family members have the opportunity to confront the information and openly air their feelings about it. Just as keeping secrets can be divisive, sharing them can build equality, respect, and trust between members of a family. (Webster, Family Secrets)*

Dysfunctional Family Rules:
1. Don't talk
2. Don't feel
3. Don't deal

chapter four

Abuse going on in a family takes emotional energy to conceal. Therefore, it's emotionally healing to talk about it. It's not private, and for the health and restoration of all involved, it shouldn't be kept private. Keeping silent about abuse is unhealthy secrecy. It's wrong for families to enact these codes of silence and to forbid its members from doing the very thing they most need to do: feel and talk about abuse.

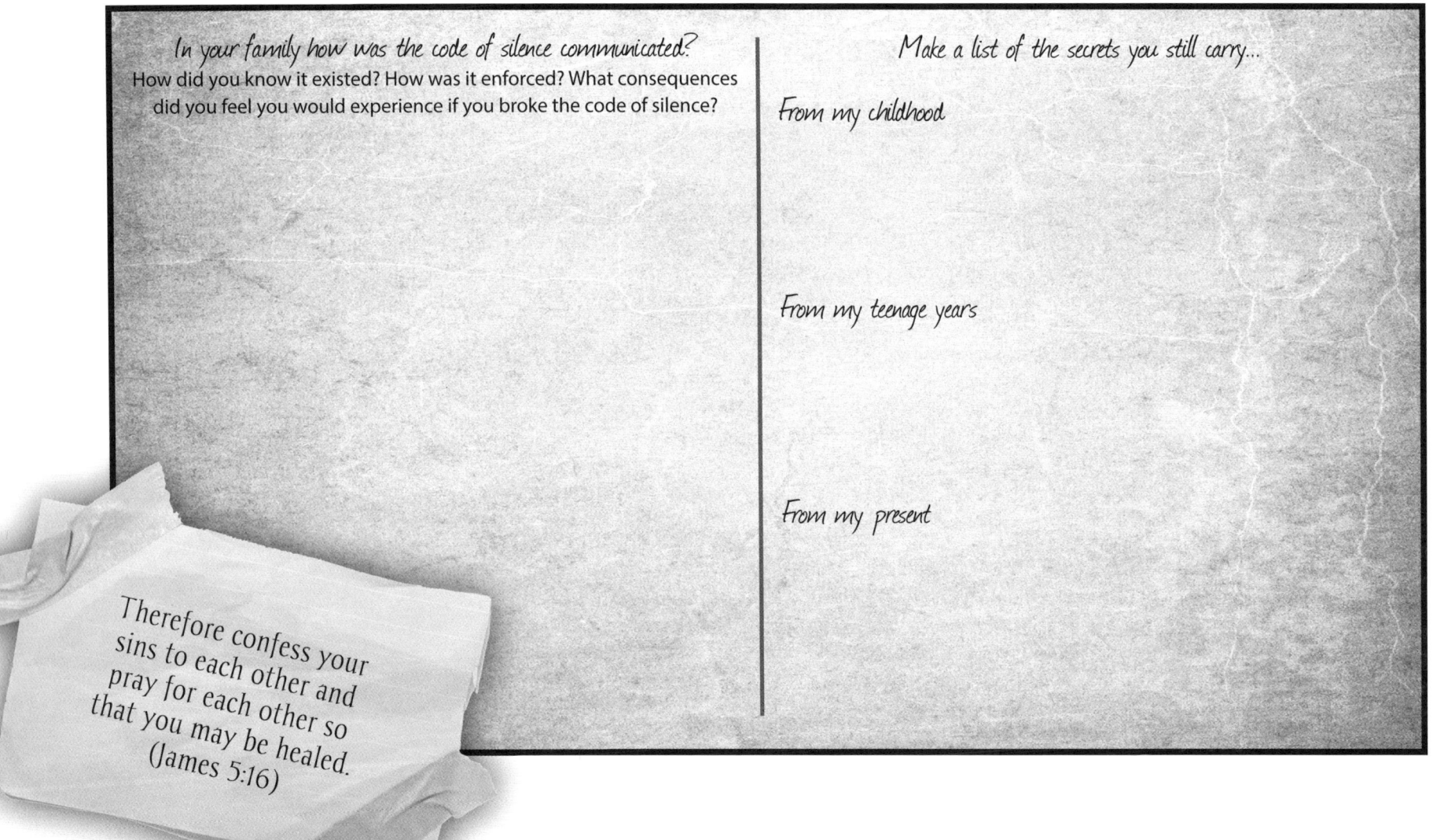

In your family how was the code of silence communicated? How did you know it existed? How was it enforced? What consequences did you feel you would experience if you broke the code of silence?

Make a list of the secrets you still carry...

From my childhood

From my teenage years

From my present

Therefore confess your sins to each other and pray for each other so that you may be healed. (James 5:16)

chapter four

My thoughts and feelings...

As a deer pants for flowing streams, so pants my soul for you, O God. My soul thirsts for God, for the living God. When shall I come and appear before God? (Psalm 42:1-2 ESV)

At that time I will deal with all who oppressed you; I will rescue the lame and gather those who have been scattered. I will give them praise and honor in every land where they were put to shame . . . I will bring you home.

(Zephaniah 3:19-20)

Chapter Five
Shame

Original Design

It's made of shame and built with lies, the mask I found I wear
It keeps me happy, laughing, safe—the truth too hard to bear
It shows the world my choice for me, not really where I've been
Those things are unacceptable; they're drenched with hurt and sin

But then my journey takes a turn. God says, "It's time to heal—
It's time to face the ugliness, it's time for you to feel"
My laughter turns to mourning, as I miss what could have been
Emotions are not those I choose as the healing begins

Little did I know that it would somehow set me free
To start again and find out who God wanted me to be
I know in time and by His grace, joy and laughter will be mine
God wants to show the world and me
His original design

—Dagny

My name is Sophia, and I'm thirty-two. I want to tell you my story...

I'm thankful for the healing I've experienced through Mending the Soul. For the first time, I felt understood. I still have a long way to go, but I never dreamed I would be where I am today. I have a husband, a daughter, and friends. My mom and I are working on our relationship. I am happy most days. That's a miracle.

Satan has used fear and shame to entrap and manipulate me. I'll never get back what I've lost, but I'm beginning to trust again and envision a future for myself. I have many memories that will never leave me, but one in particular has become my destiny. I was at my lowest point, and I remember being thrown into the back of a paddy wagon with other "prostitutes." There was a mangled, emaciated girl on the floor of the van, and she was all tweaked out. Her face was dirty and her makeup smudged—when I looked at her there was a tear on her cheek. She reached out her hand to me and said, "Help me. Please help me." I'll never forget that girl. I knew then that God would save me and redeem me so that I could help other girls like her.

My starting place has been the painful process of being honest about my life. I realize now that it was shame that kept me enslaved to the streets. I felt incredibly guilty for so many things, such as being an angry, rebellious teenager. I still don't understand why I was so mad as a kid, but I was, and I took it out on everybody in my family, especially my parents. The night I was picked up by an older man, I had sneaked out of the house to be with my high school friends who my parents didn't like. My parents would never have given me permission to be with them...Once this guy raped me (I only now can call it rape), he started giving me drugs. I liked the way they made me feel and felt guilty for that. Within weeks I had sex with two of his friends and then felt even greater levels of guilt. He would make fun of my body—degrading me and then building me up—over and over again until I believed him. I've looked demons in the face. It was so confusing because I didn't really want to be with him. Now I realize that I stayed because of the shame. I knew that I couldn't go home, because deep down I believed that I deserved the things that were happening to me—that I deserved him. Now I know that this pervasive feeling of badness and false guilt is shame. I wish I'd known then. This guy betrayed my trust and sexualized me in a way that bonded me to him.

My shame was the glue.

chapter five

LIVING SHAME FREE

Shame is a powerful emotion and is one of the primary effects of abuse. It drives us into hiding, wreaking havoc on all our relationships. Shame distorts how we perceive almost everything in life—especially ourselves. When we're filled with shame, the entirety of our experiences—no matter how positive—are experienced through the shame. Shame binds, numbs, disconnects, and destroys. Nothing seems to erase the ever-present feelings of worthlessness.

Shame can attach itself to other emotions, drives (such as hunger and sex), or needs (such as security, love, or attention). It appears at the most unexpected times. For example, it's quite common for survivors of childhood sexual abuse to experience toxic shame each time they feel sexual desire or pleasure. Sadly, the shame was activated through the original abuse and is stubbornly connected to these other natural drives and normal feelings. Until these connections are exposed, understood, and integrated, a person will feel little control over changing these negative, shame-based associations. In this chapter we'll identify six healthy responses to shame.

Task One: Know the Difference Between Shame and Guilt

The first and most challenging task in recovery is untangling the difference between healthy shame (legitimate guilt) and toxic shame. More often than not, survivors carry guilt for the things (others' sin perpetrated against them) they are not responsible for. This false guilt is in actuality their toxic shame. They can carry this shame for a lifetime if it's not dealt with and teased out from the healthy guilt they are responsible for. Typically, when a person is sinned against, it creates wounds that go very deep and, in time, can morph into sinful responses. We'll address both healthy and unhealthy shame.

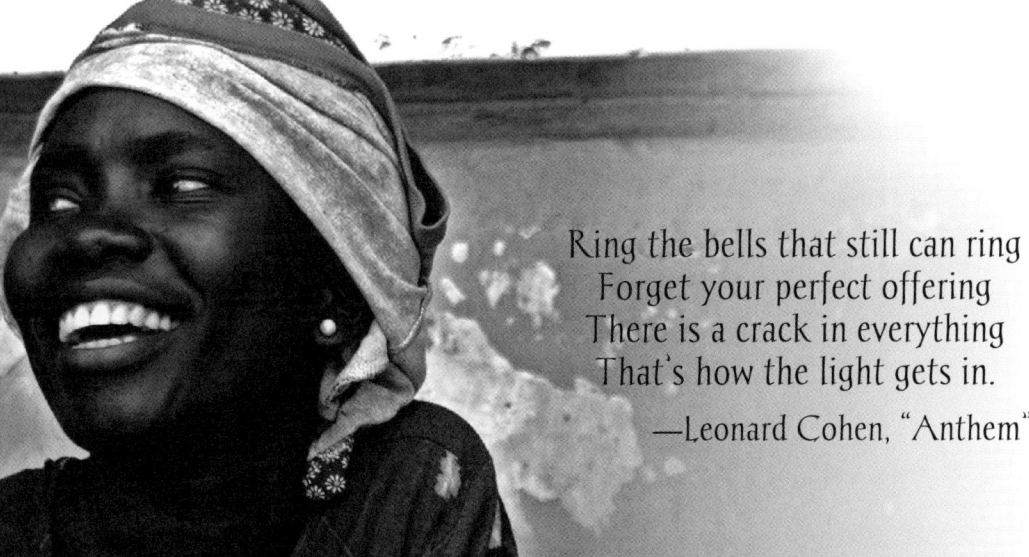

Ring the bells that still can ring
Forget your perfect offering
There is a crack in everything
That's how the light gets in.

—Leonard Cohen, "Anthem"

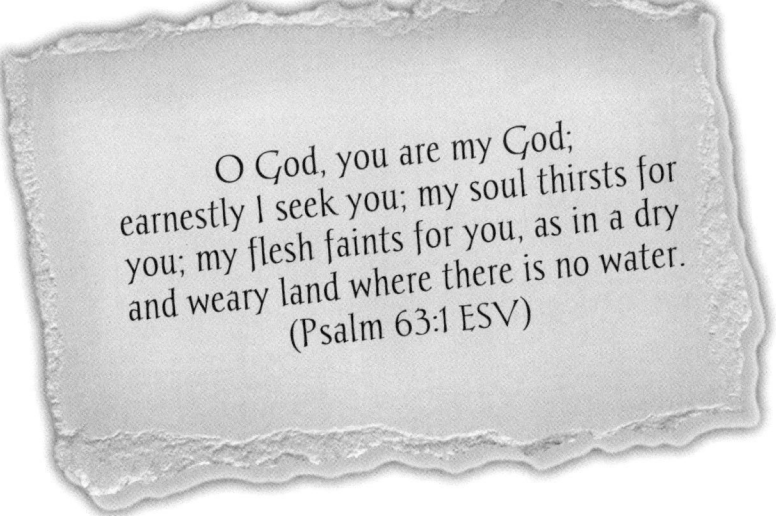

O God, you are my God; earnestly I seek you; my soul thirsts for you; my flesh faints for you, as in a dry and weary land where there is no water.
(Psalm 63:1 ESV)

chapter five

Healthy Shame

God in His pursuing love created healthy shame for a specific reason: to alert us that something is wrong, that we have done something wrong, and that we're on a pathway that will eventually lead to death. Our sin separates us from God (and others), and it's His love that triggers guilt when we've violated His ethic of love in any way. His desire is that this guilt drives us to repentance and thus life.

> As it is, I rejoice, not because you were grieved, but because you were grieved into repenting. For you felt a godly grief, so that you suffered no loss through us. For godly grief produces a repentance that leads to salvation without regret, whereas worldly grief produces death. (2 Corinthians 7:9-10 ESV)

Because of the cross and Jesus' redemptive death, the penalty for our sin (death) has already been completely satisfied, paid, taken care of! God has made us righteous by His son's death on a filthy cross so that we might stand righteous before Him. At this point, our only task is to simply confess and repent of the sin that's legitimately ours. This is a one-time act. Shockingly, once we have confessed, God removes our sin as far as the east is from the west (Psalm 103:12), never more to count it against us (Psalm 32:1-2), never more to be remembered (Jeremiah 31:34). It will be tempting to reclaim forgiven guilt. Don't! Instead, choose joy. Let it in.

Dear God,

There's quite a bit that I need to say . . .

Never believe anything about yourself or God that makes His grace to you seem anything less than astonishing.

—Randy Alcorn

chapter five

I feel healthy shame about . . .

I feel toxic shame about . . .

I feel intensely dirty when my body experiences sexual arousal. I have avoided sex with my husband for as long as I can remember.

Toxic Shame

Unlike healthy shame, toxic shame tells us that we're bad beyond repair, beyond forgiveness, beyond hope. Toxic shame often involves feeling shame and guilt for things that are not really our fault (such as being angry as a kid). Through toxic shame Satan distorts God's good gift of guilt so that we believe there's nothing we can do to get rid of it. He convinces us that we're worthless and always will be. Toxic shame robs us of hope and pushes us away from God and healthy relationships with people who are good for us and want to love us. It pushes us toward people who treat us badly; after all, that's what we think we deserve.

Stay alert! Watch out for your great enemy, the devil. He prowls around like a roaring lion, looking for someone to devour. Stand firm against him, and be strong in your faith. Remember that your Christian brothers and sisters all over the world are going through the same kind of suffering you are.

In his kindness God called you to share in His eternal glory by means of Christ Jesus. So after you have suffered a little while, he will restore, support, and strengthen you, and he will place you on a firm foundation. (1 Peter 5:8-10 NLT)

When I am aware of a need in my life, I will reach out to others who love me and ask for help. I will let myself experience joy and comfort, thanking God for His provision to me through others.

—J. Bradshaw, *Healing the Shame That Binds You*

chapter five

If you feel ready, begin to connect the dots from your original pain to the subsequent toxic shame and your present feelings, thoughts, and actions. Complete the sentence in the following exercise and continue journaling as other thoughts, feelings, or memories begin to pop up. Journal in the third person by writing about the child you were—this will help you separate who you are from who you were. Remember that you've already survived the horror of that pain. You are here . . . now, allowing God to heal and redeem your pain. Connect yourself to the present by holding onto a safe anchor (either literally or figuratively) that reminds you of His power to heal and love you. Please don't do this exercise alone—reach out to someone who feels safe, and do this section together, or do it in your group.

> Reproaches have broken my heart, so that I am in despair. I looked for pity, but there was none, and for comforters, but I found none.
> (Psalm 69:20 ESV)

> The Lord is merciful and gracious, slow to anger and abounding in steadfast love. . .He does not deal with us according to our sins, nor repay us according to our iniquities . . . As far as the east is from the west, so far does he remove our transgressions from us.
> (Psalm 103:8-12 ESV)

Do you feel shame at unexpected times?
Journal your thoughts and feelings, identifying when the shame began.

The first time I remember feeling shame for _____ was when . . .

chapter five

Task Two: Label Shame as Shame

Shame manifests in our lives in myriad ways. It's important that each of us knows how shame shows up—so that we can deepen our relationships and heal. Review the list of symptoms associated with shame. *Highlight the symptom(s) you have experienced in the past and circle the symptom(s) you're currently experiencing.*

Addictions/Compulsions
You use substances or people to numb shameful feelings and memories. You struggle with lying, avoidance, and maladaptive relational patterns.

Chronic Depression
You've struggled with a low, dark, or sad mood on most days for at least two years. You have chronic hopelessness, sleep disturbance, fatigue, and poor concentration.

Comparison/Competition
You constantly compare yourself to others in an attempt to feel superior. You're highly competitive and feel sad or angry when you fail.

Dishonesty with Negative Feelings
You learned as a child to numb feelings related to abuse or family-of-origin pain. You change your strong, distasteful feelings into more acceptable ones. You don't know your relational needs or how to advocate for them, because of emotional numbness. Chronic anxiety often results, which can produce a controlling style of relating.

External Focus
You create a perfect public persona due to fear of flaws being exposed. Your self-value depends on others' opinions, which are perceived as more valid than your own. You're achievement driven, often at the expense of others—too busy to relax and have fun.

Hypercriticism
You're cynical or sarcastic, with hatred for others who display traits you also have but don't like. Putting others down makes you feel better. You have unrealistic standards for yourself and others that can't be met, and you have difficulty forgiving.

Inability to Accept Criticism
You're unable to accept even constructive criticism. When you accept fault, it leads to shame, which keeps you from admitting and owning mistakes.

Inability to Accept Responsibility
You shift blame onto others; you can't admit fault for another's pain. You seldom say you're sorry.

Insecurity/Jealousy
You feel inferior to others, and you're prone to making comparisons. The achievements of others make you uncomfortable and defensive.

Intimacy Sabotaging
You have an intense fear of personal exposure, and you use avoidance and anger to keep others at comfortable distances. It's hard to trust people and show your real self.

Low Self-Esteem
You struggle to accept the fact that you're made in the image of God and are intrinsically worthy, regardless of achievements or others' opinions.

Self-Focus
You feel insecure, and you feel as though others are always focusing on you. It's hard to accept different opinions, thoughts, and feelings of others.

Sense of Not Belonging
You desperately long for acceptance and love, but you fear intimacy, and create a push-pull relational pattern. You constantly feel as if you don't fit in.

Shallowness
You hide your true self behind superficiality in relationships. You avoid any relational closeness, openness, or vulnerability that could lead to real intimacy. You're chronically unsatisfied.

chapter five

Shame distorts our vision of who God has created us to be. In reality, he thinks we're magnificent! The following poem expresses the truth of your original design through the playful metaphor of a crown.

On the day that we met and I put you to bed, I noticed a crown on the top of your head.
It was made up of sparkling, glimmering things like moonlight and fireflies, and dragonfly wings.
As the days came and went it was faithful and true, and it grew right along with the rest of you.
I always knew just what your crown meant. It said that you were MAGNIFICENT!

That's about as high as a word can climb! That's the top of a mountain . . . a steeple chime.
That's over the moon in a nursery rhyme . . .
And it means, like a star, YOU WERE BORN TO SHINE.

In other words, from your very first day, you were chosen to glow in a very big way!
With your crown made of glittering, high-flying things
You've got wind in your pocket, your wishes have wings.
You can run like you mean it . . . so, let the wind blow . . .
There's just no telling how high you can go!

Whatever it is you choose to do, no one can do it exactly like you.
Ride on the big slide! And if you fall down, remember your glorious, marvelous crown.
It won't flicker or fade. It won't dim. It won't leave. ALL YOU HAVE TO DO IS BELIEVE.

Do you, my child? I hope that you do . . .
Your crown is your best friend forever, by far.
It tells the true story of just who you are.
That's why every night, when I put you to bed,
I'm careful to kiss the crown on your head. You are loved.

—Nancy Tillman, *The Crown on Your Head*

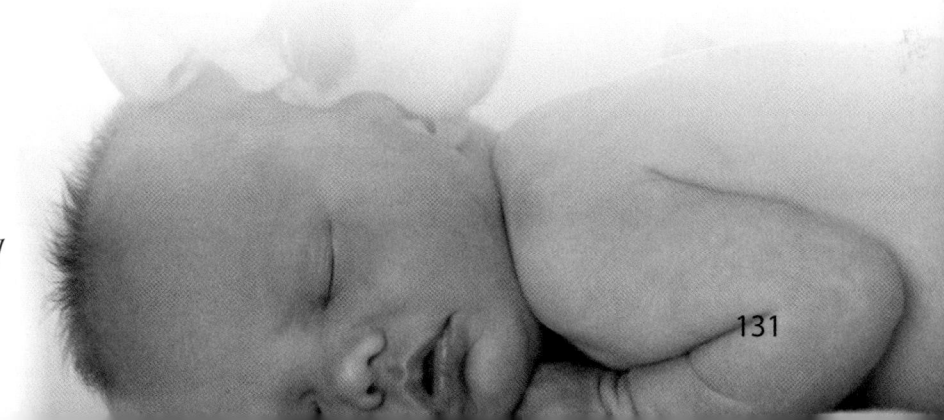

chapter five

Safe Anchor Image

In the frame below, draw, collage, or paste an image that reminds you of God's power and goodness to heal. This image will anchor your thoughts to the *truth* of who you are and who He is while you process through the memories and residually attached shame. Keep it for ready referencing as needed.

Some days I have a hard time holding onto the value of myself or seeing myself in the mirror of life with worth. I have a hard time just being me. As old days press down, I feel smaller under the weight, and I turn to see if I am still breathing after all this.

chapter five

Task Three: Talk—Feel—Deal

Facing the truth about your past is a strategic step you can't skip. God has called you to live in a real world as a real person to deal with real issues. To the degree that you've not dealt with the realities of your past and current life, you'll be unable to help others deal with theirs. Minimizing and denying your painful past will temporarily make you feel better, but shame will be growing in you like bad mold in the dark.

> *The time is ripe for looking back over the day, the week, the year, and trying to figure out where we have come from and where we are going to, for sifting through the things we have done and the things we have left undone for a clue to who we are and who, for better or worse, we are becoming. But again and again we avoid the long thoughts… We cling to the present out of wariness of the past. And why not, after all? We get confused. We need such escape as we can find. But there is a deeper need yet, I think, and that is the need—not all the time, surely, but from time to time—to enter that still room within us all where the past lives on as a part of the present, where the dead are alive again, where we are most alive ourselves to turnings and to where our journeys have brought us. The name of the room is Remember—the room where with patience, with charity, with quietness of heart, we remember consciously to remember the lives we have lived. (Frederick Buechner, A Room Called Remember)*

The apostle Paul leads the way by his example. In Philippians 3:1-13 he describes needing to first carefully evaluate his former life, including his shameful abuse of Christians, before he was able to successfully let go of those things that were in his past. We must do the same if we're to experience the same freedom.

More often than not, talented, gifted, highly successful super-achievers who have been admired and praised for their talents and achievements often struggle with feelings of emptiness and depression. Behind all this lurks a vague sense of self-alienation and a sense of meaninglessness. Once the drug of grandiosity is taken away, as soon as they are no longer the stars, they are plagued by deep feelings of shame and guilt.

—Alice Miller, *Drama of the Gifted Child*

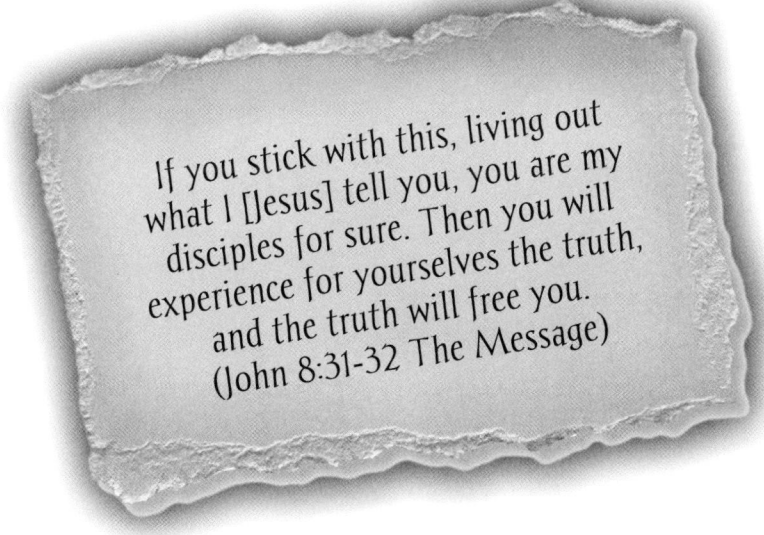

If you stick with this, living out what I [Jesus] tell you, you are my disciples for sure. Then you will experience for yourselves the truth, and the truth will free you. (John 8:31-32 The Message)

chapter five

Return to the timeline you began in chapter one. Add any memories that have surfaced since you did that first chapter. You may use symbols, pictures, or words. Remember, *you are in charge of what you share with others.* Record any feelings or thoughts after completing this exercise.

> Therefore, having put away falsehood, let each one of you speak the truth with his neighbor, for we are members one of another. (Ephesians 4:25 ESV)

Relentless

I know you...I know you by name
You plague my soul with a violent game

I recognize you by your hideous face
I know by your hunt in this maddening place

As if in the depths of the limitless sea
Relentless, you dwell inside of me

Reality beckons—it searches all parts
It peers sneeringly into hidden hearts

Reality beckons, but who can endure
Pain-saturated truths all pristine and pure

But endure it I must whether able or not
The painful reality that time has not bought

The truth that once hid behind lies so polite
It pursued without mercy endless depth, endless height

To trap me and capture any joy I once felt
To force me to look at lies where they dwelt

Deep in my heart denying the pain
Now it's free to display my bold-faced shame

How will I cope? What is my plan?
I'll hide truth again for as long as I can...

—T. Haley

chapter five

Task Four: Identify the Lies

> The original, shimmering self gets buried so deep that most of us end up hardly living out of it at all. Instead we live out all the other selves, which we are constantly putting on and taking off like coats and hats against the world's weather.
>
> —Frederick Buechner, *Telling Secrets*

Satan lies. Evil distorts. Jesus declares this about Satan: *"he was a murderer from the beginning, not holding to the truth for there is no truth in him. When he lies, he speaks his native language, for he is a liar and the father of lies"* (John 8:44). The evil embedded in Satan's lies is a distortion not only of our view of ourselves but also of others and God too. His is a power that misrepresents what's true and perverts what's beautiful. Of course, Satan doesn't have the power of God, thus he can't create. Because of this limitation, he cleverly distorts the best of what God has created. He masterfully deceives us into believing the worst about God and about ourselves so that we'll make choices accordingly.

I'll tell you a secret that will support you in quickly getting to the truth of your original design. Ask yourself—

What are the things you're most afraid of doing?
What do you secretly despise about yourself?
What are the first three negative words that come to mind for yourself?
What do you typically avoid?

Turn your answers to the above questions over, and the truth about your originally designed self will be hiding there. Lift the slime and negativity off, and you'll find beauty. Satan is working overtime to shut down the very expressions you were intended to have—the person you were created to be. When we're disconnected from our true selves, we lose our spiritual way, because God resides at the core of our being. Our return to God is a return to the center of life.

We often define ourselves in terms of the ugliness of what we have done or become rather than in terms of the essence of our life. We are made in the image of God, in the image of the One who is Beauty ... Think of a beautiful plant suffering from blight. If botanists were shown such a plant, even if they had never seen that particular type of plant before, they would define it in terms of its essential features and life-force. They would not define it in terms of its blight. Rather, the blight would be described as foreign to the plant, as attacking its essence. This may seem an obvious point botanically, but perhaps it is such an obvious point that we have missed the point when it comes to defining what is deepest within us.... Sin is attacking the essence of our being. What is deepest in us is the beauty of our origins. (J. Philip Newell, *Echo of the Soul: The Sacredness of the Human Body*)

chapter five

Lies are insidiously harmful—they're engineered by Satan and individually crafted to distort the best of what God has created in us and others. Since Satan is the "father of lies," he's a master at deception. The toxic shame that he creates in us as a result of our abuse or abandonment is pervasive and seems frighteningly real. God's Word, which contains the truth about His love for us and the beauty He has created in us, is our only guide for identifying and healing these destructive and deceptive beliefs about ourselves and others.

Place a check mark by each of the lies you have believed.

Lies about God...

- ☐ I can't trust God. He allowed me to be abused.
- ☐ God despises me.
- ☐ God is distant and uninterested in me.
- ☐ God is disgusted with me when I fail. Sooner or later He'll leave me.
- ☐ God wants to punish me and is angry with me.
- ☐ God will accept me if I'm good.
- ☐ Sooner or later God will reject me too.
- ☐ God loves others more than me. I am unlovable.
- ☐ God can't forgive some of the things I've done.
- ☐ Other: _____

Lies about others...

- ☐ Others say I'm worthless, so I must be.
- ☐ In order to be accepted by others, I must be perfect.
- ☐ Everyone always leaves me at the worst possible point.
- ☐ People will only hurt you or leave you. No one can be trusted.
- ☐ Women are all the same; they only want your money.
- ☐ No sane person would ever want me.
- ☐ Men only want me for sex.
- ☐ Sooner or later people will find out the truth about me and reject me.
- ☐ Other: _____

chapter five

As it is, I rejoice, not because you were grieved, but because you were grieved into repenting. For you felt a godly grief, so that you suffered no loss through us. For godly grief produces a repentance that leads to salvation without regret, whereas worldly grief produces death.
(2 Corinthians 7:9-10 ESV)

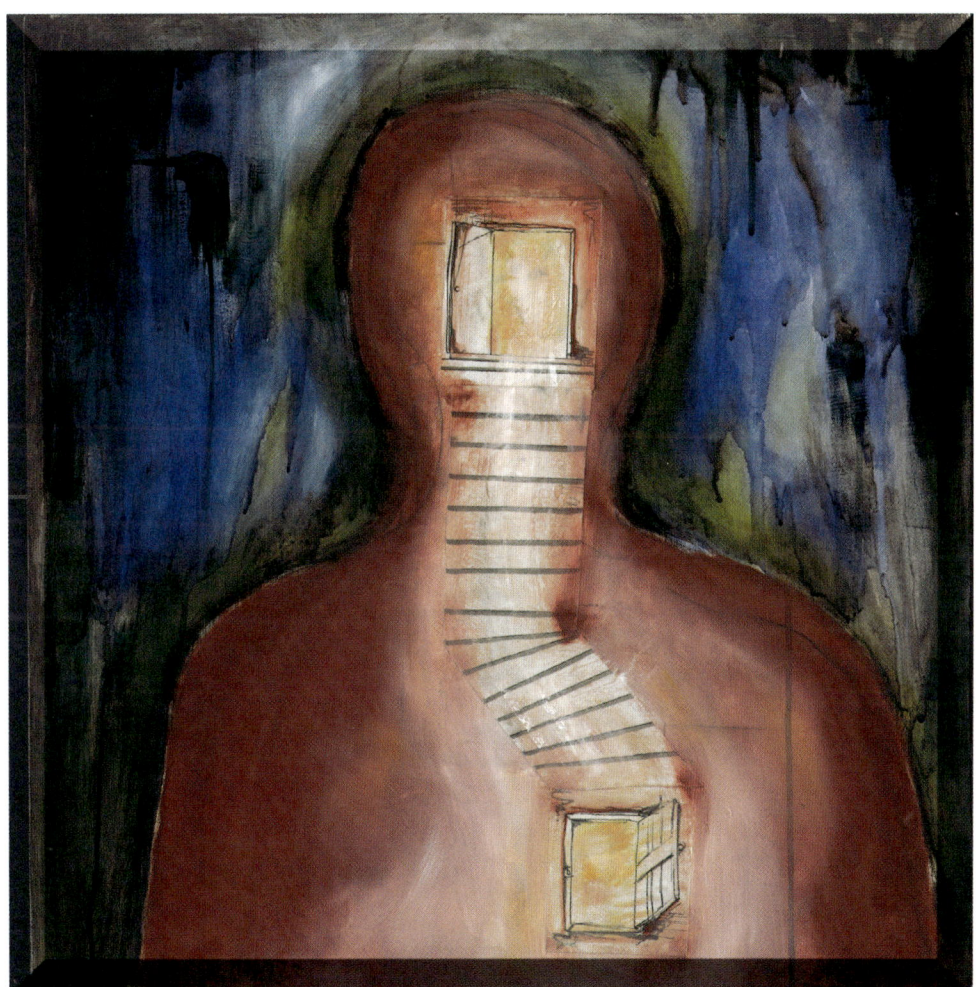

He reveals deep and hidden things; he knows what lies in darkness, and the light dwells with him.
(Daniel 2:22)

Lies about myself...

- ☐ I must have deserved my abuse.
- ☐ I have nothing to offer others.
- ☐ I'm only important if I'm beautiful, superior, and successful.
- ☐ I should never have been born.
- ☐ I must do everything right to be accepted.
- ☐ I deserve to be punished.
- ☐ I know I'll never make it to heaven.
- ☐ I'm not a Christian.
- ☐ I'm evil.
- ☐ I'm a worthless sinner.
- ☐ I'm a hopeless case; I can never change.
- ☐ I'm inferior to others and always will be.
- ☐ I'm disgusting and sinful because I have sexual desires.
- ☐ I don't deserve a great relationship; I would only ruin it.
- ☐ Other: _____

chapter five

Select a lie from each category from the previous pages and write them in the spaces below. What are the truth(s) that Satan is attempting to separate you from? If you were to act consistently with the truth instead of the lie—about God, others, and yourself—what would be different in your life?

Lies I believe about...	Truth I will believe about...	If I act consistently with truth, I will...
GOD		
OTHERS		
SELF		

Task Five: Claim Truth— God's Crazy About You!

[God is] the Father of our Master, Jesus Christ, and takes us to the high places of blessing in him. Long before he laid down earth's foundations, he had us in mind, had settled on us as the focus of his love, to be made whole and holy by his love.
Long, long ago he decided to adopt us into his family through Jesus Christ. (What pleasure he took in planning this!) He wanted us to enter into the celebration of his lavish gift-giving by the hand of his beloved Son.

Because of the sacrifice of the Messiah, his blood poured out on the altar of the Cross, we're a free people—free of penalties and punishments chalked up by all our misdeeds. And not just barely free, either. Abundantly free!
He thought of everything, provided for everything we could possibly need, letting us in on the plans he took such delight in making . . .

It's in Christ that we find out who we are.
(Ephesians 1:3-11 The Message)

chapter five

Task Six: Boldly Hand Shame Back to the Abuser!

This task will feel very empowering. Ask God to overwhelm the abuser with his or her own shame, which can lead that person to repentance. It's also biblical to ask God to destroy your abuser if he does not repent. This is a repeated refrain throughout the Bible. David, in the Psalms, often pleaded with God to shame his enemies (Psalm 35:4-8; 69:19-28) and crush those who oppressed with their power. God instructs us not to seek revenge, but instead He tells us to trust Him for justice (Romans 12:19). Christ rejected the shame of our sin as He hung on the cross. We're to do the same. We must not allow the names, evil declarations, and the contempt that has been spewed venomously upon us to stick. It doesn't belong to us!

Close your eyes and visualize your abuser sitting in a chair across from you. Now imagine yourself handing back all the shame that you've been carrying that rightfully belongs to your abuser. If you had more than one abuser, you may repeat this step as often as is necessary.

Journal the "shame attacks" with which you most often struggle.
How can you directly reject this shame?

chapter five

What are the characteristics of your original design that you are reclaiming? Include every one. You will probably need some outside voices on this one.

Satan cannot create anything. He can only distort the best of what God has created. Think about the areas of shame with which you have struggled the most. Chances are, these are the areas where God most wants to use you. I believe it is a very helpful strategy to unmask Satan. This significantly diminishes the power of shame in one's life. For example, I grew up believing I had no voice. I did not want to stand out, make a mistake, or have an opinion that might upset anyone. I worked very hard to please and comply. This strategy kept me from having the impact God had designed me to have on those around me. In my healing I became very convicted of this "hiding" of my true, God-designed self. I repented of this strategy to control my world and now use my triggers of shame to remind me of Satan's strategy to keep the best parts of me hidden. This energizes me to not allow shame to shut me down or keep me silent ever again.

The Lord your God is in your midst, a mighty one who will save; he will rejoice over you with gladness; he will quiet you by his love; he will exult over you with loud singing.
(Zephaniah 3:17 ESV)

chapter five

Draw, describe, or collage a picture of yourself that is the true image of your original design.

chapter five

My thoughts and feelings...

Let us stake out a claim for ourselves on grace. Let us make a commitment to faith a shame-free life, grace-based life, lighter life. Let's live in the lighter life of grace.

—Brennan Manning

Chapter Six
Powerlessness and Deadness

Lord, I'm desperate for you tonight
I want to hear your heartbeat
To feel your presence deep within me

I bolt and run—it's so hard to stay
I hurt deeply
What is it you want me to remember?
To feel, to know?

Tether me to yourself
While I feel this fire of deep pain
I'm desperate for you tonight
I want to feel your heartbeat
To know I'm not alone
To feel your presence deep within
To know I am alive

If I stay your Spirit will carve out
The rocky places of my heart
And grow where once there was stone
A garden, a secret garden
Where only we will go
Our place, our space
Sacred
That you and I indwell

I'm desperate for you tonight.

—Celestia

Cursed is the man who trusts in man
And makes flesh his strength,
Whose heart departs from the Lord.
For he shall be like a shrub in the desert,
And shall not see when good comes,
But shall inhabit the parched places in the wilderness,
In a salt land which is not inhabited.

Blessed is the man who trusts in the Lord,
And whose hope is the Lord.
For he shall be like a tree planted by the waters,
Which spreads out its roots by the river,
And will not fear when heat comes;
But its leaf will be green,
And will not be anxious in the year of drought,
Nor will cease from yielding fruit.

Heal me, O Lord, and I shall be healed;
Save me, and I shall be saved,
For You are my praise.
(Jeremiah 17:5-8, 14 NKJV)

PTSD: POST-TRAUMATIC STRESS DISORDER

My people are destroyed for lack of knowledge. (Hosea 4:6 ESV)

Researchers have documented the long-term emotional and physical damage created by abuse. Powerlessness and emotional numbing are the result of trauma and neglect. Webster's dictionary defines *trauma* as injury to the body or mind. Abuse is extremely traumatic to your soul because it robs you of your security and normalcy; extinguishes your hopes and dreams; and destroys your wholeness, trust, and self-esteem. During the abuse you felt powerless to stop the one who was hurting you and powerless to stop the pain. You didn't choose to be injured; you had no choice. In an effort to avoid the deepening pain, you numbed your feelings and began to die inside.

PTSD is a potentially debilitating anxiety disorder triggered by exposure to a traumatic situation such as being physically or sexually assaulted, being exposed to a disaster or an accident, experiencing childhood abuse and neglect, experiencing combat, or witnessing a traumatic event. There are three main clusters of symptoms: those related to re-experiencing the event, those related to avoidance and arousal, and the distress and impairment caused by the first two symptom clusters.

Arousal

Arousal is a state of increased psychological and physiological tension marked by such effects as reduced pain tolerance, anxiety, increased heart rate and blood pressure, nausea, exaggeration of startle response (continually looking around to ensure safety), irritability, insomnia, fatigue, and accentuation of personality traits. In chronic hyperarousal the brain and body stay continually aroused, even after the trauma has ended. Due to the neurological and hormonal changes that occur with trauma, the body will continue to react as if it's still in danger, exacerbating feelings of helplessness.

Avoidance and Numbing

Avoidance and numbing are common reactions to trauma. It's natural to want to avoid thinking about or feeling emotions about a stressful or painful event. But, when extreme avoidance is the only way to cope, it can interfere with healing and actually make a person worse. There are two kinds of avoidance: *Emotional avoidance* is when a person avoids thoughts or feelings about a painful event, shutting down all emotion related to it. Numbing can be either an involuntary response to stress or deliberately done. Numbing provides temporary relief from negative feelings yet robs a person of the positive feelings as well. *Behavioral avoidance* involves making choices to avoid anything that might remind a person of the original trauma. For example, a rape survivor may move to a rural region of the country in order to avoid memories of her rape in the city.

chapter six

Intrusion

Intrusion is the reoccurrence of unwanted memories in the form of nightmares (while asleep) or flashbacks (while awake). These memories can occur unexpectedly with no clear explanation, or they can be triggered by someone or something that reminds a victim of the original abuse or trauma. A survivor may engage in behavior that repeatedly puts him or her in traumatic situations in an attempt to reenact and thus overcome the powerlessness felt during the original abuse. A survivor vividly describes this experience below:

> *It feels as if my body and brain are conspiring against me! I'm always tired and want to sleep, but I can't. I'm mentally exhausted and want to relax, but I can't. I'm sick of my repetitive, racing thoughts and want them to stop, but I can't make them. My brain feels like the "boss" of everything—my nervous system and connected organs—making my body feel out of control! I'm constantly aware of people around me—remembering where they are or where they've moved from. At church this happens—this symptom drives me crazy. It makes me incredibly tired. I realized I was keeping track of everyone around me. I automatically mentally recorded their physical appearance. I'm sensitive to noise and light. I'm jumpy, and my legs shake. I can hear the quietest whisper. I'd make the perfect witness to a crime, because I record so much detailed information.*

After reviewing arousal, avoidance, numbing, and intrusion, describe your experience with each.

Arousal	Avoidance	Numbing	Intrusion

Comfort, comfort my people, says your God. Speak tenderly. . . (Isaiah 40:1-2)

chapter six

You came into my life on May 2...

You were just eighteen. A child really. "I'm brutal" were the words you used to describe yourself. "I don't talk to anybody!" Your tough exterior belied a vulnerable heart—a heart miraculously alive after years of brutality. You ran away for the first time with your little brother, Joey. You loved him so much and felt responsible to keep him safe. You never forgave yourself for the damage the streets exacted on him. You were in a double bind. Forced to choose between two worlds: your home, which you described as "unstable, chaotic, abusive," and the world of the streets. You grew up with a mother and step-dad, who "did drugs, fought, and abused each other." You were "taken, raped, sold, beaten, and drugged." You checked every box of trauma and abuse: emotional, physical, spiritual, neglect, and sexual molestation. You had a "history of survival sex—not seeking" you clarified. I knew that, my dear girl. No girl wants to trade her body for food, shelter, and love. No girl seeks that. "I'm starting over when released [from jail]" you wrote on your intake with a cute smiley face—you were excited to "work on your problems." The only suggestion you recorded for helping you was to "be reliable." Was I? In a hurried hand you wrote, "I need a change!"

All you had known was the repeated experience of terror and reprieve, abuse and comfort, within the isolated context of a "love" relationship. This trauma sequence powerfully bonded you to him—your "boyfriend"—with your feelings of intense, worshipful dependence. He was your all-powerful, godlike authority. You lived in terror of his wrath, but at the same time you viewed him as your source of strength, guidance, and life itself. He had seen to that. Your relationship with him took on extraordinary qualities of "specialness." You held on to your delusion, embracing his "love" for you. You worked hard to repress your own doubts as proof of your loyalty, submission, and love. You could not have known that in your relationship with him, you were similar to people who have been inducted into totalitarian religious cults.

He established control over you by systematic, repetitive infliction of psychological pain. He was organized with his techniques of disempowerment and disconnection—these successfully instilled terror and helplessness in you, which destroyed your sense of connectedness and made you increasingly numb. He used violence infrequently and as a last resort. You were gentle and loved to please—the perfect victim in your ready compliance and quick mercy. Eventually, you lived in constant fear. His threats of death or serious harm were much more successful than actually resorting to violence. He threatened others that you loved, and this was more effective than his threats against you. After these episodes of verbal abuse, he would be the one to comfort you. After his abuse, you were encouraged to return, not by further threats but by apologies, expressions of love, promises of reform, and appeals to loyalty and compassion. For fleeting moments the balance of power seemed to be reversed, just long enough for you to believe in that shift, and then the cycle of terror would be begin all over again. Abuse. Pain. Comfort. Abuse. Pain . . .

His ultimate goal was that you would believe he was omnipotent, that it was futile to resist him, that your life depended upon winning his attention through your submission and compliance. You were grateful that he allowed you to live—he was your "savior." But, in the end, he took your life, although the act was inflicted by your own hand.

This one thing I promise you, precious girl. Your death won't be in vain.

—Celestia

Menu of Feelings

Mad	Sad	Glad	Uneasy	Curious	Uncomfortable	Out of Place
Bothered	Down	At Ease	Apprehensive	Uncertain	Awkward	Left Out
Ruffled	Blue	Comfortable	Careful	Ambivalent	Clumsy	Lonesome
Irritated	Somber	Relaxed	Cautious	Doubtful	Self Conscious	Disconnected
Displeased	Low	Contented	Hesitant	Unsettled	Disconcerted	Insecure
Annoyed	Hurt	Optimistic	Tense	Hesitant	Chagrined	Unappreciated
Steamed	Disappointed	Satisfied	Anxious	Perplexed	Abashed	Invisible
Irked	Worn Out	Refreshed	Nervous	Puzzled	Embarrassed	Unwelcome
Perturbed	Melancholy	Grateful	Edgy	Muddled	Flustered	Misunderstood
Frustrated	Downhearted	Pleased	Distressed	Distracted	Sorry	Excluded
Angry	Unhappy	Warm	Scared	Flustered	Apologetic	Insignificant
Fed Up	Dissatisfied	Happy	Frightened	Jumbled	Ashamed	Ignored
Disgusted	Gloomy	Encouraged	Vulnerable	Unfocused	Regretful	Neglected
Indignant	Mournful	Tickled	Repulsed	Fragmented	Remorseful	Removed
Resentful	Grieved	Proud	Agitated	Dismayed	Guilty	Detached
Ticked Off	Depressed	Hopeful	Shocked	Insecure	Disgusted	Isolated
Jealous	Lousy	Cheerful	Alarmed	Dazed	Belittled	Unwanted
Fuming	Crushed	Thrilled	Overwhelmed	Bewildered	Humiliated	Rejected
Explosive	Miserable	Delighted	Frantic	Lost	Violated	Deserted
Enraged	Defeated	Joyful	Panic Stricken	Stunned	Dirty	Outcast
Irate	Dejected	Elated	Horrified	Chaotic	Mortified	Abandoned
Incensed	Empty	Exhilarated	Petrified	Torn	Defiled	Withdrawn
Burned	Wretched	Overjoyed	Terrified	Baffled	Devastated	Desolate
Outraged	Despairing	Ecstatic	Numb	Dumbfounded	Degraded	Forsaken
Furious	Devastated	Afraid	Confused	Ashamed	Lonely	

The feelings above are ranked from least to most severe.

What I'm feeling now...

Use the menu of feelings on the previous page and pick three feeling words that match what you're feeling now. Put each of these feeling words into a sentence. (Example: I feel _____ when _____ .) Set a timer for five minutes and write without stopping until the timer goes off. This type of journaling is called mind-streaming and is an effective way to get at your deeper feelings. Don't edit for grammar or spelling—the important thing is to expose your deeper heart's truth.

When your heart speaks, take good notes.

chapter six
FEELING AGAIN

Throughout the course of a day, we make thousands of decisions, most in the blink of an eye. These decisions are fed by our beliefs, thoughts, and feelings. Living and relating without connecting to our inner self is a bit like purchasing a new car and driving with duct tape plastered across the instrument panel. We might love the car, desire to take good care of it, and even hire the most expensive mechanic we can find. Yet, if we're making decisions about the care of the car independent of the instrument gauges, we'll eventually blow up the engine—it's just a matter of time. Loving but living disconnected from our own heart and the Spirit of God is the same. Our relationships will eventually blow up—it's just a matter of time.

Respond to the following questions using three feeling words for each question. Refer to the feeling menu on page 150.

What emotions feel unsafe or wrong to you? Why?

What emotions do you feel every day? How do you typically express these?

What emotions do you feel the least or not at all? Why?

What emotions would you like to have more of?

When do you feel most emotionally free?

chapter six

POWERLESSNESS

Powerlessness is the feeling of having no voice and no ability to choose—it's the feeling of living under the control of others. Traumatic powerlessness isn't only experienced during childhood abuse but is further experienced by the child as he or she is required to participate in the abuse or to hide the abuse. When powerlessness with pain is experienced in childhood, it becomes a learned response, which often returns at future times of stress—some call it a "learned helplessness." Real powerlessness in childhood produces a perceived sense of powerlessness in adulthood. In a very real sense, child victims will continue to put themselves into harm's way. Abuse victims become addicted to abuse: the response to abuse is to stimulate more of it. Adult victims of childhood trauma and neglect literally reenact their abuse over and over in their relationships. (For a further discussion of reenactment as a response to powerlessness see *Princess Found: A Guide for Mentors of Sexually Exploited Girls* by Tracy and Tracy, 123-126).

Imagine a baby elephant held captive in a circus by a strong chain secured to his ankle. His repeated attempts to escape consistently fail and at times even increase his suffering. In time he comes to believe that he is—and always will be—powerless and escape is futile. Even after he's grown, and is much larger than his captors, he doesn't attempt escape. Why? He has learned that there's no hope of freedom. His chains are no longer needed; he has enslaved himself.

> Listen to your life. See it for the fathomless mystery that it is. In the boredom and pain of it no less than in the excitement and gladness: touch, taste, smell your way to the holy and hidden heart of it because in the last analysis all moments are key moments, and life itself is grace.
> —Frederick Buechner, *Now and Then: A Memoir of Vocation*

As a guy, I can say that men are loath to identify with powerlessness. Those of us who admit to the frozen experience of powerlessness have been there for some time. The longer we've been there, the thicker the walls around us. This is often the reason why many men begin using drugs or alcohol. Yet, I have found that a safe group—more than anything else—allows men to learn that powerless feelings and emotional deadness do not equate with man-lessness. Men need a group, because they just don't talk about this stuff on their own.

> The world is unprincipled. It's dog-eat-dog out there! The world doesn't fight fair. But we don't live or fight our battles that way—never have and never will. The tools of our trade aren't for marketing or manipulation, but they are for demolishing that entire massively corrupt culture. We use our powerful God-tools for smashing warped philosophies, tearing down barriers erected against the truth of God, fitting every loose thought and emotion and impulse into the structure of life shaped by Christ. Our tools are ready at hand for clearing the ground of every obstruction and building lives of obedience into maturity.
> (2 Corinthians 10:3-6 The Message)

chapter six

DEADNESS

Abuse creates deeply embedded pain that we'll do anything to deaden. This unrelenting pain feels unbearable, and thus we numb it to survive—dying to our dreams, desires, and to life itself.

Death to Reality

When you don't accept the truth but instead pretend that everything is perfectly normal, you're living in denial. This response to pain can be an automatic coping mechanism or can be consciously enacted by a survivor. Either way, it's unhealthy.

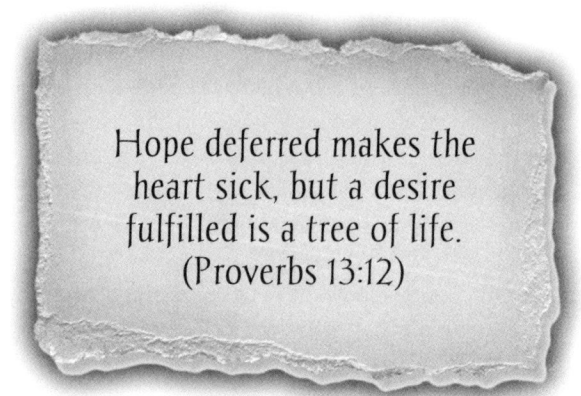

Hope deferred makes the heart sick, but a desire fulfilled is a tree of life. (Proverbs 13:12)

One Woman's Story

I couldn't face the fact that my husband was abusive. I had come to believe that I would if I faced the truth. I thought I would die without him, so I allowed the abuse to happen. I knew he would leave me if I stood up for myself. Each time he told me I deserved it, his words felt more and more true. I believed no one else would want me. I tried to hide by only having shallow relationships. This way no one would know how disgusting I was and that I deserved to be punished. I thought I would die under the weight of a relationship gone bad. I'd been taught that I had to be perfect to be accepted. So I pretended everything was wonderful. I felt like I was in control once I decided to deny the damage being done. Of course, my pretending just confirmed the false image of a perfect relationship.

When the abuse escalated I tried hard to keep it a secret. Eventually I became so depressed that I began to see a Christian counselor. I learned that my denial was enabling my husband to keep sinning and abusing me. My denial was keeping him from being accountable for what he was doing, and it was killing me. This was not what God wanted for my life. I came to know that denying reality is a way to protect myself from painful truths. Because my husband was everything to me—my entire life—there was no more me. I also came to know that putting my husband in first place in my life was idolatry. God was supposed to have that spot in my life. When I repented of this, I felt hollow and gutted inside, like a house that had burnt down with the wind whistling through. But as I began to trust God, I asked Him to take up residence there, and a feeling of being complete soon followed. It's a struggle sometimes to live in reality since I spent so many years in a fantasy world that I created; but with God's help I'm choosing to live in a healthy, godly way.

One Man's Story

Dad, I was your only son, and I needed you. When I was little I wanted to be like you—be you. I'm so angry at you today! You sat back, worked late, served at church, watched TV—anything but deal with Mom. All the while she raged and shamed you. Shamed me. Even when we were out as a family, she was in control and you allowed it. You saw her two faces: the public smiling one and the face we got. You saw but did nothing. I'm just now figuring out what I feel about her. About you. Why didn't you do anything? Didn't you see what she was doing to me? Didn't you feel it? I did! You were silent Dad—you did not speak truth that would have protected us. Your silence was your abuse of me.

chapter six

Death to Desire

An abuse survivor may attempt to protect him or herself from future pain by shutting down the desire for intimacy and relationship. When hope is lost, desire is seen as the enemy.

One Woman's Story

I was abused as a child and I learned not to hope for a loving relationship, because I believed I didn't deserve one. I went through counseling, received God's healing from the abuse, and finally met a wonderful man—only to find out that I was sabotaging the relationship. I wasn't even aware of the things I was doing to make the relationship fail. My counselor helped me to see that I was afraid of my desire to be loved. I was desperately afraid that this man would abuse me or leave me when he found out who I really was. This fear of rejection and discovery of how defective I was drove me to protect myself against hoping for love that would never come—or love that might come and then be jerked out of my reach. After discovering that I was trying to die to my desires (again), I asked God to help me live and to experience my desires in spite of the fear and risk involved. I had to push through the fear and choose life. It has been worth every risk. I'm not saying I don't struggle with this anymore, but it has really been worth taking the risks, because I'm now beginning to live.

One Man's Story

I'm a thirty-five year old single man. If you knew me you would say, "He's completely laid back. Chill." In reality, I'm not! The truth is, I'm scared relationally. I've never seen a good marriage—at least not one that I'd want—and I'm terrified of having a relationship like my parents had. You know what's crazy? Deep down I want to be married. I think I fear rejection most of all. That's why I do the rejecting. I never put myself in a relationship where I'm vulnerable. If a chick wants to do a lot of talking, I'm out of there! I was in this seminary class where I had to do a sexual history. Wow, was that ever eye-opening!

chapter six

Death to Relationship

Hope is lost when abandonment and abuse are unacknowledged. We *are* responsible for each other; and God has mandated that we see, hear, and feel each other—that we comfort each other. We're only able to comfort others with the comfort we've received. God's design is that we experience His comfort through each other.

When I was a child, my father cruelly abused me. I was removed from my home, and from there I spent the remainder of my childhood in a series of foster homes. Because of my abuse, I'd learned that I couldn't trust anyone. I spent a lifetime being a loner. I felt extremely uncomfortable around people.

As an adult I started attending a church in my community and put my faith in Christ. I was uncomfortable with the friendliness of the members. After weeks of giving excuses for not attending activities with the other young people in my class, I began to wonder what was wrong with me. I began to feel a loneliness in my soul that deeply disturbed me. I began to pray about it, asking God to help me. That next Sunday the church bulletin announced that there was a support group for those who were confused about life and wanted answers. I knew this was where God was directing me because of my prayer, but the thought of sharing with others was extremely scary. I eventually decided to try it, and even though I didn't share much, I somehow felt comfortable for the first time in my life. It seemed that those people accepted me and didn't expect anything from me. They encouraged the new people to come for a few sessions before deciding if working through a workbook was something we wanted to make a commitment to do.

I'm glad I stayed even though it was uncomfortable at first, because I eventually came to know myself and even started seeing a Christian counselor. I learned that I had died to any hope of having intimate relationships. I had surrounded myself with a barrier that kept me safe yet also kept others outside and at a distance. I had lost a lifetime of love because of my abuser. With God's help I slowly began to take small risks in the group and began to trust the group members with bits and pieces of my story. The support and acceptance helped me to learn to trust others, and now I'm on my way to a healthy life—one I've learned is worth living.

Which of the previous stories do you relate to the most?

Compassion is sometimes the fatal capacity for feeling what it is like to live inside somebody else's skin. It is the knowledge that there can never really be any peace and joy for me until there is peace and joy finally for you too.

—Frederick Buechner

chapter six

Two Different Lives, Same Pain

Everywhere I go I see a bitch and the pimp team.
They are quiet: lay low, trying not to make a scene.
I know how the bitch feels: tongue tied, she can't scream.
They got the bitch hooked on cocaine amphetamines,
They got her staying up cookin' crack for the pimp fiends.
Put your shoulder in it—you won't lose even a small percentage.
Now look your daddy in the face; tell him how good do he taste.
Forced to spread your legs, while he collects the john's pay.
Not allowed to take no breaks, especially on holidays.
I know how the bitch feels—she thinks she's going crazy.

Feeling this tightness in my throat, every spoken word almost makes me choke. I've hit bottom smacked with consciousness,
Racing thoughts giving symptoms of dizziness
Hanging by a thread—I'm losing hope
I need to forget my past before I act on impulse.

For my mind there is no sleeping,
Haunting memories are always creeping,
My eyes see more than one perspective—
Experience made me too protective. Constant thoughts, my head is throbbing. Too many weak spots, I'm always sobbing.
How is it that I still have hope? The reason is, I've learned to cope.

No hostage has been held like
I've been held in mine. But I'm just fine.
No prisoner can climb up these walls
that I've built up in my mind.
And I'm just fine. I'm just fine.

—Sixteen-year-old trafficked girl
Juvenile correction facility

That one. She lies awake; a soft spot in her heart is awake also. I don't want to pray. I don't want to feel. I'm sick of being fake. Those people—the ones with the advice—they've never had a conversation with God in their life. My Bible is lying under my bed. Uninviting. When the words have been used as ammunition against you, how do you take them back?
So I pray then. My words are simple and commonplace. I'm broken—I hate this! I hate picking up the pieces over and over and over. I can't stand living to please everyone, God. I can't do it anymore. My soul is wounded and weary! I see something in my mind's eye.
God is handing me a rose. The very gift of my salvation. I grab on to it and smile, and I realize that its thorns have pierced my hand. I'm bleeding. God, do you not see that I'm wounded? The very gift you've given me has been the source of so much pain!

"Do you think that it didn't pierce me?" His answer brought me to my knees. I saw him standing as if He was just flogged. I saw myself on my knees at his side—his hand gently placed on my head. He looked strong, and He was smiling. The blood was pouring out of Him and on to me. I was crying. So was He. But His tears were joyful tears, and as He looked down on me with His sorrow-tinged smile, I cried more. As they took Him away, I saw the thorns pierce His brow. I saw the nails in His hands and feet. I saw the blood and water pour from His side as His stone cold body hung lifeless. Dead.

And I saw Him coming up out of the wilderness—riding forth victoriously. He always came back for me. He always invited me to ride with him. I felt that age-old wound, the lie that said, "God cannot fill the hole in your heart." I felt it fading as I leaned upon Him. I let my face sink into His back, and I let myself breathe in his fragrance. This is my Jesus. He has the power over death and Hades. And he rides forth in victory with me.

—Twenty-one-year-old pastor's daughter

chapter six

WAKING THE DEAD

For most of us, waking the deadness in our souls can be a scary thing. Living brings risk. We run the risk of being wounded again. But the risk is necessary for you to begin to heal, grow, and someday thrive. Below are four necessary steps to conquer deadness:

1. Create Safety

You must feel safe before you can begin to think about taking the risks that are needed to build trust and bring healing. This is understandable since the abuse diminished your ability to trust. When you feel safe it will then be possible to begin the work of healing, which requires vulnerability, feeling, and sharing. Safety involves not only physical safety from danger, but also requires a place where you feel free to express emotions (no matter how strong) without fear of harsh judgment, retaliation, or rejection. In a place of safety, you'll receive unconditional acceptance as well as validation, empathic listening, and supportive encouragement.

2. Integrate the Abuse

The tasks of integration include—

- Feeling the appropriate emotions associated with the abuse.
- Mourning your losses—expressing your feelings.
- Repenting of your sinful choices in response to the abuse.
- Taking steps to stop deadening yourself.
- Accept your abuse as part of your history—your unique story.
- Discover God's plan for you (2 Corinthians 1:3-7).

The story of Joseph is told in Genesis 37-50. He was betrayed and abused by his brothers, who sold him into slavery. He was then taken to Egypt, where he suffered even more. He was deceived, betrayed, and unjustly imprisoned.

Joseph went on to save his brothers from dying during a severe famine and still they didn't trust him. Dr. Steven Tracy describes Joseph's response to his brother's mistrust in the following way:

Joseph wept and grieved their failure to recognize his love. While Joseph was attuned to his own feelings of grief and loss over his brothers' past abusive behavior and their present distrust, he was able to integrate the abuse into his life as a whole. This is reflected in Joseph's summary statement regarding his brothers' abuse. He had come to believe that God used his abuse for much bigger, ultimately good purposes. This integration of his abuse with the whole of his life and with God's redemptive purposes is what allowed him to be gracious to his brothers in spite of their ongoing mistrust. (MTS Basic Training)

3. Repent of Idolatrous Deadness

Idolatry means choosing something over God. Idolatrous deadness is choosing death and a false reality over intimacy with God. Much of the time deadness is a conscious choice—an attempt to protect oneself and decrease pain. It's an understandable option for the abuse survivor, but if you're isolating yourself from others, denying the truth, and deadening yourself to your desires, you must realize that these choices are sinful. Ask God to deepen your understanding of the way in which you might be controlling pain and managing your life apart from Christ.

chapter six

Describe the person who makes you feel emotionally safe. What do you admire about this person? How do you feel in his or her presence?

How can you relate to Joseph's story? How has your abuse impacted your life? How are you different? What has the abuse taken from you? Record your honest feelings here.

> My people have committed a compound sin: they've walked out on me, the fountain of fresh flowing waters, and then dug cisterns—cisterns that leak, cisterns that are no better than sieves.
> (Jeremiah 2:13 The Message)

chapter six

Who among you fears the Lord and obeys the voice of his servant? Let him who walks in darkness and has no light trust in the name of the Lord and rely on his God. Behold, all you who kindle a fire, who equip yourselves with burning torches! Walk by the light of your fire, and by the torches that you have kindled! This you have from my hand: you shall lie down in torment. (Isaiah 50:10-11 ESV)

How have you tried to control pain and manage life apart from Christ?

Be merciful and gracious to me, for my soul takes refuge and finds shelter and confidence in You; yes in the shadow of Your wings will I take refuge and be confident, until the calamities and destructive storms are passed. I will cry to God Most High, Who performs on my behalf and rewards me, [Who brings to pass His purposes for me and surely completes them]! He will send from heaven and save me from the slanders and reproaches of him who would trample me down or swallow me up and He will put him to shame. (Psalm 57:1-3 AMP)

Use Psalm 57 as a structure for your own psalm. Write honestly, boldly, and with longing.

God is working His plan in your life. Continue to do the work of awakening your heart to fully feel. Trust Him and talk honestly to Him now . . .

chapter six

If the Holy Spirit has given you a vision . . . you will have to pay to the last farthing in concentration along that line until all you saw in vision is made actual. By prayer and determination we have to form the habit of keeping ourselves soaked in the vision God has given. The difficulty with the majority of us is that we will not seek to apprehend the vision, we get glimpses of it and then leave it alone.

—Oswald Chambers

Chapter Seven
Isolation

This is the love story we must know to tell...

[He] will gather them and will watch over his flock like a shepherd.
For the Lord will deliver . . . and redeem them
from the hand of those stronger than they.
They will come and shout for joy on the heights . . .

They will rejoice in the bounty of the Lord.
They will be like a well-watered garden,
and they will sorrow no more.
Then young women will dance and be glad,
young men and old as well.
I will turn their mourning into gladness;
I will give them comfort and joy instead of sorrow.
I will satisfy them with abundance,
And my people will be filled with my bounty.
(Jeremiah 31:10-14)

chapter seven

Isolation occurs when we maintain relational distance in order to feel safe. The trauma of abuse and the emotional damage of neglect create isolation in myriad ways. The unhealthy relational patterns you learn when you're a child stay stubbornly with you into adulthood. If you have a history of broken relationships, you may feel safer keeping others at a distance—both longing for, and fearing intimacy: that vulnerable joy of being known and knowing another. We're drawn to each other because this is how God created us. In Genesis 2:18 God said, "It is not good for the man to be alone. I will make a helper suitable for him." Scripture describes intimacy between man and woman as "one flesh" because they become as one person, naked without shame (Genesis 2:25). But Adam and Eve sinned (Genesis 3:6-13), and the perfect connection between man and woman—as well as the perfect connection between them and God—was severed. Experiencing shame for the first time, they hid from God, and blame shifting began: Adam blamed God and then Eve for his choices, and Eve blamed the serpent.

God said, "It's not good for the Man to be alone; I'll make him a helper, a companion." So God formed from the dirt of the ground all the animals of the field and all the birds of the air. He brought them to the Man to see what he would name them. Whatever the Man called each living creature, that was its name. The Man named the cattle, named the birds of the air, named the wild animals; but he didn't find a suitable companion.

God put the Man into a deep sleep. As he slept he removed one of his ribs and replaced it with flesh. God then used the rib that he had taken from the Man to make Woman and presented her to the Man.

The Man said, "Finally! Bone of my bone, flesh of my flesh! Name her Woman for she was made from Man."
Therefore a man leaves his father and mother and embraces his wife. They become one flesh. The two of them, the Man and his Wife, were naked, but they felt no shame. (Genesis 2:18-25 The Message)

> I watched her at night. My mother, in her Christian Dior nightgown. She could never sleep. Her whole life she had fought to stay on the surface of things—to not argue with my father in public, to cover her emotions with a flashy smile—and it showed in her face, where lines of deep fatigue were grooved beneath her makeup. "Mom Mom," I whispered. I always wanted to cry for her. I always will.
>
> —L. Slater, *Lying*

chapter seven

The woman was made of a rib out of the side of Adam; not made out of his head to rule over him, nor out of his feet to be trampled upon by him, but out of his side to be equal to him, under his arm to be protected, and near his heart to be beloved.

—Matthew Henry

What does this quotation prompt you to feel, think, or remember?

Record your thoughts and feelings toward the opposite sex. Think about your relational behavior that flows out of these thoughts and feelings. Describe.

> . . . And the man and his wife hid themselves from the presence of the Lord God among the trees of the garden.
> (Genesis 3:8 ESV)

chapter seven

ISOLATION RESULTS FROM THREE DAMAGING CORE BELIEFS

I'm Shameful

Toxic shame drives us into hiding, because we believe we'll never be loved or forgiven. Shame tells us we'll be rejected if we're real and honest. So, like Adam and Eve, we withdraw and hide from God, others, and even ourselves.

I'm Shattered

Children learn whether or not to trust others within the first few years of life. If a child's needs are responded to in loving and consistent ways, she internalizes positive beliefs about herself and her relationships: my parents love me, I'm good, people like me, people are good, etc. Neglect and abuse shatter these positive core beliefs, convincing the victim that the world is a dangerous place. If the abuse or neglect was perpetrated by someone the child trusted, the damage is even more severe, debilitating and paralyzing the child or adult and furthering their relational isolation.

Reading about Jeremiah's feelings helped me understand that godly men are not immune to crushing self-doubt and regret.

> O Lord, you have deceived me, and I was deceived; you are stronger than I, and you have prevailed. I have become a laughingstock all the day; everyone mocks me. Cursed be the day on which I was born! The day when my mother bore me, let it not be blessed! Cursed be the man who brought the news to my father, "A son is born to you," making him very glad. Let that man be like the cities that the Lord overthrew without pity; let him hear a cry in the morning and an alarm at noon, because he did not kill me in the womb; so my mother would have been my grave, and her womb forever great. Why did I come out from the womb to see toil and sorrow, and spend my days in shame? (Jeremiah 20:7, 14-18 ESV)

Jeremiah endured spiritual, physical, and verbal abuse from his countryman (Jeremiah 20).
What was Jeremiah's response to God and to himself? Can you relate to his feelings?

chapter seven

I Can't Trust and Am Untrustworthy

Relational distrust flows out of our assumptions about life and others. *I'm safer not trusting others*, we assure ourselves. Abuse destroys trust. For example, a boy who experiences the pain of emotional and verbal abuse from his mother learns not only to distrust her, but he probably distrusts all women. His distrust manifests in different ways as he develops. Let's imagine that when he was a child, he was compliant and pleasing, desiring to "stay under the radar" so as not to trigger her tirades. He seemed the perfect child. But as he grew into puberty, he began to change. The once happy and obedient child turned into a sullen and angry teenager—disappearing within himself, he became quiet and emotionally numb. Over time, without nurture or parental protection and guidance, he was irresistibly drawn to pornography, powerfully attracted to the images of male domination and control and female desire. He felt safe and desired without having to take relational risk or responsibility. Pornography soon became his drug of choice, zapping what was left of his interest or ability to enter into a real relationship with a girl. He's now trapped in a shamed, numb, isolated world. Each time he uses pornography he becomes more isolated.

Can you relate to this story?	When did you begin feeling this way?	How isolated do you feel?

chapter seven

Relational Hiding <<<

I have a history of leading women on—allowing them to think that I'm seriously interested in pursuing a relationship with them. They affirm who I am as a man, but I feel torn apart and exposed. It's easier for me just to ignore them for a while until they get the hint. I feel bad, but I can't face explaining myself.	*I'm being challenged to open my heart in ways that I know will make me feel vulnerable and weak to important people in my life. I need to trust more like the child Jesus referred to by stepping out from behind my superficiality to take a risk. I want to be authentic and genuine, but I'm not really sure what it looks like. Maybe I just need to say that.*	*As a single person, I long for the touch of another—even just a soft touch on the shoulder. I long to be wanted and cared for. I'm praying that God will one day fulfill this God-given desire as I wait on Him and find satisfaction in Him; I'm opening my heart to life-giving community.*
I was horribly sexually abused by the two most significant men in my childhood: my dad and my brother. Now I realize that it's because of the sexual shame I carried from this original abuse that I became disrespectful and haughty toward the guys that I dated. I kept them from getting close by making fun of them or by seducing them. Either way I felt in control.	*I'm chronically lonely. I work as a counselor, treating traumatized and marginalized women. I feel very isolated in my church, and people don't seem to understand me or my work. I dreamed last night that I was standing by myself on a concrete slab surrounded by three tall brick walls. I moved robotically as I trowelled cement on bricks one at a time, walling myself inside.*	*This is a difficult conversation for me to have with you, but it's important to me that I'm honest. I have a history of lying in order to avoid uncomfortable conversations, and I'm not going to do that this time . . .*
I'm a pastor's wife and thus always felt I was in the public eye. I hid from my husband by being as "perfect" as I could be at church, but then at home I isolated. I avoided sex, watched TV, refused to resolve conflict, and kept myself as busy as possible with church activities. There were many difficult conversations my husband and I needed to have, but it was always easier not to. As the years went by, the wall between us grew. I was good at keeping him at arm's length.	*I've learned to cope by shutting off my phone. If I'm not reliable, people won't call and expect me to come around. I have a lot of friends, but only because one group assumes that I'm with the other when really I'm home alone. I'm learning that love initiates and pursues. This is why I've starting texting people to let them know I care about them. It may not be the best communication method, but it's a start.*	*I'd kneel down to pray, believing God wanted me for Himself. But my relationship with Him was disrupted in the weirdest ways. I could be praying when suddenly I felt as if God were laughing. Many times I allowed this to make me stop. Now I know that when this happens, I must be honest and keep right on praying!*

>>> # Respectful Honesty

chapter seven

Mind-Streaming...

Set a timer for five minutes and write very quickly from a place of feeling. Don't edit or check your work. Write without stopping until the timer goes off.

chapter seven
thorns

A rose of love bloomed inside of him
A deep-seated affection for the woman of light
His thoughts were consumed by her tenderness
Desire awakened

He considered the days in which he was living
And decided to pursue wholeheartedly
For love was not left to the faint or the slow
Desire commissioned

She received not the pitiable tries
Her heart and her eyes were simply unmoved
Fear gripped her because she knew
Desire unrequited

She knew that those roses do not remain so
Locked in a cage of unreturned trust
The roses turned into thorns
Desire devastated

The thorns could consume anything in their path
No, not of love, but of undeserved wrath
Her response was not unkind but wise
Desire dismantled

She fled to the mountains in utmost retreat
A Bible in tow and a song so sweet
Only for her Maker she desired to sing
Desire awakened

"I see the thorns that He himself hath borne
Like a rose in bloom, how beautiful is the bridegroom.
He is coming with fire to burn up the chaff
The dawning of a new age is hidden in his staff."

"Sing, for the King is ready to wage war
Against the abusers, all evil and sin
Put on the crown of the covering blood.
For we all harbor thorns deep within."

—Mandy

chapter seven

> Repent therefore and be converted, that your sins may be blotted out, so that times of refreshing may come from the presence of the Lord. (Acts 3:19 NKJV)
>
> *What would it look like if you were to claim Acts 3:19 today?*

His habit of reading isolated him: it became such a need that after being in company for some time he grew tired and restless... and he had not the skill to hide his contempt for his companions' stupidity... But though he did everything to alienate the sympathy of other boys he longed with all his heart for the popularity which to some was so easily accorded. These from his distance he admired extravagantly; and though he was inclined to be more sarcastic with them than with others, though he made little jokes at their expense, he would have given anything to change places with them.

—W. Somerset Maugham, *Of Human Bondage*

re·pent·ance
(noun)
1. Deep sorrow, compunction, or contrition for a past sin, wrongdoing, or the like.
2. Regret for any past action.
3. Returning to God.

chapter seven

My child,

I am with you and for you. You face nothing alone. I'm faithful to you and will establish you—guarding you from the evil one. I will direct your heart into the love of God and into the patience of Christ. When you feel anxious, fix your eyes on Me and not the world around you. Verbalize your trust in Me. Look to Me and know that I'm restoring your health and healing your wounds.

I know what it is to be an outcast—humiliated, scorned, and ignored. I know what it means to be rejected, isolated, alone. I hung on a cross in a public square so that you would not be forsaken. I gave everything for you. My comfort, My position, My dignity . . . Think of Me when you feel alone. Remember how you are loved! You are not on your own, no matter what you feel. Trust in the strength of My words, My love, My Presence. Trust Me to be with you.

I will turn your mourning into joy, your sorrow into worship, your isolation into comfort. I will satiate your soul with abundance and satisfy you with My goodness.

I love you so.

Your Savior

Reflect on God's promises and record His words to you here.
2 Thessalonians 3:3, 5 and Jeremiah 31 are full of promises.

Isolation

Here I sit,
ready to swallow
the red sunset
of the earth
all the while
knowing
that I shouldn't.

It is melodious
the torrent of
the rain, but
it is disturbing—
different from
what I know
to be real.

I exist in a
half-world—one
that is known
only to me,
surrounded by
desert and mountains
my valley is barren.

The dwelling is dusty and dark—it has no
windows only doors.
Doors everywhere
leading nowhere.

The wooden planks of
the porch scream
for the weight of footsteps
they will never know.

Only mine—only mine . . .
echoing forever
in the landscape
of my mind.
My cluttered, dull mind.

Here I stand,
able to swallow
the yellow sunrise
of the earth.
My night is over.
My day begun.
Which is worse?

—T. Haley

chapter seven

I WANT TO KNOW GOD

The very language in Scripture of God as our Father is based on our human understanding of our relationship with human parents. God planned for us to feel love, protection, and care in our families of origin so that we could have a healthy script for knowing and trusting God. Can you relate to any of the following unhealthy responses to God?

Rejecting God

This response concludes that God doesn't exist—that He couldn't possibly have allowed the terrifying abuse you experienced. Therefore, there cannot be a God. A God who was absent during the evil of abuse may be seen as absent altogether, like a nonexistent parent.

Withdrawing from God

This response concludes that God can't be trusted because He didn't stop the abuse. Oppression is an exercise of power over another person, so it's understandable that a survivor might wrongfully concludes that an all-powerful God is frightening and therefore must be avoided. This is particularly true if your abuser was a spiritual leader. A person can withdraw from God in numerous ways that don't look like spiritual avoidance. For example, a highly religious person who turns his or her spirituality into a list of religious behaviors and beliefs may be avoiding real intimacy with God.

Cowering from God

This response incorrectly concludes that God can't possibly love you because of your past sin and brokenness. Maybe you believe in a loving God but not in a God who really enjoys you. Your abuser taught you to cower and to expect rejection. In the same way, you shrink before God, believing you'll experience—and thus deserve—His rejection too. Sadly, some believe that it's impossible for them to be a true child of God because of the abuse in their past. This belief is satanic in its origins and stems from toxic shame. Of course, these distorted perceptions of self and God are lies, but they can feel very true. Only under the light of God's truth and in safe community can these lies be dispelled.

chapter seven

Abuse sabotages your relationship with God. Describe how you've responded to God (past and present) by rejecting Him, withdrawing from Him, or cowering before Him because you believed He couldn't love or accept you.

Past	Present

Jesus don't want me for a sunbeam.

—The Vaselines

You can only afford to be generous if you actually have some money in the bank to give. In the same way, if your only source of love and meaning is your spouse, then anytime he or she fails you, it will not just cause grief but a psychological cataclysm. If, however, you know something of the work of the Spirit in your life, you have enough love "in the bank" to be generous to your spouse even when you are not getting much affection or kindness at the moment.

—Timothy Keller

chapter seven

Abuse sabotages your relationships with others. Describe how you've responded to others (past and present) by rejecting them, withdrawing from them, or cowering before them. What would you like to change?

Past	Present

Early on I knew that women were mysteriously different. I felt intimidated in their presence. They seemed powerful. I used to wonder what it would take for me to get close to a girl. Would I need to match her power with mine and win, or would it be better to be submissive?

chapter seven

Write a response from God to you using portions of Scripture you've connected to from the previous chapters.
What do you imagine He's saying to you? Tell Him how you're feeling right now—be honest about your thoughts and feelings.
He knows them already and will never be surprised by anything you say. Finally, ask Him for specific support and clarity as you move on from here.

If we love one another, God dwells deeply within us,
and his love becomes complete in us—perfect love!
(1 John 4:12 The Message)

chapter seven

How to Journal

Journaling is an effective method for rebuilding intimacy with God. Just as we make appointments to meet with others we care about, so we must make appointments to meet with God. Select a time and prepare a place for these meetings. Make this time intentional, and purchase a notebook to record both your lament and God's words to you.

Open your journal, and on the right-facing page, date the entry. In two sentences or less, record the event, interaction, or painful memory. Don't spend time recording the details. Instead, focus your energy on describing your feelings and thoughts as responses to the precipitating event. Write without filtering—let your mind stream until you're done. Don't be concerned with grammar, spelling, or punctuation. You may need several pages. If so, continue to write on the right-facing pages until you're done. When you're finished, make some very specific heart-focused requests of the Lord. These are requests for your heart, not requests about changing your circumstances to alleviate your pain. Make requests for comfort, reassurance, wisdom, or conviction if you're thinking or responding in an ungodly manner.

Now turn to God's Word. If you're not reading through the Bible in a systematic way, begin with the Scriptures from the chart on pages 173-174 of Mending the Soul. Read until one of the verses or passages stands out to you—record this Scripture on the left-facing pages that you've left blank. Copying Scripture is one of the best ways I know to slow down and meditate on the words, concepts, and truths God wants you to have for that particular day. The God who spoke the universe into existence is speaking just to you. Listen for His voice and record every bit of it. There are times that I don't receive anything specific from the Lord, and when I don't I just leave these left-facing pages blank until I do. Sometimes I receive something weeks after recording my requests of God, and when I do I go back to that section of my journal and layer it there. By the time I've completed a two hundred page journal, I've recorded one hundred pages of God's Word. God promises that His word will not return empty but will accomplish its intended purpose.

God delights in making himself intimately known to you. Your job is to show up, be honest, and listen as you record His Word. His job is the miracle of healing—making His love your reality, His face the face you see, His power your redemption, His truth your truth, His voice yours.

—Celestia

chapter seven

My Thoughts and Feelings...

Meditate on these things; give yourself entirely to them, that your progress may be evident to all. (1 Timothy 4:15 NKJV)

Chapter Eight
Facing the Brokenness

You're always remembered . . .

Can a mother forget the baby at her breast
and have no compassion
on the child she has borne?
Though she may forget,
I will not forget you!
See, I have engraved you
on the palms of my hands;
your walls are ever before me.
(Isaiah 49:15-16)

. . . never forgotten

chapter eight

> Run, John, run, the law commands.
> But gives us neither feet nor hands.
> Far better news the gospel brings:
> It bids us fly and gives us wings.
>
> —John Bunyan

Facing your brokenness and the truth of your past and present is necessary in order for you to *really* move on from your past. It's also essential that you integrate your past experiences and pain in order to heal the ongoing effects of trauma and neglect. Thus, facing your brokenness is an exquisite expression of your trust in a healing God!

Philippians 3:13 is often quoted in order to convince us that we're to ignore the events of the past and look only to the future. However, when we look at the broader context of Paul's statement, we begin to understand how this verse has been misused to distort Paul's meaning and thus hinder the healing of many. Paul understood not only the scope of his sinful past but also the lies that had energized his sin. Through a ruthless pursuit of truth, he identified his need. In other words, you can't put your painful past behind you until you have fully considered the effects of your abuse. Paul also had to face the reality that he had been abusive toward others. This was painful but necessary to make him useful for the work God had called him to do. Like Paul, you must confront both the pain of the ways in which you've been sinned against and the pain of your unhealthy responses and sin toward others. This must happen before you can experience the intimate relationships God has created you for. This painful journey will activate previously deadened parts of your heart and set you free to live out your redemptive destiny.

My thoughts...

> Not that I have already obtained this or am already perfect, but I press on to make it my own, because Christ Jesus has made me his own. Brothers, I do not consider that I have made it my own. But one thing I do: forgetting what lies behind and straining forward to what lies ahead, I press on toward the goal for the prize of the upward call of God in Christ Jesus.
> (Philippians 3:12-14 ESV)

Whatever happens, my dear brothers and sisters, rejoice in the Lord. I never get tired of telling you these things, and I do it to safeguard your faith. Watch out for those dogs, those people who do evil, those mutilators who say you must be circumcised to be saved. For we who worship by the Spirit of God are the ones who are truly circumcised. We rely on what Christ Jesus has done for us. We put no confidence in human effort, though I could have confidence in my own effort if anyone could. Indeed, if others have reason for confidence in their own efforts, I have even more!

I was circumcised when I was eight days old. I am a pure-blooded citizen of Israel and a member of the tribe of Benjamin—a real Hebrew if there ever was one! I was a member of the Pharisees, who demand the strictest obedience to the Jewish law. I was so zealous that I harshly persecuted the church. And as for righteousness, I obeyed the law without fault. I once thought these things were valuable, but now I consider them worthless because of what Christ has done. (Philippians 3:1-7 NLT)

How does Paul describe his persecution of Christians?

Why did Paul persecute Christians?

If Paul hadn't reflected on his past and identified his incorrect beliefs, would he have recognized his abusive behavior and unhealthy responses?

Such is the confidence that we have through Christ toward God. Not that we are sufficient in ourselves to claim anything as coming from us, but our sufficiency is from God. (2 Corinthians 3:4-5 ESV)

chapter eight

FACING BROKENNESS: FOUR STEPS

Step One: *Surrender my false reality!*

The Lord is near to the brokenhearted and saves the crushed in spirit. (Psalm 34:18 ESV)

When we refuse to face our brokenness, we're essentially saying that God isn't powerful enough to heal us. "Denial is an affront to God. It assumes that a false reality is better than the truth" (Dan Allender, *Wounded Heart*). Denial assumes that God must be a liar too—that His promises are not real and that He is not good enough, or strong enough to be with us through the pain of recall and recovery.

In the case of trauma, out of sight is not out of mind. Just because one has been able to repress past trauma does not mean it is no longer embedded in the brain, having significant impact. (Mending the Soul, 136)

Step Two: *Expose my lies—surrender to God's truth*

Investigate my life, O God, find out everything about me; cross-examine and test me, get a clear picture of what I'm about; see for yourself whether I've done anything wrong—then guide me on the road to eternal life. (Psalm 139:23-24 The Message)

As we begin to live in truth, we become aware of the lies that were created by the shame of past abandonment or abuse. Often these distortions are deeply embedded in our personalities and—for the most part—lie outside of our awareness. Careful reflection and prayer is therefore necessary to uncover and expose these distortions (about ourselves, others, and God) so that we can regain both a proper sense of empowerment in our relationships and a deepened ability to love humbly as Christ directs us to do.

Check the distorted core beliefs you've experienced.

- ☐ I'm not good enough the way I am.
- ☐ I say what I think others want to hear.
- ☐ I wear masks (or create an image) to make sure no one ever knows what's inside me.
- ☐ My happiness depends on others.
- ☐ I'm responsible for the feelings and behaviors of others.
- ☐ If something bad happens, I immediately think it's my fault.
- ☐ I worry when things occur that I can't control.
- ☐ I allow others to control me.
- ☐ I'm looking for something or someone to fill my emptiness.
- ☐ I tend to be a perfectionist.
- ☐ I'm good at repressing my feelings.
- ☐ I'm a caretaker. I often attract needy people.
- ☐ It makes me happy when I fix someone's problem.
- ☐ I don't ask for help. I'm self-sufficient.
- ☐ I don't think much of myself: I have low self-esteem.
- ☐ I'm in a great deal of denial about my problems
- ☐ I stay busy or rely on addictions to stay in control.
- ☐ I often use humor when things get too serious.
- ☐ I don't have close friends or share what's going on in my life.
- ☐ I stir up trouble when bored or to feel that someone cares.
- ☐ I'm too serious and can't have fun—there's too much to do.
- ☐ I rarely say what I'm thinking for fear of rejection.
- ☐ I would never admit I have a need, because I'm afraid the need won't be met. Sometimes I don't know what normal is.
- ☐ I'm constantly trying to make others happy—I'm always seeking approval.

chapter eight

Pray and reflect on the events in your past that caused you the most pain—enter these on the timeline on page 36. Then, in the first box here record the memories you've felt and shared with a safe person. In the second box record the memories you haven't disclosed yet. This week consider sharing these with someone safe enough and competent enough to comfort you.

Previously disclosed painful memories

Undisclosed painful memories

What am I feeling now?

What do I need now?

What requests do I need to make now? To whom?

surrender

chapter eight

Pray and ask God to help you trust His Spirit's prompting in the following exercise. Don't over think this one. Instead, write the first thoughts that come, even if they seem inconsequential. God is bringing them to mind for a reason and is wanting you to trust Him. In the first box, record three of the distorted core beliefs you struggle with the most. In the second box record the first memory from your past that comes to mind in association with the distorted belief. In the third box record God's truth and claim it as your truth. This truth can be a Scripture that God has given you or something someone has shared. Walk away from this exercise aligning your behavioral choices with the truth.

My Lies	My Memories	God's Truth
1. 2. 3.		

Step Three: *Surrender to the work of healing*

Heal me, O Lord, and I shall be healed; save me, and I shall be saved, for You are my praise. (Jeremiah 17:14 NKJV)

Our pasts affect how we think, feel, and behave in the present. An intentional person is one who has integrated the past with the present and can live and love from a connected, self-aware place. The same tools used to integrate your past pain are the tools you'll use to maintain your self-awareness and relational connectedness with God and others. The reward of this endeavor will be a deeply intimate and satisfying relationship with Jesus Christ. You won't regret this journey! Because it's necessary to face past abuse in order to heal the ongoing effects of trauma, it's important to make the connection between your past pain (trauma) and your current physical, emotional, and spiritual condition.

> *Revisit your timeline on page 36* and fill in any additional memories—positive and negative—you've had since beginning the workbook. Remember to add the secondary effects of the abuse to your timeline as well. For example, this would include any addictive behaviors or patterns you've experienced. Use a separate color to identify connections between your original abuse and current destructive patterns and symptoms.

Strengthen me according to Your word. Remove from me the way of lying, and grant me Your law graciously. I have chosen the way of truth; Your judgments I have laid before me. (Psalm 119:28-30 NKJV)

chapter eight

This watercolor heart was painted by a little girl who had experienced sexual abuse and, as a result, was behaving sexually toward other children. She felt great shame for her behavior. She painted this picture to describe the damage done to her heart.

You also have in your heart black holes from the sins committed against you and gray holes from your sins. Identifying these holes, sharing them in safe community, and feeling the ensuing pain is part of the healing process. This will empower you against the hidden effects of trauma.

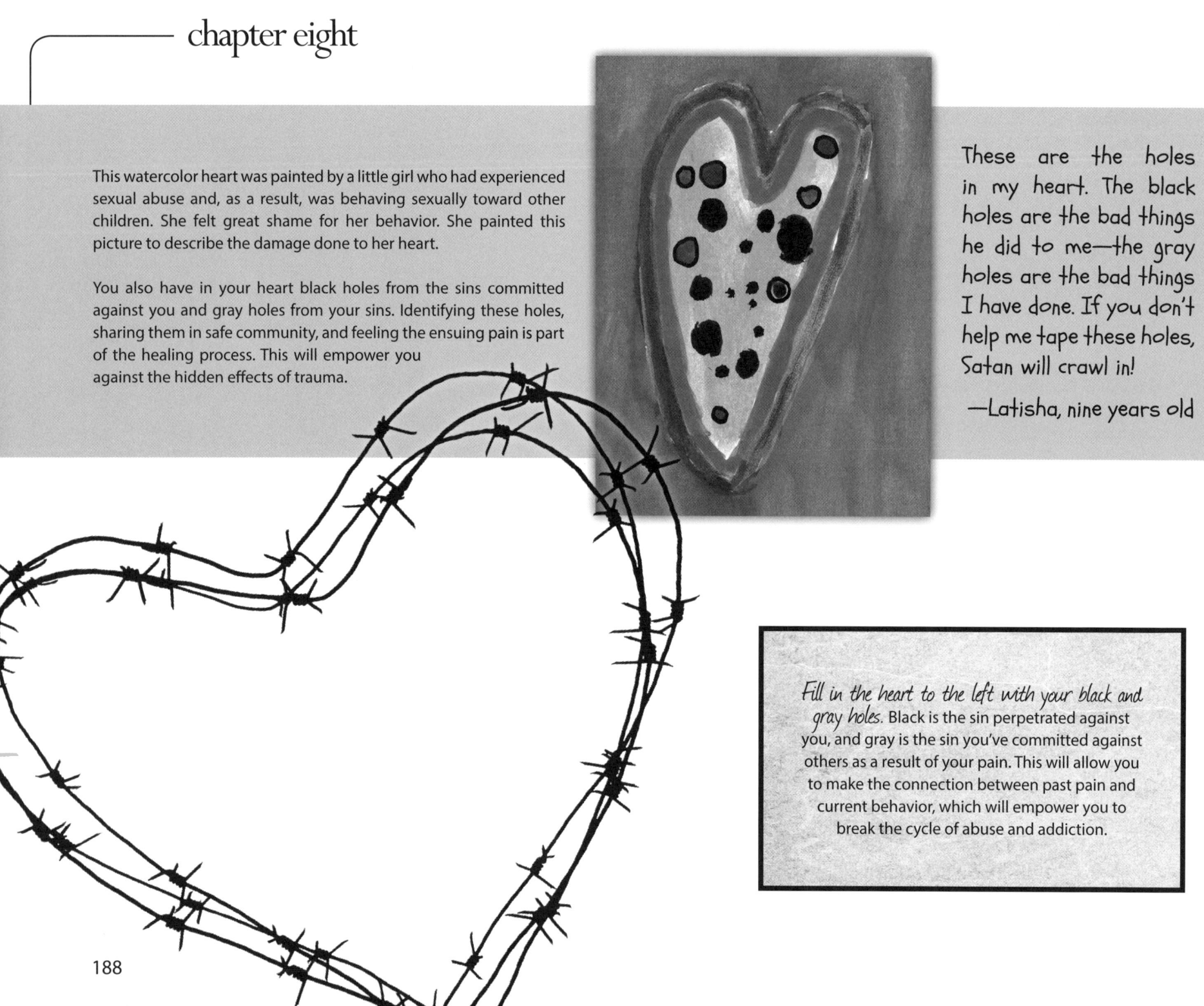

These are the holes in my heart. The black holes are the bad things he did to me—the gray holes are the bad things I have done. If you don't help me tape these holes, Satan will crawl in!

—Latisha, nine years old

Fill in the heart to the left with your black and gray holes. Black is the sin perpetrated against you, and gray is the sin you've committed against others as a result of your pain. This will allow you to make the connection between past pain and current behavior, which will empower you to break the cycle of abuse and addiction.

My Black and Gray Holes...

O Lord, do not put me to shame! I will run the course of Your commandments,
for You shall enlarge my heart. (Psalm 119:31-32 NKJV)

chapter eight

Step Four: *Surrender to healthy relationships*

Love has been perfected among us in this: that we may have boldness in the day of judgment; because as He is, so are we in this world. There is no fear in love; but perfect love casts out fear. (1 John 4:17-18 NKJV)

For full healing to occur, you must thoroughly examine your significant relationships, focusing on the roles you play in them. Depending on your personality, you'll be prone to either a passive, codependent style of relating or a controlling, dominating relational style. The best way to get clear about which one you are is to ask the person closest to you!

Love and acceptance are expressed inconsistently in dysfunctional families; therefore, children in these families don't learn healthy ways to resolve conflict. As children, we may have been either aggressive in relationships or very passive and withdrawn. We may have displayed sexual behavior with other children as well. In short, child abuse victims often fail to develop the relational skills necessary for healthy, intimate, adult relationships.

In the box to the right, draw your family of origin in stick figures. Under each person, describe the role they played in the family. For example, *My sister was the perfect one—she always got good grades, my brother was the angry one—he was always getting into trouble,* or *my brother was the liar—he was always weaseling his way out of trouble.* Be sure to include yourself.

My role in my family of origin . . .

chapter eight

How did your role in your family affect you?

Did you carry any of this same role into adolescence?

How would you describe your style of relating today? How has it changed from when you were a child?

What do you want to change about how you relate to others?

> My unprocessed past led to today's lies and random notions about reality—which led to my current behavior—which was based on yesterday's experiences.

chapter eight

What can you learn about safe, loving relationships and comfort from the following Scriptures?

1 Samuel 19-20

Acts 9:1-30

What can you do to deepen your current relationships?

Peace is first of all the art of being.
—Henri Nouwen

You made us for yourself [O Lord] and our hearts find no peace until they rest in you.

—Saint Augustine

Facing brokenness feels like I'm wimping out. It's like selling when the market is down. It's not easy to cut your losses even if it's the right thing to do. Surrender—even if it is surrender to healing—isn't easy for me. After all, I invested in my efforts to conceal the secondary effects of abuse: sinful behavior, patterns of avoidance, and secrets. But it's time to drop my hands and let go.

Peace I leave with you, My peace I give to you; not as the world gives do I give to you. Let not your heart be troubled, neither let it be afraid.
(John 14:27 NKJV)

chapter eight

IDOLATROUS HABITS OF THE HEART

As men and women created in God's image, we're called to pursue relationships with others in ways that express God's love. These relationships must be founded on an intimate relationship with God. In other words, we can only love and be loved in healthy ways when we have absorbed the truth of God's penetrating and pursuing love for us. Further, we must have absorbed this love in a way that redeems our shame. This gives us the ability to love in bold ways: with truth, grace, and forgiveness.

Satan's strategy is to substitute people or things for God. When we succumb to Satan's influence, we attempt to get satisfaction, security, and fulfillment from sources that ultimately cannot meet our needs. When we grow up feeling empty and starved for love, we can easily make the object of our love another human being. In our shame-filled unhealthiness, we rely on other people—especially family members or lovers—to fill our souls in ways that only God can. The longer we continue in these codependent patterns, the more enslaved to them we become.

This helps us understand how young Christian women with strong biblical values can become "stuck" in destructive relationships where they're not only treated disrespectfully but are also sexualized and abused. These young women are often strong spiritual leaders within their Christian communities, but their relational and sexual lives are split from their public personas. As a therapist, I've worked with hundreds of men and women who didn't understand the profound sense of powerlessness and the sexual compulsivity that drove their relationships.

Hosea gives us a graphic picture of this compulsive and destructive pattern in the life of a woman named Gomer. She left her loving husband to pursue other lovers and was eventually sold into slavery. God was always there, supplying her with the good gifts of provision and love, yet she couldn't see Him. Scripture tells us that Gomer is a picture of us. She demonstrates our human propensity to pursue that which will not satisfy or fulfill us.

The longer Gomer pursued these men, the more wounded she became. Yet God continued to pursue and provide for her. In her compulsive state she was blinded to the truth of God's love for her and of her beauty in God's eyes. She couldn't see or feel His presence. Despite her unfaithfulness, God remained faithful to her. He allured her with His patience, kindness, goodness, and mercy. He eventually created a hedge of thorns around her to bring her to Himself. When she tried to run away from Him and His love, the hedge of thorns pricked her, causing her pain for the sole purpose of bringing her back to Him.

Absorb the poignant picture of God's love. Continue to read Hosea 2 until you get it. He loves you because you are His—in spite of what you have done or where you've been. In fact, this passage of Scripture suggests that in your woundedness you can know an even deeper sense of His love toward you.

Therefore I will hedge up her way with thorns, and I will build a wall against her, so that she cannot find her paths. She shall pursue her lovers but not overtake them, and she shall seek them but shall not find them. Then she shall say, 'I will go and return to my first husband, for it was better for me then than now'...

"Therefore, behold, I will allure her, and bring her into the wilderness, and speak tenderly to her. And there I will give her her vineyards and make the Valley of Achor [trouble] a door of hope. And there she shall answer as in the days of her youth, as at the time when she came out of the land of Egypt.

And I will betroth you to me forever. I will betroth you to me in righteousness and in justice, in steadfast love and in mercy. I will betroth you to me in faithfulness. And you shall know the Lord.
(Hosea 2:6-7, 14-15, 19-20 ESV)

They called her Abia...

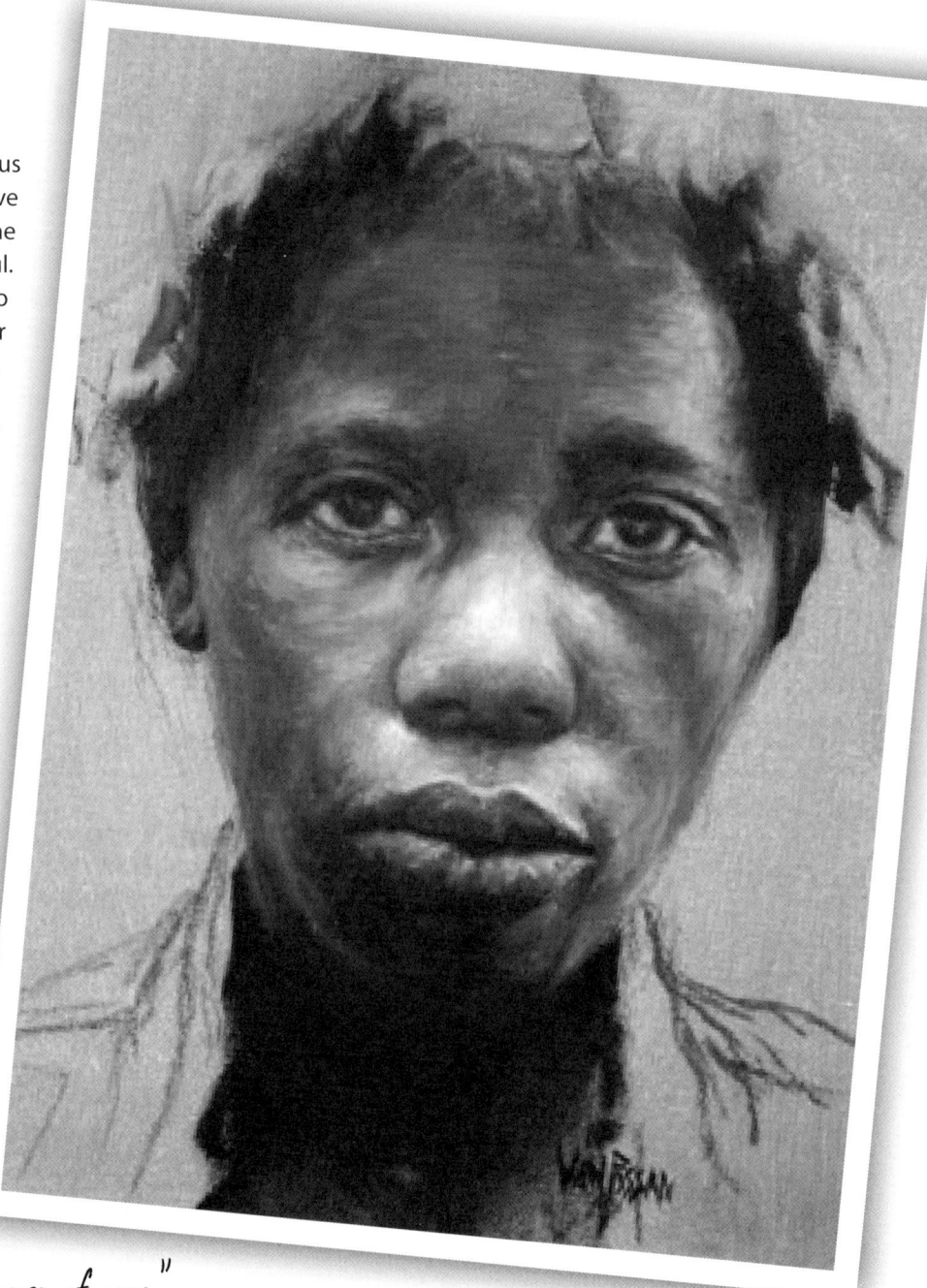

...an outcast, a German Muslim prostitute, untouchable. She told us she wanted the bus destined for the witch doctor's village to remove her "demons." Angry, bitter words spewed from her mouth as she declared her contempt for us, for herself, and Mending the Soul. "Take me back!" She demanded. "We cannot," we explained, "It's too far." God had brought her here: to a power—His power—that far exceeded that of the witch doctor and to a love she'd never known.

Her eyes narrowed in rage as she threw herself heavily upon a dusty bench in the back. She angrily folded her arms across her chest—like two fierce soldiers guarding her heart's door. I didn't leave her side. Throughout that extraordinary day we prayed, trained, ate, worshiped; and then, as the sun set and the room darkened, I began packing my things to go.

She grabbed my hand and begged me not to leave. She pulled me down beside her. Abia opened her book to a picture she had drawn during the training—it was the face of Jesus. "This is the man sitting with me," she explained with tears flowing down her cheeks. "He loves me and I want Him." Without prompting, she lifted her face to heaven and shouted her desire for a Lover whom she had never known before; her shirt was soaked with tears.

She was set free, and claimed in faith the newness of her name and identity. That night, after leaving the conference, she was in the hospital with her sick baby who desperately needed medicine and care. A man came up to her and offered to save her child if she would sell herself to him for the night. She declared,

"I cannot, sir! I'm a new child of God. I am His now! He will take care of me."

Not an actual picture of Abia

chapter eight

Who or what have you given the highest priority in your life?

Ask God to reveal the truth to you now. He wants to set you free from whatever is keeping you in bondage. God is a jealous God; He wants to be central in your heart and life. (Isaiah 45:20-22, Matthew 22:37-38)

How do you feel about letting go of this person, place, or thing?

Have you compromised yourself (your values, beliefs, or morality) to keep this relationship? Be very honest with yourself.

Talk honestly to God now.

Write a prayer expressing your thoughts and desires.

His was the holiest face I ever saw. My very name turned holy on his tongue. If he had bade me rise and follow to the end of time, I would have gone. If he had bade me die for him, I would have died. When I deserved it least, God gave me most. I think it was the savior's face I saw.

—Frederick Buechner, *Godric*

Write your own poem. Use the scriptural metaphors that are most redemptive for you.

We Will Not Forget

Your courage to survive, a solid, stoic stance
Against forces that would destroy you

Your children kept close, wrapped with cautious watch
Babies swaddled severely on your back
Beads of sweat like tiny pearls

Your eyes, vigilant and guarded
Pools of pain and hunger
Full of story, ache

Your hands, worn, tired and reaching
Your words, "Don't leave me,"
"Stay"

Your pure salvation, fixed, steadfast, and resolute
The first certain Love you have ever known
Faces turned heavenward, tears washing, Gospel
All for you

—Celestia

Fifty-seven prostituted women eagerly accepted Christ in one day.

O death where is your victory, O grave where is your sting? Once you held such power o'r me but now my heart can sing. The hurt that sat like granite rock upon my chest is gone; My view once darkened with a mist now beholds the dawn. Meaning and purpose grace my thoughts; love wells up within where once an angry ogre lived bound up in chains of sin. And as my eyes behold the cross, I see a treasure there; I hear Love's call—it bids me near, by grace I enter in.

chapter eight

SETTING HEALTHY BOUNDARIES

Boundaries are limits we set for ourselves and others. They serve as the relational expression of who we believe ourselves to be. For instance, if I believe that I'm inferior or worthless and that others are superior, I'll exhibit minimal personal boundaries in areas of self-respect. I'll probably allow others to interrupt me, talk over me, talk down to me, and disrespect me in various ways. Allowing this unhealthy behavior will fit with my distorted perception of myself and others.

Make a list of all the people you have daily contact with. Briefly describe how you feel about these relationships; include what you enjoy about them as well as what you wish were different.

What are the sinful, disrespectful, or abusive behaviors, you're currently experiencing and thus allowing? List them here.

What are the sinful, disrespectful, or abusive behaviors, you're currently initiating in your relationships? List them here.

What steps are you ready to take to set boundaries that are founded on God's truth of your actual value in relationships?

Painting by James Van Fossan

Chapter Nine
Surrendering to God's Love

So, what do you think? With God on our side like this, how can we lose? If God didn't hesitate
to put everything on the line for us, embracing our condition and exposing himself to the worst
by sending his own Son, is there anything else he wouldn't gladly and freely do for us?
And who would dare tangle with God by messing with one of God's chosen?
Who would dare even to point a finger?

The One who died for us—who was raised to life for us!—is in
the presence of God at this very moment sticking up for us.
Do you think anyone is going to be able to drive a wedge between us and Christ's love for us?
There is no way! Not trouble, not hard times, not hatred, not hunger, not homelessness,
not bullying threats, not backstabbing, not even the worst sins listed in Scripture.

. . . I'm absolutely convinced that nothing—nothing living or dead, angelic or demonic, today
or tomorrow, high or low, thinkable or unthinkable—absolutely nothing
can get between us and God's love because of the way
that Jesus our Master has embraced us.
(Romans 8:31-39 The Message)

Tell me now how this story ends.

I want to read the last page,
 just to know that all this is worth second pain.

Oh, Lord, press this assurance into my heart,
 and let it become me.

Let me hear this voice of comfort,
 whispering into my broken places,
  wiping tears that I feel desperate to
  hide.

Let there be kindness in the healing,
 sure and tender hands, Oh, Lord,
 some gentle hold about me.

Let the wound dissipate
 as voices calm and old danger
 shifts to light.

Let the pain come again,
 this time turning to its end, and
 let the healing be bearable.

Artwork by James Van Fossan

chapter nine

REBUILDING INTIMACY WITH GOD

Our most basic need is relational—we were designed to be in intimate relationship with God. The greatest tragedy in human history is that sin alienated us from God our Creator and separated us from each other. We were doomed, but God sent Christ into our world in order to bring us back to Him (2 Corinthians 5:19). God so values intimacy with us that He was willing to pay the greatest imaginable price in order to meet our greatest imaginable need. God did this in spite of the fact that we can't give Him anything—He lacks nothing. He has enjoyed perfect intimacy in His own divine Being since before the beginning of time. Such is the incomprehensible beauty of God's love: He delights in intimacy with us—no matter how messed up and mixed up we are.

Because God created us in and for Eden, we search for that perfect relationship in which we're unconditionally loved. The world we live in is nothing like Eden, but we still long to be perfectly known and to perfectly know another—yet we're afraid to trust, because we've been hurt. The only way out of this dilemma is to focus on healing our relationship with God until we know and feel His delight in us. This spiritual reconciliation must take place so that we can know His perfect love and then be freed to love others. Only when we've internalized our Father's love for us can we push past our reluctance to trust, embracing our new identity that comes when we see ourselves through His eyes of love. (For further discussion see *Forever and Always: The Art of Bonding* by Tracy and Tracy).

> *My gift to you is love, but worship is your gift to Me. And oh, most glorious it is! Worship always calls Me "Father" and makes us both rich with common joy. Worship Me, for only this great gift can set you free from the killing love of self, and prick your fear with valiant courage to fly in hope through moments of despair. Worship will remind you that no man knows completeness in himself. Worship will teach you to speak your name, when you've forgotten who you are. Worship is duty and privilege, debt and grand inheritance at once. Worship, therefore, at those midnights when the stars hide. Worship in the storms till love makes thunder whimper and grow quiet and listen to your whispered hymns. Worship and be free!"*
> (Calvin Miller, *A Requiem for Love*)

In this chapter we'll explore the process of creating a more intimate and dynamic relationship with Christ. We'll reflect on the ways in which parents shape a child's view of God and unintentionally create a script for how a person relates to Him. Once you can identify any negative messages you've received, you'll be able consciously to embrace God as an attentive "parent" and let His love in.

chapter nine

Re-Imaging the Parenthood of God

When we experience the pain of abandonment and abuse, it can be difficult to understand how a loving God could allow this suffering. As a result, we reject God, avoid God, or cower in fear before Him. These responses reflect the spiritual damage that occurs when God's perfect plan for intimacy is disrupted by neglect and abuse. The good news is that God is invested in healing us so that we can trust Him again!

Best memory of my father	Best memory of my mother	What I learned about God from these memories
Painful memory of my father	Painful memory of my mother	What I learned about God from these memories

chapter nine

Describe your relationship with God. What would you like to change? What do you long for?

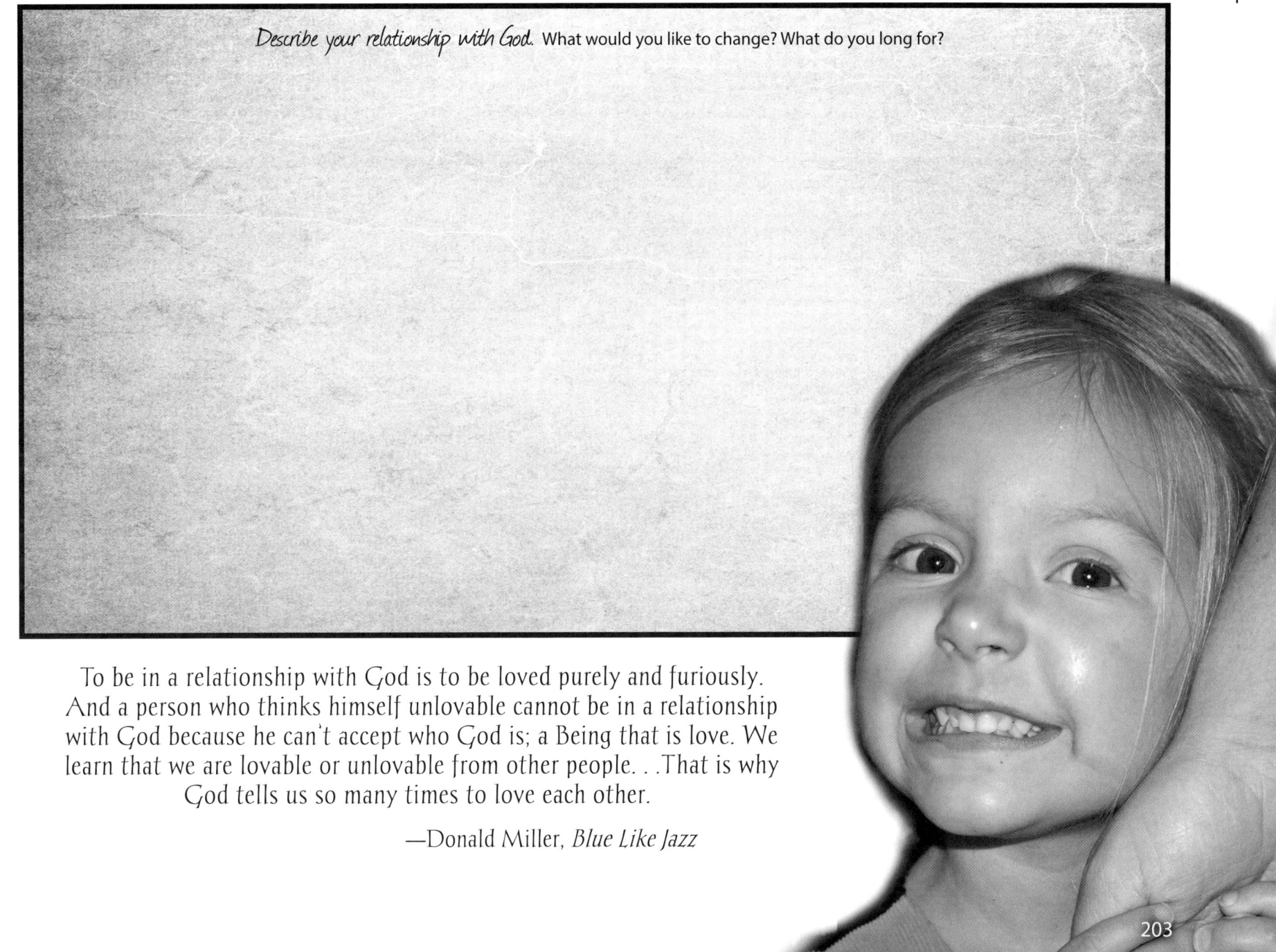

To be in a relationship with God is to be loved purely and furiously. And a person who thinks himself unlovable cannot be in a relationship with God because he can't accept who God is; a Being that is love. We learn that we are lovable or unlovable from other people...That is why God tells us so many times to love each other.

—Donald Miller, *Blue Like Jazz*

chapter nine

Embracing the God of Scripture

It's important to remember Satan's strategy: he can't create anything, so he distorts the best of what God offers us. He distorts God's character, causing us to disbelieve and misconstrue God's attributes: who God really is and how He relates to his creation. These are precious aspects of God we deeply need to understand, for such an understanding leads to healing and growth. Reread pages 166-179 in *Mending the Soul* before filling in the following chart.

God's Truth	Scripture about His Character	My New Image of God
Psalm 91:1-2	He who dwells in the shelter of the Most High will rest in the shadow of the Almighty. I will say of the Lord, "He is my refuge and my fortress, my God, in whom I trust."	You shelter me and offer refuge for me at all times.
Deuteronomy 32:18		
Psalm 131:2		
Isaiah 49:15		
1 Peter 2:2-3		
Jeremiah 1:5		
Luke 13:34		

chapter nine

Circle the words below that come to mind when you think of God. Highlight the words that come to mind when you think of your father.

Answer honestly. It's important to uncover any distortions about God that have crept into your thinking as a result of your history.

Gentle	Peaceful	Harsh	Generous
Loving	Gracious	Miserly	Unreasonable
Kind	Tender	Nurturing	Just
Caring	Joyful	Cherishing	Loathing
Disciplining	Manipulative	Emotional	Abusive
Interested	Indifferent	Tense	Patient
Affectionate	Encouraging	Sensitive	Angry
Trustworthy	Depressed	Mean	Cursing
Good	Anxious	Supportive	Addicted
Reliable	Forgiving	Sarcastic	Holy
Passive	Absent	Bitter	Providing
Apathetic	Unavailable	Humble	Delightful
Stern	Close	Unstable	Strong
Aloof	Intimate	Friendly	Protective
Distant	Disapproving	Wise	Unpredictable
Demanding	Compassionate	Guiding	Unforgiving

chapter nine

There is a place in me that shifts and bends almost to breaking, touching down to soil and dampness. Breathing is difficult, all bent to the ground. A shifting that sounds like ice breaking on the lake when days stretch, when black ice begins to move just enough, moaning as it sheds its own weight. Simple, pervasive darkness begins to lift. There are early spring days to remember—a sweet popping of the warmth into the banks of old snow and hope of the first flower, standing bright against winter's endless white—iris, crocus, wild violets—all of these—the better part of spring just starting.

How has my earthly father shaped my view of God?

What do I want to keep from his legacy?

How has my mother shaped my view of God?

What is my new image of God?

chapter nine

Wrestling with God—Feeling Again

Our spiritual pilgrimage will often lead us through dark valleys of doubt and frustration—especially for abuse survivors. In fact, when survivors begin to heal, they often find that their anger and doubts intensify toward God. Before healing, survivors are often quite emotionally numb and cut off from their negative feelings and doubts. This may manifest as a legalistic, mechanistic spirituality. Quiet times with God are done out of a sense of duty and checked off as an external measurement of religiosity. Christianity is lived out of the head rather than the heart. To many, this can look like an enviable form of spirituality; however, it's actually quite unbiblical. As evidence to the contrary, Dr. Tracy notes that *"David, Jeremiah, Job, and Habakkuk were among the godliest people described in the Bible. They suffered excruciating verbal, physical, and spiritual abuse. They walked with God. They became intimate with God. But their path to spiritual intimacy led through dark valleys of doubt and struggle."* (Mending the Soul, pg 161) Our spiritual journey will probably be the same.

Emotional numbing is expressed in myriad ways. In adults, chronic or explosive anger can be a manifestation of emotional numbing. Men and women also differ in the experience and expression of emotion. Men, on one hand, take six to eight hours to process hard emotive data, while women are quick to feel, think, connect, and express—virtually all at the same time. When men experience relational pain, most have an automatic fight-or-flight response, making it difficult for them to resolve emotional ambivalence or conflict well in real time. A male survivor describes his experience with anger below:

> *I thank God for anger. Anger appears throughout the Bible, and I see it as a great emotional gift—especially to those of us with power (physical or otherwise). That's one of the things I appreciate about being a physically able man. Although age will eventually catch up with me, for the time being I have the God-given means to protect those who can't protect themselves. But with great power also comes great responsibility; and, as a fallen and sinful man, my strengths come with certain weaknesses. Anger can become a man's primary tool for dealing with perceived threats (real or imagined), consequently overriding other mental, emotional, and spiritual problem-solving resources. When that happens I'm no longer using anger—it's using me. My verbal communication shuts down, I lose the ability to understand what's really happening, and I can no longer think of creative win-win solutions. It's like trying to fix a car with only a sledgehammer. Sure, the problem stops making noise, but many important things get damaged in the process. Anger comes from an immature part of the brain (what we often think of as our "heart"), so when we're angry, we rarely take into account long-term consequences, the most appropriate target, or what healthy limits look like. Learning to control anger is like learning to use the right tool for the right job—even when I'm itching to loose the sledgehammer. When I do this, my adult-functioning mind remains in charge and allows me—if I'm ready—to begin exploring the even deeper question of why I feel so threatened.*

In summary, it's quite easy to repress negative feelings. Therefore, we must strive toward connection every day—so that our relationships with God and others don't suffer. Remember that we can only feel another's pain if we feel our own. Emotional constriction produces dangerous consequences if it's not identified and mediated.

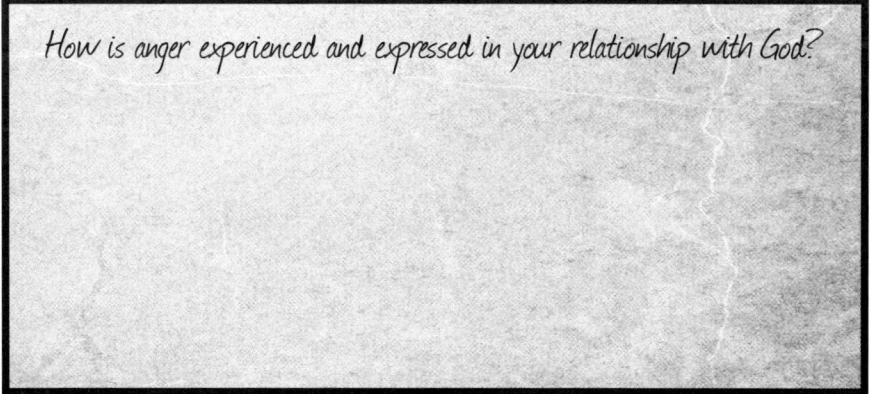

How is anger experienced and expressed in your relationship with God?

chapter nine

How do you act when you're emotionally numb?
Seek feedback from others in order to answer this question.

Do you see the effects of emotional numbing in someone you love?
How do they make you feel when you're with them?

Whom have I in heaven but you? And earth has nothing I desire besides you. My flesh and my heart may fail, but God is the strength of my heart and my portion forever.
(Psalm 73:25-26)

Every Day

Every day it's a fight to get through. Every day.
Some days more than others. Often in different ways.
Always challenging. Usually painful. Often masked. So I can get through.

But it's when the mask gets lowered
That the deepest of healing begins.
It's overwhelming. It's too much to bear.
It never should've been this way. But it is.
And these things are true.

So, I cannot walk this path alone.
I look to my God, my Savior, my Lord.
Whose Word is TRUTH and Whose promises never fail
Though my human reality may be far different, this is the Truth of Christ.

And as I look to my left and to my right,
In front and behind, I will see those people
In human flesh He is giving me to be His hands and feet,
His legs and arms, His mouth and ears so that I do not walk alone

And I heal from the damage that was done
And am loved and touched and accepted and valued and respected
And honored as our Heavenly Father intended for me to be.
He knows it is too hard, too painful, too ugly, too heavy to bear

And always has been so He gave us Himself
in His Son Jesus Christ, and He gave us each other
That we may walk together with Him through the destruction and despair
To wholeness and abundant life:
The life that was His original design.

Wrestling with God—Overcoming Passivity

If we believe we're powerless, we'll act powerless, manifesting a passive, overly submissive, and non-initiating relational style. The more powerless one believes him or herself to be, the more anxious and depressed that person will feel—the more "victimized" by circumstances and people around them. The more powerless a person feels, the more passivity he or she will present—both in relationship with others and in relationship with God. God is pursuing you with His love and desires intimacy with you. Wrestling with God means you refuse to give up on Him—holding on until you hear Him, see Him, feel Him.

How has powerlessness impacted your relationship with God?

How would others describe your relationship with God?

I lived as a shell of a man. For years I was unable to cry, though I began to think it might be good for me. As a junior in high school, I made a commitment to conceal my vulnerable side—and I did for fifteen years. Then, somehow, the ideas of suffering and love converged on me as I watched a film about the life of C.S. Lewis. While driving home I had to pull over twice because I couldn't drive while weeping. The floodgates opened, and fifteen years of tears washed over me. Another fifteen years would go by before this chapter would help me absorb the truth that the object of God's love was me.

The Incredible Shrinking Woman

I am yelling inside again
I am louder than ever
More persistent
Angrier than the last time I spoke up

I am yelling, but you hear nothing
You see nothing, you feel nothing
All that is bad is left for me to deal with
That is my role: to absorb all that feels bad
So that you only feel good

I am slipping away at your words
At the hardness of all that sounds holy
Coming from deep within you

From a place that feels hostile and hurtful
Yet somehow sounds holy
As you draw back your frustration
And control your breathing

I wonder if I'm going deaf inside
All the noise of my words
neither said nor heard

The ones I yell inside
At the top of my lungs
Drowning out so much
A sustained silence

chapter nine

Are you honest when you talk to God? Talk to Him now—finish the following sentences with your raw responses.

Dear God,

I feel confused by . . .

I feel frustrated when . . .

I feel angry about . . .

I'm most discouraged by . . .

I need You most when . . .

Thank You for . . .

I love You because . . .

> Awake, Lord! Why do you sleep? Rouse yourself! Do not reject us forever. Why do you hide your face and forget our misery and oppression?
> (Psalm 44:23-24)

> My soul thirsts for God, for the living God. When can I go and meet with God? My tears have been my food day and night.
> (Psalm 42:2-3)

chapter nine

Wrestling with God—Embracing the Cross

The fullest divine response to suffering and evil is the cross of Christ. On the cross Christ suffered the most excruciating physical, emotional, and spiritual torture to deliver us from the curse of sin. Jesus understands the horrors of abuse. He was publicly mocked, stripped naked, slapped, whipped, spit on, shamed, and eventually tortured to death. Christ isn't indifferent to our suffering. He experienced that suffering for us—with us—and promises to redeem every bit of our pain. He is God with us, Emmanuel.

> He was despised and rejected by mankind, a man of suffering, and familiar with pain. Like one from whom people hide their faces he was despised, and we held him in low esteem. Surely he took up our pain and bore our suffering, yet we considered him punished by God, stricken by him, and afflicted. But he was pierced for our transgressions, he was crushed for our iniquities; the punishment that brought us peace was on him, and by his wounds we are healed.
> (Isaiah 53:3-5)

How can you identify with the suffering Christ did on your behalf?

How is God manifesting Himself to you now?

> Only the suffering God can help.
> —Dietrich Bonhoeffer

chapter nine

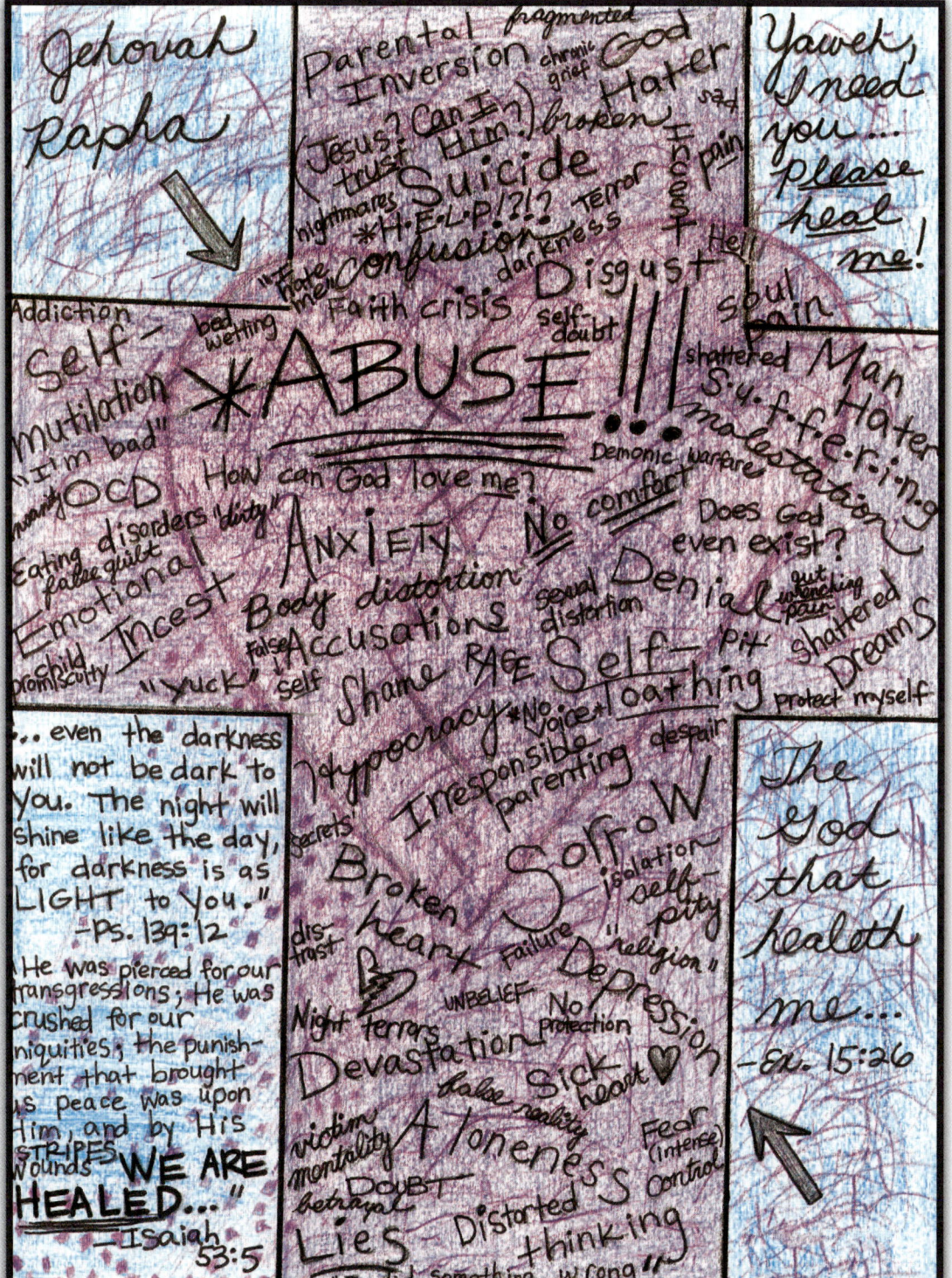

I created this cross...

during a desperate time in my healing journey, when I was truly making the transition of giving every bit of my pain to Him. I was suicidal and desperate for more of the Lord. I was desperately crying out to Him for whatever I needed. I drew a picture of the cross and put all my pain on it. Everything my abuse caused I heaved onto the Cross, as a heavy burden now off of my shoulders and safe with Jesus.

I look at this cross to remember that He died on the cross to carry these effects for me. I have many slash marks all across it to represent the stripes on Jesus' back, by which I AM BEING HEALED! As I made this picture, I almost broke the colored pencil by slash-slash-slashing the thing so much. I was healing as I did that, envisioning His healing stripes. I was brutally honest about all I had experienced and all I was feeling. This picture is very important for me to use as an...

anchor for my heart.

"You'll forget all about the humiliations of your youth, and the indignities of being a widow will fade from memory. For your Maker is your bridegroom, his name, God-of-the-Angel-Armies! Your Redeemer is The Holy of Israel, known as God of the whole earth. You were like an abandoned wife, devastated with grief, and God welcomed you back, like a woman married young and then left," says your God. "It's with lasting love that I'm tenderly caring for you."
(Isaiah 54:4-6,8 The Message)

How does this Scripture make you feel? What's your truth?

God's love is beginning to feel like a place for me and less like an emotion. I mean, I feel as if I belong. I have a place among others and there's this sense of community. I feel validated and at home. I neither have to bear the burden of the spotlight nor be lost in the crowd. I'm welcomed into close proximity to God even as others are also welcomed.

chapter nine

Wrestling with God—Holding on to Him

Jacob gives us a powerful model of holding on to God until we experience His love and goodness. Jacob was desperate for God's blessing. So much so, that he chose to wrestle all night with an angel until God promised to bless him. From that point forward Jacob walked with a limp as a reminder of his commitment to wrestle with God until he experienced His goodness. Following this incident God affirmed this choice by changing Jacob's name from "trickster" to Israel which means "one who struggles with God" (Genesis 25:26; 32:28). God honors your commitment to radically pursue intimacy with Him.

> So Jacob was left alone, and a man wrestled with him till daybreak. When the man saw that he could not overpower him, he touched the socket of Jacob's hip so that his hip was wrenched as he wrestled with the man. Then the man said, "let me go, for it is daybreak." But Jacob replied, "I will not let you go unless you bless me." The man asked him, "What is your name?" "Jacob," he answered. Then the man said, "Your name will no longer be Jacob, but Israel, because you have struggled with God and overcome." Then he blessed him there. (Genesis 32:24-29)

What do you need to hear from God?

Are you committed to holding on to Him until you experience His goodness and love? Tell Him.

chapter nine

I've been reflecting on God's good and sovereign hand upon me. My primary request of Him is wisdom and stamina to do the healing ministry He has called me into. He hears me, and at a time when I need more anointed direction than ever, He is giving it. Because of pain, I'm awake and up many nights. This is unexpected time with my precious Savior—I now have hours of time that I would not ordinarily take when I pour my raw and honest pain into His hands and then sit desperately needy until He fills me with Himself. I call these "sit-outs." If I wait, Christ is the prize in my pain, my severe mercy. I am fully aware that if I had a strong body and robust health, I would be doing more and more of my life and ministry in my own strength—out of my flesh—which would be to greatly diminish the power within it. God loves me too much to allow me to settle for "lesser things." I'm thankful He loves me like that.

What does He want to do in your pain?

Just as we like for others to be honest with us, so does God. Throw at him your grief, your anger, your doubt, your bitterness, your betrayal, your disappointment—he can absorb them all. As often as not, spiritual giants of the Bible are shown contending with God. They prefer to go away limping, like Jacob, rather than shut God out . . . God can deal with every human response save one. He cannot abide with the response I fall back on instinctively: an attempt to ignore or treat him as though he does not exist. That response never once occurred to Job.

—Philip Yancey, *Disappointment with God*

Lord, I have survived ugliness. You could have stopped it—but chose to walk it with me. Lord, fully sovereign, I am that willful child even now, seeking desperately to yield.

Suffering—that irreconcilable know, pain upon pain, wound and pulled tight. Bruising, numbness, silenced heart—buried deeper than I know. This is the ugly I survived.

The untangling begins when I least expect, a strange surfacing of bad water from deep—it comes rushing, rising up, always unbidden, spreading along the surface, oily and leaden, shrouding me in familiar dullness.

I have learned your unseen law of recurrences, and through it, to pursue freedom. There's intimacy on the other side.

chapter nine

Dear God,

I'm holding on to You for . . .

He has made my teeth grind on gravel, and made me cower in ashes; my soul is bereft of peace; I have forgotten what happiness is. But this I call to mind, and therefore I have hope: The steadfast love of the Lord never ceases; his mercies never come to an end; they are new every morning; great is your faithfulness. "The Lord is my portion," says my soul, "therefore I will hope in him." The Lord is good to those who wait for him, to the soul who seeks him.
(Lamentations 3:16-17, 21-25 ESV)

Chapter Ten
Forgiveness

chapter ten

Often when we share our stories of abuse with others, the first thing we're told is that we must forgive our abusers. However, although forgiveness is essential, it must come at the end of our healing rather than at the beginning. Forgiveness in the face of abandonment, abuse, and sexual exploitation is not as simple a biblical concept as some believe and teach. Many are taught that the Greek word for *forgive* means to "let go." Although this definition is accurate, it's often mistimed and misapplied. What about the family whose child has been molested by a member of the extended family and is now expected to let go and not disclose the abuse or notify authorities? What does letting go mean for this child at family gatherings? For her parents? For others? In this chapter we'll explore the biblical concept of forgiveness.

> My friends, we will not go again or ape an ancient rage. Or stretch the folly of our youth to be the shame of age. . .For there is good news yet to hear and fine things to be seen, Before we go to Paradise by way of Kensal Green.
> —G.K. Chesterton

Knowing what you know about God's love for you, do you think He would expect you to "let go" of your abuse in a way that would expose you or others to further abuse?

I was always in denial and forever minimizing my feelings, so it was difficult to forgive. Forgive what!? It doesn't matter . . .It's not a big deal. No wonder I so readily forgave yet remained resentful—I didn't know what it was that I was forgiving!

The weak can never forgive. Forgiveness is the attribute of the strong.
—Gandhi

chapter ten

HARMFUL TEACHING ON FORGIVENESS

There is widespread confusion in the community of faith about the relationship between forgiveness and abuse. Some Christians claim that biblical forgiveness means letting go of the offense so that there is no longer any fear, anger, or mistrust toward the one who hurt you. This, however, is a harmful, incomplete, and unbiblical model of forgiveness. Scripture *does* describe forgiveness as letting go of a debt, but it also demonstrates that there are consequences for the offender. Nowhere does the Bible say that trust and reconciliation will always be granted. It's important to realize that trust cannot be demanded—it's earned.

God said, "I forgive them . . . But as I live and as the Glory of God fills the whole Earth—not a single person of those who saw my Glory, saw the miracle signs I did in Egypt and the wilderness, and who have tested me over and over and over again, turning a deaf ear to me—not one of them will set eyes on the land I so solemnly promised to their ancestors. No one who has treated me with such repeated contempt will see it." (Numbers 14:20-23)

What consequences did the Israelites experience after God forgave them for their rebelliousness?

"You're the man!" said Nathan [the prophet to King David]. "And here's what God has to say to you: I made you king over Israel. I freed you from the fist of Saul. I gave you your master's daughter and other wives to have and to hold. I gave you both Israel and Judah. And if that hadn't been enough, I'd have gladly thrown in much more. So why have you treated the word of God with brazen contempt, doing this great evil? You murdered Uriah the Hittite, then took his wife as your wife. Worse, you killed him with an Ammonite sword! And now, because you treated God with such contempt and took Uriah the Hittite's wife as your wife, killing and murder will continually plague your family. This is God speaking, remember! I'll make trouble for you out of your own family. I'll take your wives from right out in front of you. I'll give them to some neighbor, and he'll go to bed with them openly. You did your deed in secret, I'm doing mine with the whole country watching!" (2 Samuel 12:7-13)

What consequences did David experience after God forgave him for his sexual sin?
Can you relate to anything in this passage? Explain.

chapter ten

THREE TYPES OF FORGIVENESS

Judicial Forgiveness

Judicial forgiveness is a complete pardon of all sin, granted only by God. God's forgiveness is available to all sinners, but can only be granted after a person has confessed and repented. Only God can grant judicial forgiveness. It's not for us to forgive another so that person can go to heaven or stand in right relationship with God. This is between that person and God. We're also to hold our abuser accountable, not make excuses for them, or take their responsibility—when we do these things, we actually can hinder them from knowing God's forgiveness. Our only job is to speak truth about our abusers' behavior.

> He who covers his sins will not prosper, but whoever confesses and forsakes them will have mercy.
> (Proverbs 28:13 NKJV)

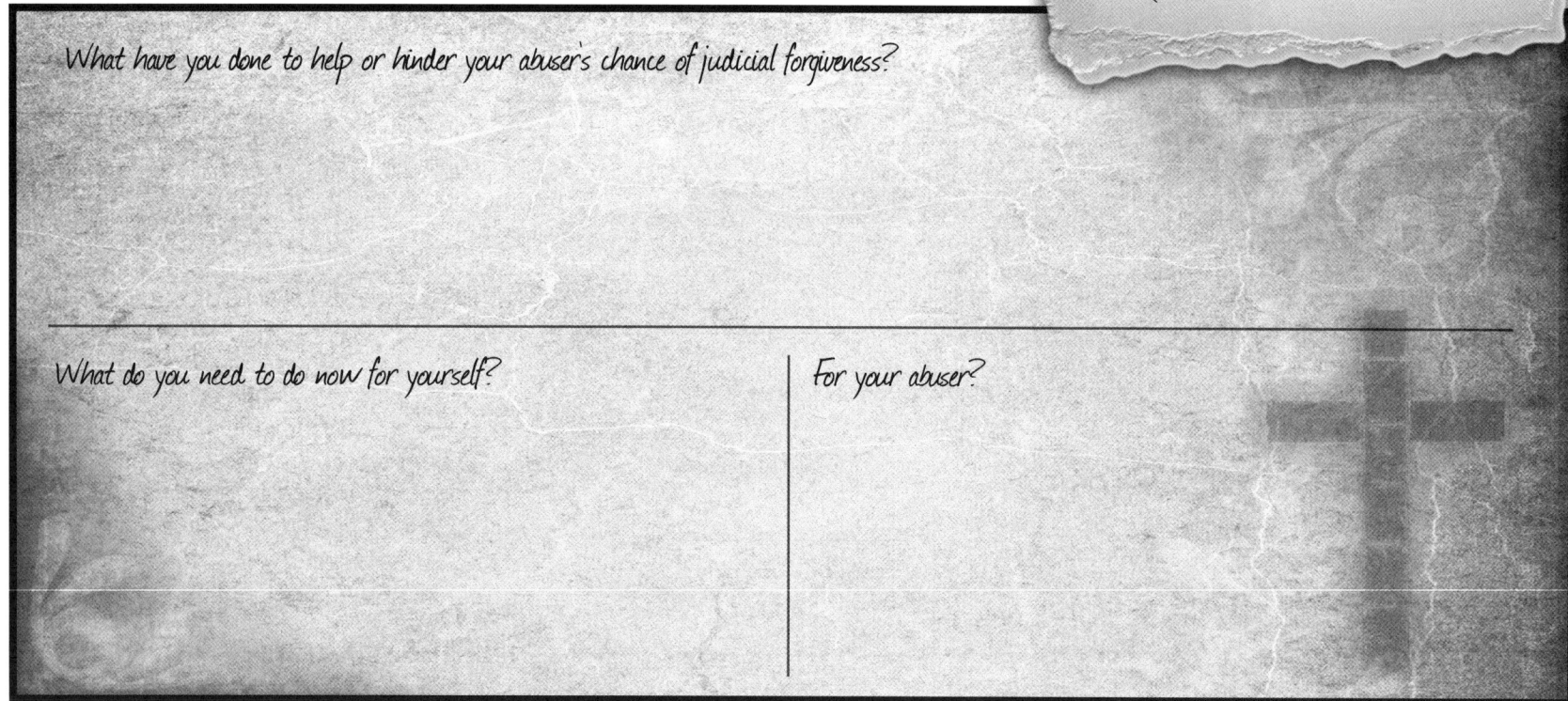

What have you done to help or hinder your abuser's chance of judicial forgiveness?

What do you need to do now for yourself?

For your abuser?

[We can] hinder abusers from finding God's forgiveness when [we] fail to press offenders for full ownership of their behavior.
—Steve Tracy, *Mending the Soul*

David's Prayer of Repentance–God's Forgiveness

Blessed is the one whose transgressions are forgiven, whose sins are covered. Blessed is the one whose sin the Lord does not count against them and in whose spirit is no deceit.
When I kept silent, my bones wasted away through my groaning all day long.
For day and night your hand was heavy on me; my strength was sapped as in the heat of summer.

Then I acknowledged my sin to you and did not cover up my iniquity.
I said, "I will confess my transgressions to the Lord."
And you forgave the guilt of my sin. Therefore let all the faithful pray to you while you may be found; surely the rising of the mighty waters will not reach them. You are my hiding place; you will protect me from trouble and surround me with songs of deliverance.

I will instruct you and teach you in the way you should go; I will counsel you with my loving eye on you. Do not be like the horse or the mule, which have no understanding but must be controlled by bit and bridle or they will not come to you. Many are the woes of the wicked, but the Lord's unfailing love surrounds
the one who trusts in him. (Psalm 32:1-11)

Write your own prayer of repentance...

chapter ten

Psychological Forgiveness

Psychological forgiveness is an inner (intrapersonal) process, which extends mercy by surrendering our right to retaliate against our offenders. In order to take this step, you must thoroughly process the sin that has been committed against you as well as the impact of it. Anger is a *very* appropriate response to the evil of abuse. God demonstrates this anger at unrepentant abusers throughout the Old and New Testaments. The Gospels recount multiple instances where Christ became angry at people who defamed God and hurt people made in God's image (John 2:13-17; Matthew 21:12-13; 23:1-36; Mark 3:1-5). Scripture warns us against holding on to resentment in order to enact revenge. God is the only one powerful enough to make wrongs right. That's His job, not ours.

When we psychologically forgive our abusers, we're not letting go of our desire for justice, we're letting go of our right to take revenge. God's judgment toward unrepentant evil will be perfect. Any attempts we make at revenge will be insignificant compared to what God has planned. When we cling to our right to take revenge, we distance ourselves from God. Essentially, we're telling Him that we need to step in because He can't execute justice as well as we can. Ask God to deepen your faith in His goodness and power to redeem the pain you've experienced. He's our suffering Savior, and He will free us.

Remember, you must feel and express negative emotion (including anger) in order to heal. If you don't give yourself this permission, you're at risk of developing deep roots of bitterness and passive resentment that will eventually morph into myriad relationally destructive patterns.

> Some things are intolerable and nobody should tolerate them—they violate the law of life. It is precisely because they are intolerable that such a radical remedy as forgiving had to be found for them.

What losses have you experienced as a result of your abuse or neglect?

How does listing these losses make you feel?

What stages of grief are you experiencing now? Describe.

Stages of Grief

> Elisabeth Kübler-Ross, M.D. (July 8, 1926 – August 24, 2004) was a Swiss American psychiatrist and a pioneer in near-death studies. She is the author of the book *On Death and Dying* (1969) where she first introduced what is now known as the Kübler-Ross model of grief. Her model consists of five stages: **denial, anger, bargaining, depression, acceptance.**

The stages of grief were originally applied to people suffering from terminal illness. She later expanded her theoretical model to apply to any form of catastrophic personal loss: death of a loved one; end of a relationship through divorce, drug addiction, or incarceration; onset of a disease or chronic illness; and the effects of abuse and abandonment. Kübler-Ross claimed that these stages don't necessarily come in order, nor are all stages typically experienced. The research suggests that people will experience the stages in a roller-coaster effect by switching between two or more stages at one time before working through their grief. We also know that women are more likely than men to experience all five stages. Individuals differ in the time they will take to move through the grief process.

Because our western culture doesn't place much emphasis on grieving in general, it's very important that you validate for yourself the losses you've experienced as a result of your abuse and express these fully to the Lord. This will move you through the stages of grief and assure that you don't get stuck. He will show you His purposes in your pain and help you move to a place of acceptance. He promises to redeem every bit of your pain as you surrender to Him.

chapter ten

Ultimately, psychological forgiveness is expressed by our desire for our abuser's healing. No sin is too big for God to forgive—He just requires repentance. Carol's story gives a picture of what it looks like to desire healing for someone who has hurt us deeply.

For our entire thirteen-year marriage, our goal was to have big houses in at least two states, nice cars, and enough money to do whatever we wanted, whenever we wanted. We believed that once we had achieved this goal, we would finally be truly "happy." Yet the closer we came to this goal, the more miserable we became. Through marriage counseling with a highly regarded biblical counselor, it was exposed that not only were we worshiping the wrong god, but also that Joe was being unfaithful and had a sexual addiction. I may never know the extent to which he betrayed me, but what I did know left me feeling as if my heart had been ripped out of my chest, brutally beaten, and handed back to me.

For me there was only one place to turn, and that was the cross of Christ. Joe saw two choices: He could either turn to Christ, repent of his sins, seek help for his addiction, and work toward restoring our marriage; or he could turn to the young woman at his office who was pursuing him in her attempt to escape her drug-addicted, physically abusive boyfriend. The choice that Joe made left me as a single mother and our two boys victims of divorce at two and four years. Samantha, the young woman from Joe's office, now had a "savior" for herself and a daddy for her baby girl.

Four years have now passed, and I'm happy to say that I have joy in my heart that I never had before. God has provided for us in ways I never could have imagined. The boys and I have a new life in a wonderful community and a home that's modest but perfect for us. I graduated from college last year, am currently working toward becoming a public school teacher, am starting a ministry in our church to help women heal from abuse, and I hope to attend seminary in the near future. Although I still long for a godly man with whom I can have a loving, committed relationship, I'm content and confident that God is faithful with his promises. Right now I'm right where He wants me.

As for Joe, each weekend when I drop off the boys, I see his big house and nice cars, and I know that he's well on his way to having the financial "freedom" he's always longed for. How sad it makes me to see that nothing has changed. Under the façade of success lies a man whose every thought is consumed with sex and money. This is a bright man with a sensitive, giving heart who has the potential to be a dynamic witness for the healing love of Christ, yet he is still so lost and confused that he has nothing of real value to offer anyone. If only he were willing to push past the fear and pride that keep him from turning to the only One who can truly free him. I pray that someday he will find the joy I have found through my relationship with Christ. I feel scared for Samantha. She doesn't see that she has simply walked out of one abusive relationship and into another. She believes that Joe has saved her. My prayer for her is that the Lord will bring someone into her life who will help her to realize that Jesus is the only one who can truly save her.

Repentance is—

1. Acknowledging the widespread and extensive damage done to the victim and demonstrating remorse for the harm done.

2. Taking full responsibility for the abuse—by confessing.

3. Establishing new boundaries that demonstrate respect for the victim and help ensure that the abuse will not reoccur.

4. Taking active steps to change the sinful pattern of behavior that led to the abuse.

5. Making restitution to the victim.

Bear fruits in keeping with repentance. (Luke 3:8 ESV)

MY PRAYER OF FORGIVENESS FOR MY ABUSER

Listen to my cry for help, my King and my God,
for to you I pray . . . In the morning, O Lord,
I lay my requests before you and wait in expectation.
You are not a God who takes pleasure in evil;
with you the wicked cannot dwell.
The arrogant cannot stand in your presence;
you hate all who do wrong.
You destroy those who tell lies;
bloodthirsty and deceitful men the Lord abhors . . .

Lead me, O Lord, in your righteousness
because of my enemies—
make straight your way before me.

Not a word from their mouth can be trusted;
Their heart is filled with destruction.
Their throat is an open grave . . .
Declare them guilty, O God!
Let their intrigues be their downfall.
Banish them for their many sins,
for they have rebelled against you.

But let all who take refuge in you be glad;
let them ever sing for joy.
Spread your protection over them,
that those who love your name may rejoice in You.
For surely, O Lord, you bless the righteous;
you surround them with your favor as with a shield.
(Psalm 5:2-12)

MY PRAYER OF FORGIVENESS FOR MYSELF

He does not deal with us
according to our sins,
nor repay us according to our iniquities.
For as high as the heavens are above the earth,
so great is his steadfast love
toward those who fear him;
As far as the east is from the west,
so far does he remove
our transgressions from us,
As a father shows
compassion to his children,
the Lord shows compassion
to those who fear him.
For he knows our frame;
He remembers that we are dust.
Bless the Lord, O my soul!
(Psalm 103:10-14, 22 ESV)

chapter ten

Relational Forgiveness

Relational forgiveness is reconciliation—it's always desirable but not always possible. Reconciliation is a restoration of relationship with the abuser after he or she repents (Matthew 3:8, Acts 26:20, 2 Corinthians 7:9-10). The responsibility for reconciliation rests *solely on the abuser*. Since abusers are rarely willing to do the hard, humiliating work of repentance, it's often not possible to restore the relationship. Only when an abuser has genuinely evidenced repentance are we to offer this final aspect of forgiveness.

It's vital that we not confuse a manipulative apology with genuine repentance. A simple apology doesn't mean that the offender has truly repented. Nor are tears or any display of grief necessarily an evidence of genuine repentance either (see the example of Esau in Hebrews 12:15-17). In Greek, the word for *repent* comes from the words for *change* and *mind*, and so indicate a radical change of perspective regarding one's sin. In the New Testament, repentance also involves complete ownership of one's sin (Jonah 3:4-9; Matthew 12:41). In order to offer relational forgiveness, an abuser should be expected to "produce fruits in keeping with repentance" (Luke 3:8). This means that the abuser will take full responsibility for what he or she has done as well as recognize how destructive these actions were. Additionally, the abuser will make radical behavioral changes in order to safeguard against any similar abusive actions in the future. This is true repentance: owning and grieving over sins one has committed, completely forsaking those sins, and turning to God. It's thus an action with tangible evidences, or as the Bible describes it, "fruit." Laurie Hall describes genuine repentance as follows:

> Just as forgiveness isn't cheap, repentance isn't cheap. Repentance isn't just being sorry we got caught. Repentance is learning from our mistakes. Repentance is walking a mile in the shoes of the one we've wounded. Repentance demands that we lie for a time in the bed we have made. In real repentance, we feel the pain we have cause others and ourselves. (An Affair of the Mind)

Describe a time when you were instructed to forgive someone who apologized without repentance—how did you feel?

Based on what you have learned, how would you respond today if you were in that same situation?

Pay attention to yourselves! If your brother sins, rebuke him, and if he repents, forgive him. (Luke 17:3 ESV)

chapter ten

Have you relationally forgiven (reconciled with) your abuser?
Why or why not?

We will not take healing action against unfair pain until we own the pain we want to heal. It is not enough to feel pain. We need to appropriate the pain we feel: Be conscious of it, take it on, and take it in as our own. We need to acknowledge our pain, admit that we feel it, admit it to ourselves and to anyone else who wants to know. We need to name the pain we feel: Identify it for what it is and what it is not. We need to evaluate the pain we feel: Ask ourselves whether the pain we feel matches the kind of wrong we were done. And, finally, we need to take responsibility for the pain we feel: Decide what we are going to do with it hold onto it, get even for it, or heal it. When we have owned our pain, we are ready to do something else with it.

—Lewis B. Smedes, *The Art of Forgiving*

All praise to the God and Father of our Master, Jesus the Messiah! Father of all mercy! God of all healing counsel! He comes alongside us when we go through hard times, and before you know it, he brings us alongside someone else who is going through hard times so that we can be there for that person just as God was there for us. We have plenty of hard times that come from following the Messiah, but no more so than the good times of his healing comfort—we get a full measure of that, too. When we suffer for Jesus, it works out for your healing and salvation. If we are treated well, given a helping hand and encouraging word, that also works to your benefit, spurring you on, face forward, unflinching. Your hard times are also our hard times. When we see that you're just as willing to endure the hard times as to enjoy the good times, we know you're going to make it, no doubt about it. (2 Corinthians 1:3-7 The Message)

Stepping into Freedom!

In order to be at peace with your past pain, you must grant forgiveness. Even if your abuser hasn't repented or owned his or her sins of abuse, forgiveness allows you to experience emotional and spiritual freedom. There are five main steps you must take as you seek to forgive those who have harmed you. Place yourself upon the stair that you are processing at this time.

5. Extend appropriate grace:
Pray for his or her repentance and healing (Romans 12:17, 21).

4. Reevaluate the abuser:
Discover his or her humanity (Colossians 3:12).

3. Release your right to get even:
Exercise faith in a good and just God (Romans 12:19).

2. Set boundaries:
Check evil and stimulate repentance (2 Thessalonians 3:14).

1. Clarify the offense and consequences:
Feel and express the emotion resulting from the abuse (Psalm 55: 1-5).

chapter ten

Draw or describe your journey.
Where did you begin and where are you now? Where do you want to be?

chapter ten
My Thoughts and Feelings. . .

chapter ten

Congratulations!

You have finally finished. That's one big accomplishment, and I think you should celebrate! Remember—healing and forgiveness are not one time events, but instead are pathways you will walk for the duration of your life...

As you step away from these pages, be patient with yourself and commemorate your victories along the way. God has big plans for you and a unique redemption of every bit of your pain. Trust Him. Follow Him. And fly...

Celestia

We Want That Something

We don't know how to ask for your help;
We don't understand our need for deep healing.
Would you be willing to seek us out? Would you hold on to us and not let go
Until you know we're safe—even if we fight against your loving grip?

Our feet hurt from walking all day, trying to find a place to rest.
Our bodies ache from the damage the world has done to us—the damage we've done to ourselves.

We've not tasted the moment that takes place
When a mother cradles her baby and whispers love.
We've not experienced the joy that comes when a father
Tosses his child in the air and catches him with laughter.
We don't know the peace that comes when a mother and father
Read His words of love and fall asleep in a warm, purified bed.
When you say *family*, we think of nothing but a void. Will you show us what these things are?

What is the space shared between two lovers blessed by God?
What is the space between a loving father and mother and their children?
Between a brother and sister? A grandparent and their grandchildren?
What does it look like, feel like? Somehow, we know that we're missing out on something,
but we don't know what it is. We want that something! How do we get that something?

At first, don't toss Scripture at us. Show us through demonstration
Lay your Holy-Spirit-filled hands upon us and petition the King for our healing.
Cry out to Jesus and don't stop until you see us respond.
Continue to pray for us before you sleep.
Will you show us that we matter and that you love us?
Place your hands gently over us, and anoint us with His peace.
Tell us that He loves us. Show us how to set safe boundaries around our hearts and bodies.

Stand with us while this healing takes place
And let us know you'll stay—no matter how long it takes.
Tell us you'll walk this long journey with us.

Copyright © 2012, Celestia G. Tracy
This material may not be copied or altered in any manner without express written consent of Mending the Soul Ministries.

Epilogue

I want you who are reading this to know that no matter how badly you've been abused, healing is possible when you're surrounded by healthy, trained people and good resources. I'm currently employed at City Hall as staff assistant for Commissioner Saltzman. I'm currently working on issues that pertain to youth who have aged out of the foster care system. I speak on behalf of the abused and of those who've cried out for help while their bodies were exploited. Those of us with deeply wounded souls know that we're missing out on something, and we yearn to have it. We need someone to show us what it looks like and feels like to be loved.

The state found me on the streets alone when I was two years old. I had lice, was suffering from malnutrition, and cigarette burns covered my body. While in the foster care system, I went through seven foster homes in which I continued to endure abuse. When I was four, a loving family adopted me. Because of my abuse, I had severe scarring all over my body, and my adoptive parents had to put vitamin E oil on me each night before I went to bed. As I got older, the state provided information regarding my abusive family history, but by that time my heart was hardened and guarded. When I became a teen, my parents were unable to emotionally reach me. They sent me to boarding school, but I left and ended up on the streets. I was commercially sexually exploited—I worked the streets so my girlfriends wouldn't have to. I'm now thirty-seven years old, and I've been healing with the help of mentors trained by Mending the Soul.

Since beginning my healing journey, I've learned that in America only 3% of survivors who've been in my situation graduate from college, which makes permanent well-trained mentors so critical. I'm among the exception. Because of people who cared and reached out to me, I finished college and was inducted into the National Honor Society of Phi Kappa Phi, which boasts such members as former President Jimmy Carter, a United States National Security Advisor, and a two-time Nobel Laureate. Other victims of abuse can have the same opportunities to achieve—if the cycle of healing continues.

epilogue

I wrote the words below in order to thank those within the Mending the Soul community who have been trained to help survivors heal. This community stood fearlessly around me, fighting on my behalf in the name of the Holy One, King Jesus, the healer. They fought and fought, despite what seemed to be the endless torment of the evil one. Finally, God's healing hand reached through, slowly pulling me out of darkness and into the healing love of His presence. After twenty years of what seemed like hopelessness on the streets, I can finally say that help has arrived in abundance. I'm seeing hope that I've not seen before—something glorious is slowly piercing the darkness. How blessed are the feet of those who carry His wellspring of life!

My body is lying before you, torn apart and broken on the inside. My eyes and heart are darkened—I'm in utter disrepair.

I hear the sound of joyful singing as you place your hands on and over me; your faces are shining with peace. As you gently rest your Spirit-filled hands upon my head, you whisper about perfect love that comes from heaven—your words to me taste like warm honey and feel like a peaceful, cool breeze. Something like hope fills the air around us.

You continue to speak this foreign truth to me. My body begins to succumb to peace. Something like the smell of honeysuckle sinks into my flesh, my blood, and my bones. I feel this peace, and I'm perplexed. I reach toward the heavens and ask, "What is this thing I feel?" I reach out my arms towards heaven, because I can no longer see any other way to survive. I see a hand reaching down, grasping mine, and pulling me up…up…up… In a gentle, still voice, you continue to whisper love into my ear. I feel a coolness that spreads into my innermost self. I breathe deeply as this healing wave covers my heart.

Slowly my eyes begin to open as if for the first time—everything looks clearer and brighter. I'm in the middle of that something: that sacred space shared with Holy love. I hear the words of deep love from those who've been blessed by the God of heaven and earth. I've been introduced to joy, hope, healing, and peace. These things have become tangible to me. I can sing and dance with laughter before my enemies. I'm being filled with His wellspring of sustainable life.

I am becoming whole.

You're the ones who carry a banner of joy, hope, healing, and peace. Thank you, my shining, gloriously regal ambassadors of the Holy One, King Jesus.

—Alexander Villarreal
Staff Assistant to City Commissioner Dan Saltzman
Portland, Oregon

epilogue

The Lord shall preserve you from all evil;
He shall preserve your soul.

These flowers are sketches Alex created as a young adolescent just before he ran away to the streets because of the effects of his early childhood abuse. When he sent them to me, he said, "I can't believe these came from me. Sometimes I look at them and am surprised that I created them. It shows that the Lord has kept some parts of me safe . . ."

He does that Alex—for all of us. He protects His original created design in us from every form of abuse and evil. He preserves our souls.

The Lord shall preserve
your going out and your coming
in from this time forth,
and even forevermore.
(Psalm 121:7-8 NKJV)

Appendices

APPENDIX ONE: FOR CLERGY OR CAREGIVERS
How to Respond When a Child Is Sexually Exploited

1. Prayerfully gather your thoughts. Sexual abuse is a most disturbing disclosure that creates fear, anger, or panic, causing leaders to react in unwise, even ungodly ways. Specifically seek to discern the truth and ask God to give you wisdom and courage (1 Corinthians 16:13; James 1:5).

2. Contact law enforcement and report the abuse immediately. If the suspected perpetrator is a family member or if the family was negligent in protecting the child from a non family member, Child Protective Services should also be contacted. In many states, clergy and even Sunday school teachers are mandated reporters. That is, they are required by law to report any suspected child abuse or any abuse disclosure. Scripture is quite clear that we are to obey our governing authorities because they are ordained by God to impede and punish evil (Romans 13:1-7).

3. Do not interrogate the child. Abused children feel great shame, so we must be very gentle and careful in talking to them about the abuse. Furthermore, it is the job of trained law enforcement, mental health, and social workers—not church workers—to conduct forensic interviews and gather the details of the abuse, which will hold up in court.

4. Do not confront the perpetrator. For the sake of the legal investigation, it is important for law enforcement to be the first ones to interview the perpetrator. In time, God might give you the opportunity to talk to the perpetrator, but that should not happen at the outset of the abuse disclosure.

5. Assure the child that the abuse is not his or her fault. Shame causes children to innately feel they are responsible for the abuse. Additionally, perpetrators often tell the child it is his or her fault. It may take a very long time for the child to truly believe the abuse wasn't his or her fault, so repeated verbal assurances from respected leaders can be very helpful.

6. Assure the child that you take his or her story very seriously and that you are sorry for the abuse. Let the child know that you and the church take abuse very seriously because God takes it seriously (Psalm 5:6; Matthew 18:5-7). Reassure the child that you love him or her and will be praying.

7. Assure the child that you and the church will work to get help. The kinds of help needed by an abused child and his or her family are quite varied, but some of the most common needs include referrals for Christians counselors experienced in treating abuse; financial assistance with professional counseling; education and coaching of church workers on how to respond to the abused child; Christian books, ministries, and web resources to educate the child and the family on abuse. Ask the child and the family what the church could do (or not do) that would be most helpful.

8. Recognize the complexity of abuse and gather various professional and community resources. One of the most common mistakes pastors make when confronted with abuse is to try to "take care of everything in house." Abuse is an astoundingly complex problem that defies quick, simple solutions. The dynamics of abusers are complex and well hidden, making it very difficult for outsiders to know the truth, let alone offer a wise response. Hence, ministering to abuse survivors, their families, and abusers calls for a partnership with various agencies, wise Christian leaders, and professionals.

9. Protect the child from the perpetrator and from others who seek to blame the victim and minimize the abuse. God unequivocally calls spiritual leaders to confront abuse and to protect and aid those who are abused, especially children (Isaiah 1:17; Jeremiah 22:3, 15-17; James 1:27). Denial and victim blame are some of the most common responses to sexual abuse; however, these responses are most strongly condemned by God (Proverbs 17:15) and must be boldly resisted by church leaders.

APPENDIX TWO: IS A.A. FOR YOU?

Only you can decide whether you want to give A.A. a try—whether you think it can help you. We who are in A.A. came because we finally gave up trying to control our drinking. We still hated to admit that we could never drink safely. Then we heard from other A.A. members that we were sick. (We thought so for years!) We found out that many people suffered from the same feelings of guilt and loneliness and hopelessness that we did. We found out that we had these feelings because we had the disease of alcoholism. We decided to try and face up to what alcohol had done to us. Here are some of the questions we tried to answer honestly. If we answered YES to four or more questions, we were in deep trouble with our drinking. See how you do. Remember, there is no disgrace in facing up to the fact that you have a problem.

Answer YES or NO to the following questions.

1. Have you ever decided to stop drinking for a week or so, but only lasted for a couple of days?   Yes   No
    Most of us in A.A. made all kinds of promises to ourselves and to our families. We could not keep them. Then we came to A.A.
    A.A. said: "Just try not to drink today." (If you do not drink today, you cannot get drunk today.)

2. Do you wish people would mind their own business about your drinking—stop telling you what to do?   Yes   No
    In A.A. we do not tell anyone to do anything. We just talk about our own drinking, the trouble we got into, and how we stopped.
    We will be glad to help you, if you want us to.

3. Have you ever switched from one kind of drink to another in the hope that this would keep you from getting drunk?   Yes   No
    We tried all kinds of ways. We made our drinks weak. Or just drank beer. Or we did not drink cocktails. Or only drank on weekends.
    You name it, we tried it. But if we drank anything with alcohol in it, we usually ended up getting drunk.

4. Have you had to have an eye-opener upon awakening during the past year?   Yes   No
    Do you need a drink to get started, or to stop shaking?
    This is a pretty sure sign that you are not drinking "socially."

5. Do you envy people who can drink without getting into trouble?   Yes   No
    At one time or another, most of us have wondered why we were not like most people, who really can take it or leave it.

6. Have you had problems connected with drinking during the past year?   Yes   No
    Be honest! Doctors say that if you have a problem with alcohol and keep on drinking, it will get worse—never better. Eventually,
    you will die, or end up in an institution for the rest of your life. The only hope is to stop drinking.

7. Has your drinking caused trouble at home?   Yes   No
    Before we came into A.A., most of us said that it was the people or problems at home that made us drink. We could not see that our
    drinking just made everything worse. It never solved problems anywhere or anytime.

8. Do you ever try to get "extra" drinks at a party because you do not get enough? Yes No
   Most of us used to have a "few" before we started out if we thought it was going to be that kind of party. And if drinks were not served fast enough, we would go some place else to get more.

9. Do you tell yourself you can stop drinking any time you want to, even though you keep getting drunk when you don't mean to? Yes No
   Many of us kidded ourselves into thinking that we drank because we wanted to. After we came into A.A., we found out that once we started to drink, we couldn't stop.

10. Have you missed days of work or school because of drinking? Yes No
    Many of us admit now that we "called in sick" lots of times when the truth was that we were hung-over or on a drunk.

11. Do you have "blackouts"? Yes No
    A "blackout" is when we have been drinking hours or days which we cannot remember. When we came to A.A., we found out that this is a pretty sure sign of alcoholic drinking.

12. Have you ever felt that your life would be better if you did not drink? Yes No
    Many of us started to drink because drinking made life seem better, at least for a while. By the time we got into A.A., we felt trapped. We were drinking to live and living to drink. We were sick and tired of being sick and tired.

Did you answer YES four or more times? If so, you are probably in trouble with alcohol. Why do we say this? Because thousands of people in A.A. have said so for many years. They found out the truth about themselves—the hard way. But again, only you can decide whether you think A.A. is for you. Try to keep an open mind on the subject. If the answer is YES, we will be glad to show you how we stopped drinking ourselves. Just call. A.A. does not promise to solve your life's problems. But we can show you how we are learning to live without drinking "one day at a time." We stay away from that "first drink." If there is no first one, there cannot be a tenth one. And when we got rid of alcohol, we found that life became much more manageable.

ALCOHOLICS ANONYMOUS is a fellowship of men and women who share their experience, strength and hope with each other that they may solve their common problem and help others to recover from alcoholism.

- The only requirement for membership is a desire to stop drinking. There are no dues or fees for A.A. membership; we are self-supporting through our own contributions.
- A.A. is not allied with any sect, denomination, politics, organization or institution; does not wish to engage in any controversy; neither endorses nor opposes any causes. Our primary purpose is to stay sober and help other alcoholics to achieve sobriety.

Copyright © by The A.A. Grapevine, Inc.; reprinted with permission.

appendices

APPENDIX THREE: EATING DISORDER SCREENING (SCOFF)

This eating disorder screen (SCOFF) can assist you in determining if you may have a problem. If you have any concerns about yourself or someone you know, seek professional help immediately.

Take this brief yet accurate screen:

1. Do you make yourself sick because you feel uncomfortably full?
2. Do you worry you have lost control over how much you eat?
3. Have you lost more than fifteen pounds in a three-month period?
4. Do you believe yourself to be fat when others say you are too thin?
5. Would you say that food dominates your life?

Understanding the Results:

Any person answering "yes" to two or more of these five questions is quite likely to have an eating disorder.

What Should I Do?

If you or someone you know is possibly suffering from an eating disorder, please call Remuda Ranch at 1-800-445-1900. Our friendly, professional staff will answer all of your questions and can help you determine what your next step should be. All calls are confidential.

There is hope and help at Remuda Ranch. 1-800-445-1900

© 2004. ALL RIGHTS RESERVED. PRIVACY POLICY USED BY PERMISSION COPYRIGHT DR. JOHN F. MORGAN, 1999.
Note to Healthcare Professionals:
The screening test above, called the SCOFF, has been validated in a primary care setting, but may also be administered in other settings. Oral and written administrations are both valid. The SCOFF picks up nearly 100 percent of anorexia and bulimia cases. It has a small false positive rate. It is therefore an excellent, rapid, and cost-effective screening tool for identifying eating disorders.

1. Morgan, J.F., Lacey, J.H., & Luck, A. (2002, April). *Validation of the SCOFF questionnaire for case detection of eating disorders in primary care. Paper presented at the International Conference on Eating Disorders of the Academy for Eating Disorders, Boston, MA.*

2. Perry, L., Morgan, J., Reid, F., Brunton, J., O'Brien, A., Luck, A., and Lacey, H. (2002). *Screening for symptoms of eating disorders: Reliability of the SCOFF Screening Tool with written compared to oral deliver International Journal of Eating Disorders, 32, 466-472.*

APPENDIX FOUR: DEPRESSION INVENTORY

1. Are you experiencing a "down" or depressed mood?

2. Do you have trouble getting to sleep? Do you wake up frequently? Or, on the other hand, do you sleep excessively (more than ten hours a night)?

3. In recent months, have you experienced less interest in your daily activities than you did previously?

4. Are you experiencing feelings of guilt or worthlessness?

5. Are you experiencing a decreased level of physical energy that is not attributable to a physiological cause?

6. Do you have trouble maintaining your powers of concentration? (In other words, are you able to stay focused on a task requiring mental energy such as reading a book?)

7. Are you experiencing an increase or decrease in your appetite? Have you gained or lost ten pounds or more in recent months without trying?

8. Are you experiencing increased or decreased levels of physical motor activity (agitation or lethargy)?

9. Have you had any thoughts of suicide?

If you answered the first question and four others in the affirmative and you are not experiencing normal bereavement, you should receive an evaluation for clinical depression.

If you answered the last question in the affirmative, seek help immediately.

appendices

APPENDIX FIVE: FEELING CHARTS

… appendices

Menu of Feelings

Mad	Sad	Glad	Uneasy	Curious	Uncomfortable	Out of Place
Bothered	Down	At Ease	Apprehensive	Uncertain	Awkward	Left Out
Ruffled	Blue	Comfortable	Careful	Ambivalent	Clumsy	Lonesome
Irritated	Somber	Relaxed	Cautious	Doubtful	Self Conscious	Disconnected
Displeased	Low	Contented	Hesitant	Unsettled	Disconcerted	Insecure
Annoyed	Hurt	Optimistic	Tense	Hesitant	Chagrined	Unappreciated
Steamed	Disappointed	Satisfied	Anxious	Perplexed	Abashed	Invisible
Irked	Worn Out	Refreshed	Nervous	Puzzled	Embarrassed	Unwelcome
Perturbed	Melancholy	Grateful	Edgy	Muddled	Flustered	Misunderstood
Frustrated	Downhearted	Pleased	Distressed	Distracted	Sorry	Excluded
Angry	Unhappy	Warm	Scared	Flustered	Apologetic	Insignificant
Fed Up	Dissatisfied	Happy	Frightened	Jumbled	Ashamed	Ignored
Disgusted	Gloomy	Encouraged	Vulnerable	Unfocused	Regretful	Neglected
Indignant	Mournful	Tickled	Repulsed	Fragmented	Remorseful	Removed
Resentful	Grieved	Proud	Agitated	Dismayed	Guilty	Detached
Ticked Off	Depressed	Hopeful	Shocked	Insecure	Disgusted	Isolated
Jealous	Lousy	Cheerful	Alarmed	Dazed	Belittled	Unwanted
Fuming	Crushed	Thrilled	Overwhelmed	Bewildered	Humiliated	Rejected
Explosive	Miserable	Delighted	Frantic	Lost	Violated	Deserted
Enraged	Defeated	Joyful	Panic Stricken	Stunned	Dirty	Outcast
Irate	Dejected	Elated	Horrified	Chaotic	Mortified	Abandoned
Incensed	Empty	Exhilarated	Petrified	Torn	Defiled	Withdrawn
Burned	Wretched	Overjoyed	Terrified	Baffled	Devastated	Desolate
Outraged	Despairing	Ecstatic	Numb	Dumbfounded	Degraded	Forsaken
Furious	Devastated	Afraid	Confused	Ashamed	Lonely	

The feelings above are ranked from least to most severe.

FEEDBACK FORM

Please take time to reflect and give honest answers on how the Mending the Soul Workbook was helpful to you and areas for improvement.

Date:_____

1. How did the Mending the Soul Workbook impact your healing and your walk with God?

2. Before working through the workbook or attending an MTS group, how much professional counseling have you experienced that focused on the issues raised in the workbook or group?

3. How would you compare the healing you experienced during the MTS process or group to healing experienced from previous individual, professional counseling?

4. How did the exercises in the workbook help to personalize the book (*Mending the Soul*) and make it relevant to your life experiences and abuse?

5. Were there any exercises that were unclear to you? How could the questions have been more clear and helpful? Please explain.

6. What was the experience of journaling like for you?

7. How did the Scriptures in the workbook affect you?

8. Do you have any specific suggestions for improving the workbook?

9. If you were involved in a group, what did you like about the way your facilitator used the material from both the book and workbook? What did you dislike?

10. Do you have any specific suggestions for how facilitators could better utilize the material?

Thank you for taking time to share your feedback and experiences. Your feedback form can be returned to your facilitator or to:

Mending the Soul Ministries, Inc.
P.O. Box 97636
Phoenix, AZ 85060
www.mendingthesoul.org